D1335363

MATTHEW

Text copyright © John Proctor 2001

The author asserts the moral right to be
identified as the author of this work

Published by
The Bible Reading Fellowship
15 The Chambers, Vineyard
Abingdon OX14 3FE
United Kingdom
Tel: +44 (0)1865 319700
Email: enquiries@brf.org.uk
Website: www.brf.org.uk
BRF is a Registered Charity

ISBN 978 1 84101 191 2

First published 2001
Second reprint 2010
10 9 8 7 6 5 4 3 2

Acknowledgments
Scripture quotations from The New Revised Standard Version of
the Bible, Anglicized Edition, are copyright © 1989, 1995
by the Division of Christian Education of the National Council
of the Churches of Christ in the United States of America, and
are used by permission. All rights reserved.

Scripture quotations from The Revised Standard Version of the
Bible are copyright © 1946, 1952, 1971 by the Division of
Christian Education of the National Council of the Churches
of Christ in the United States of America, and are used by
permission. All rights reserved.

p. 239 Extract from *Common Order* is copyright © Panel on
Worship of the Church of Scotland, and is used by permission.

A catalogue record for this book is
available from the British Library

Printed in Singapore by Craft Print International Ltd

MATTHEW

John Proctor

THE PEOPLE'S BIBLE COMMENTARY

A devotional commentary for study and preaching

PREFACE

This commentary was written with churches and church people in mind. Some Christians have followed it in their daily Bible reading. Others have used it to help them lead Bible study. Preachers have turned to it, as they think about their sermons for Sunday. All of that is exactly what we hoped for when BRF asked me to write this commentary. It is a joy to know that it is being reissued. I hope it will help many people to grasp the good news of Jesus and to follow it in their own living.

There are some excellent big commentaries on Matthew's Gospel, some stretching to several volumes. I have learned a lot from these. Yet for many people a big commentary would be no help at all—they would find it too costly or too heavy. So this much smaller commentary aims to digest the insight into Matthew that specialists can give, and to reflect on Matthew's message for today. What does it mean in the 21st century to hear the good news, to welcome God's kingdom and to be a disciple of Jesus? What can we receive from this Gospel for Christian living in our times and among our neighbours?

God has surely given us four Gospels for a good reason. Each of the four is unique. They tell of the same Lord, but in different ways. Each has its own angles and emphases, as it shares the message of Jesus. Here are some of Matthew's:

- Roots and continuity were important to Matthew. He wanted to connect the Christian good news with the past, with the story of God's work in the Old Testament. He believed that history pointed forward to Jesus, and that the New Testament story is rooted in the Old. To read Matthew is to be reminded of a God who works through the generations, and to think again about our own debt to the past.

- Matthew's Gospel follows a sandwich pattern. Word and deed alternate. Blocks of Jesus' teaching are interleaved with blocks of action, with reports of things he did and people he met. Action and teaching mesh with one another, and in the mesh is a message. Belief in Jesus and practical Christian living are linked. True Christian living should be an integrated whole, where faith and conduct nourish one another.

- Matthew is a demanding Gospel. It takes Christian commitment seriously—commitment to Jesus, to discipleship, to high standards of conduct, to one another. To read with care is likely to be quite a searching experience. Yet Matthew was realistic. He knew that Christians are fragile, vulnerable and fallible. His Gospel urges us to be patient with one another, and to find gentle ways of supporting each other in the Church and in the Christian life.

- Matthew is a Gospel of hope. He believed in the lordship of Jesus Christ, in Jesus' authority and presence in the Church's mission, and in his coming to judge the world. To follow Jesus is to be in his company, under his command and within his care. Matthew wrote to give Christians confidence as they served Jesus in a complex world and in difficult times. We may read this Gospel, and share its message, with that same aim. We too can be confident in the Christ who is with us always, whose word and presence we proclaim and enjoy.

Some people who use this commentary may worship in churches that use the Revised Common Lectionary. This calendar of Bible readings runs over three years of Sundays. In Year A of the three-year cycle —starting in Advent 2010, 2013, 2016 and so on—most of the Gospel readings come from Matthew. Roughly half of this Gospel will be read in main Sunday services, but it is not followed in precise Gospel order, because we cover the sweep of the Gospel story from Jesus' birth to resurrection in the four months from December to Easter. This involves a very selective approach to Gospel readings in these months. The rhythm of the church year, rather than the flow of Matthew's text, sets the tone and context for these.

Once we come into the weeks after Trinity Sunday, from June to November, however, the Gospel readings run steadily through Matthew from chapters 7 to 25, sometimes skipping a slice but always moving forward. Many of Matthew's main themes figure plain and large: miracles and mission, preaching and parables, crisis and controversy, fellowship and following. For churches who want to trace the movement and message of a big biblical book, the Revised Common Lectionary offers a great deal. Listen to Matthew's Gospel in worship, and live by it through the year.

John Proctor

Contents

PBC Matthew: Introduction

Jesus of Nazareth has a strong claim to be the most influential person who ever lived. Two thousand years after his own time, hundreds of millions of people in every part of the world are glad to be known as Christians, as his friends and followers. The life he lived, the things he said and did, how he died and what happened afterwards, make a remarkable story. Christians have always wanted to know about Jesus, to understand the Lord who launched our faith.

Why write Gospels?

That is why we have Gospels. Probably they arose something like this. For a few years after Jesus' time, people remembered what he had said and done. Memories were good in the ancient Middle East, as they have to be in any culture where paper is expensive. But the people who remembered gradually died out, and Christians wanted a record of Jesus that they could keep. So about a generation after Jesus' lifetime, the Gospels started to appear.

That is very approximate. Nobody really knows when Matthew was written. Guesses vary from about AD40 to AD100. Many scholars come down in the middle of that range, between about 60 and 90. Around that time, the record of Jesus' life that we call Matthew's Gospel was put on to paper.

Global or local?

For whom was the Gospel written? Two answers are popular today. One says that Matthew (and Mark, Luke and John) always meant their Gospels to be widely read. The Church of that day was spread across much of southern Europe, western Asia and northern Africa. There were good communications between various Christian centres. The Gospels were bound to travel. The Gospel writers believed that Jesus' story was worth telling and wanted to preserve it for their own generation and those who would follow. From very early on, the four Gospels belonged to the whole Church.

A second approach suggests that the four Gospels were written for Christians in different local areas. Each of the writers was trying to help the Christians he knew best. So each Gospel is angled differently, to reflect the needs and circumstances of the writer's own local church. If we follow that sort of tack, we may try to read between the lines of each Gospel to find out about the needs and situation of the first readers, as well as about Jesus himself.

I think there is some truth in both those theories. The early Christians were interested in Jesus. They thought his life was important. They wanted to preserve their memories of him, so that others could know about him too. Jesus is the main focus of the whole gospel story and of Christian faith. But the four Gospels do have different selections of material and different emphases. They are portraits, not engineers' drawings. To some extent they each reflect their own author's perspectives on Jesus and the questions and concerns of four different groups of early Christians.

Why read four Gospels?

So I take a positive approach to the Gospels. I value the material they contain, and I believe they give a true picture of Jesus. But none of them gives the whole truth. All of the Gospel writers had to choose what to include and how to present it. Let me mention four reasons why it is helpful to have several Gospels.

Selection: Some material in other Gospels is not in Matthew. For example, Matthew only shows Jesus making one journey to Jerusalem, at the end of his ministry. Jesus goes with grim foreboding, expecting to suffer. His enemies there act quickly and harshly against him, very soon after he arrives. That sequence of events is easier to understand if we connect it to John's Gospel, which shows Jesus making several visits to Jerusalem. By the time of the last Passover visit he was known in the city and was a marked man. Both he and his enemies were ready for trouble. The accounts in two different Gospels mesh together, to give a fuller and clearer picture of Jesus' career.

Order: Some material in Matthew is in a different order in other Gospels. For example, much of the teaching in Matthew 5—7 (the Sermon on the Mount) is scattered through Luke. Matthew seems to have a tendency to collect material on a similar theme and include it in one place in his Gospel. There is something similar in Matthew 8 and 9, which shows a series of miracles in quick succession, whereas in Mark the same material is spread more widely, across Mark 1—5.

Detail: Some material in Matthew is briefer than in other Gospels. Mark reports action at length. Matthew cuts to the main point.

Compare Mark 5:21–43 with Matthew 9:18–26, for example. Mark shows each scene very closely and clearly; Matthew makes an impact by moving swiftly from one incident to the next.

Angle: Some material in Matthew is told a bit differently in other Gospels. Look at the comment on Matthew 26:26–30, for example. Jesus' words at the Last Supper vary a little as we move from one Gospel to another. The main lines of the incident are very clear, but each Gospel has its own emphasis and angle.

So for many reasons it is helpful to have four different Gospels. But in some vitally important ways they are closely similar, both in broad outline and even in some fine details. Why is this? Why in particular are Matthew, Mark and Luke so very like each other at so many points?

Identify your sources

Most people who study the Gospels think that Matthew knew Mark's Gospel, or something very like it. The two Gospels have a great deal of material in common. Most of that material—indeed all of it after Matthew 13—is in the same order, and much of it has very similar wording. So the thought that Matthew knew and used Mark, and adapted Mark's material into his own Gospel, has become wide-spread in modern study of the Gospels.

However, a lot of Matthew's material is missing from Mark. About half of that extra material, almost all of it sayings of Jesus, is very like parts of Luke's Gospel. This raises the suspicion that Matthew and Luke both had the same source for this stuff. This source has been named 'Q', which is the first letter of the German word for 'source', and a suitably mysterious title for a shadowy body of material about which we really know very little indeed.

Everything in the two paragraphs above is sensible guesswork; we cannot be certain. Matthew, like many a modern journalist, does not identify his sources. Even so, something like the above may very well explain Matthew as we now have it. But as we read Matthew, it is important to hear the way he tells the story of Jesus, to listen for his own emphases, and trace his own plan.

Matthew's plan

Have you ever been in an old building that was converted from one use to another during its lifetime? Both the original design and the later modifications contribute to the ground plan and the shape of the rooms. Some people think that has happened to Matthew. At any rate there seem to be two plans, dovetailed into each other.

The 'Jesus began' plan: The first three or four chapters of Matthew are a sort of preface to the main action. Jesus is born; later on he is baptized and tempted. Then he is ready to start his ministry, and at 4:17 it says, 'From then on Jesus began to preach.' The Gospel then shows Jesus making God's kingdom known, in word and action, in and around Galilee.

Gradually we see a very mixed response arising, and there is a hint that serious difficulties may be emerging, when we read in 11:20, 'Then he began to speak against the places which had not heeded his word.'

Opposition now starts to sharpen, and at 16:21 we realize where this will lead: 'From then on Jesus began to show his disciples that he must go to Jerusalem, suffer and die.'

By using the word 'began' as a milestone, we have found the route the Gospel takes. By that plan, Matthew's Gospel has twelve chapters about the mission of Jesus in Galilee (4—16), and twelve chapters leading to the Passion of Jesus in Jerusalem (16—27). Once we pass chapter 16, the story is drawn to the cross like a moth to a lamp. Opposition steadily advances, the moment of destruction is inevitable, and there is a deepening mood of sorrow and fear. Only at the very end does hope return, with Easter and resurrection and a completely new beginning.

The 'Jesus finished' plan: The first plan has picked out the action of the Gospel—what Jesus did. The second plan picks out what Jesus said. The words 'When Jesus had finished these sayings' come five times in Matthew (7:28; 11:1; 13:53; 19:1; 26:1). Each one ends a major block of teaching, the five great sermons of Matthew's Gospel. Each of the blocks has a main theme running right through:

- Chapters 5—7, the Sermon on the Mount, about practical living.

- Chapter 10, about mission and evangelism.

- Chapter 13, a long string of parables about God's kingdom.

- Chapter 18, about Christian community and relationships.

- Chapters 24 and 25, about the future.

So the teaching and action are interspersed, like a giant multi-decker sandwich. Each section of teaching connects with the action around it, and carries the story forward.

Why two plans? Many people answer something like this. Mark used the first plan: half of his Gospel is about Jesus' mission in Galilee, and half is about Jesus' journey to Jerusalem and his suffering and death there. Matthew adopted Mark's plan. But Matthew also knew a good deal of Jesus' teaching, most of which Mark had missed (including the so-called 'Q' material), and wanted to highlight this. So the second plan, overlaid on the first, draws attention to Jesus as teacher. The Church remembers and trusts the Lord who lived, died and rose again. The Church also values and follows what he taught. Both aspects are important to Matthew.

Who was Matthew?

Jesus had a follower called Matthew, a former tax collector, whom he had called and who belonged to the circle of twelve disciples. We meet this man at Matthew 9:9, and there is an ancient tradition that his personal reminiscences of Jesus have come into this Gospel. But did he actually write it? Many people think it would be odd if Matthew, who was one of the Twelve, copied from Mark, who was not.

Matthew's Gospel also shows a close acquaintance with Jewish religious lore and custom, and tax collectors were not very religious Jews. Some of the style in the Gospel seems to be much more like that of a Jewish religious teacher. So could Matthew the tax collector be the source for some of the information, but someone else be the writer? And is there a trace of that writer—rather like a film director appearing for a moment in the film—in Jesus' saying about the 'scribe trained for the kingdom' (13:52)? None of the other Gospels has this saying, but the writer of Matthew feels it describes his own calling, and is glad to include it.

If we take that approach, whom shall we mean when we say 'Matthew': the tax collector, or the writer of the Gospel? I shall use the name 'Matthew' to refer to the person who wrote the Gospel, and to the way he tells the story of Jesus.

Matthew and Judaism

In many ways, Matthew is the most Jewish of the Gospels. It shows a strong acquaintance with Jewish customs and laws (for example,

5:23; 17:24; 23:5). It stresses how the ancient law of the Old Testament is fulfilled in the teaching of Jesus (5:17), and how the prophecies come to fulfilment in his life and work (1:23; 12:17). In some sections it presents Jesus as a new Moses (see comment on 2:13–23, pp. 28–29).

Yet Matthew also includes some very sharp criticism of Jewish leaders. This is clearest in chapter 23. We also read that 'the kingdom of God will be taken away from you and given to a people that produces the fruits of the kingdom' (21:43). Some of Israel's ancient privileges are being taken over by the community that Jesus is founding. So Matthew's Gospel is very Jewish in its background and atmosphere, but it also tells of Judaism being split by the coming of Jesus.

At the start of Matthew's Gospel, we see Jesus' mission focused on Israel. But Israel divides: there is a core of opposition among the nation's leaders, yet many of the ordinary people are warm and receptive. Although Matthew does not directly mention this, the Christian gospel made great strides among the Jewish people in the years after the resurrection, as the Church began to grow. But it was never accepted by the nation's official leadership.

Matthew's Church

The strong Jewish flavour to Matthew's writing suggests that he was writing for a Jewish audience, probably for a group of Jewish people who had accepted and believed in Jesus. He believed that their faith was a true fulfilment of their ancient Jewish heritage. Prophecy and law found their focus and completion in Jesus. Jesus was their Messiah, and God's ancient purpose was being carried forward through him.

Yet Matthew's first readers may have had very awkward relations with some of their neighbours, who did not share their beliefs. Jews who had accepted Jesus would have been suspect, seen as a fringe group within Israel. That may be the reason Matthew included so much controversial material, involving disputes and criticism between Jesus and his opponents. All the Gospels show some of this, but it is clearest in Matthew, and it may have been especially relevant to his readers' own situation. (The comments at the start of chapter 23 discuss this point further.)

But Matthew did not expect Christianity to get stuck within a Jewish horizon. He was convinced that the Church's mission should include Gentiles too. Jesus sometimes met Gentile people during his mission in Galilee. When he saw their faith, he recognized and welcomed it. Those contacts were a hint of what was ahead. Once Jesus is risen, the horizon is the world. After the resurrection the Christian message spreads out to all the nations.

Matthew and Christian living

Three major emphases stand out when we compare Matthew with other Gospels.

- Matthew's is the only Gospel to use the word 'church' (16:18; 18:17). He shows very clearly that Jesus is gathering and shaping a community.

- There is a lot of material in Matthew about practical living. Jesus' teaching about lifestyle and relationships has a very prominent place. Matthew obviously believes that faith must show itself in everyday life.

- Matthew includes a great deal of Jesus' teaching about judgment. God weighs and measures the way people live. Faith that does not show itself in deeds is hollow, and will never be able to bluff God. God is rich in forgiveness, but that does not give Christians the right to be casual or complacent about how we live.

So Matthew's Christianity is church-centred: we belong to one another. It is practical: we aim to express our faith in love and action. And it is serious: we trust God's mercy, but we must not be careless in how we serve him.

Text and translation

Have you ever noticed a footnote in your Bible saying, 'Some manuscripts have...' or 'Other ancient authorities read...'? We do not have the original manuscript of any book of the Bible. Thank God, the early Christians copied out the biblical books, by hand. But some of the first copies got lost, or decayed, or were destroyed in persecutions. So when we want to find out what Matthew wrote, we use the earliest copies we have. But these manuscripts come from several generations after Matthew's own time.

These manuscripts do not agree with each other precisely. That can always happen with copying by hand. Where we meet disagreements in wording, we have to work out as well as we can which version is original—what Matthew actually wrote. Very rarely those differences affect a whole verse—included in some manuscripts, missing from others. Examples of this are 6:13; 16:2–3; 17:21; 18:11; and we now doubt whether those five verses were actually written by Matthew. Yet much, much more often we have no serious disagreements in the manuscripts: what we read in our 21st-century English Bibles is based on a very solid knowledge of what Matthew wrote in the first century.

Matthew did not write in English. He used Greek, though not exactly the language spoken in Greece today. In some places it has been hard to translate the Greek into English, and English Bibles show different meanings. One example is in 28:17: the last few words could mean 'but they doubted' or 'but some of them doubted'. Were all the disciples hesitant, or just a few of them? We do not know. That sort of problem is occasionally to be expected when we use a very old piece of writing. It is hard to know fully and exactly what the ancient language meant. But most of the time we can be confident in our modern translations. In our day, as for the last two thousand years, Christians are happy to use the four Gospels because they were written close to the time and place where Jesus lived, and give us the best information we have about his life and work.

Matthew's good news

So Christians read Matthew as an introduction to Jesus. That was Matthew's main motive, to present Jesus clearly and helpfully, so that his readers would understand and trust Jesus. The word gospel means 'good news', about Jesus and about the life he invites people to live.

So listen to the teaching of Jesus in Matthew, take it seriously, and try to apply it in your own life. Value your Christian relationships with the brothers and sisters who help you to follow this way. And treasure above all your relationship with Jesus who is 'with you always, to the end' (Matthew 28:20).

The Bible quotations included in the commentary are usually taken from the New Revised Standard Version; occasionally I have used a translation or paraphrase of my own.

Some further reading on Matthew

A lot has been written about Matthew's Gospel in recent years, and I have learned much from these books. This list aims to give credit for that. It also suggests books that might help you to explore Matthew further.

Shorter commentaries on Matthew

W. Barclay, *The Gospel of Matthew*, The Daily Study Bible (2 volumes), St Andrew Press, revised edition 1975. A commentary written to support and encourage daily Bible reading. Accessible to lay people, beautifully clear, now dating a little.

M. Davies, *Matthew: Readings*, Sheffield Academic Press, 1993. Looks at the Gospel as a piece of literature, and at how Matthew presents his material.

R.T. France, *Matthew*, Tyndale New Testament Commentary. IVP, 1985. Explains the meaning of the text. Very clear, careful and well-informed.

E.M.B. Green, *The Bible Speaks Today: The Message of Matthew*, IVP, 2000. A clear, practical commentary.

I.H. Jones, *The Gospel of Matthew*, Epworth Commentary, Epworth Press, 1994. Written by a very able Matthew scholar, in a series designed for Methodist preachers.

J.P. Meier, *The New Testament Message: Matthew*, Veritas, 1980. By a leading Roman Catholic Gospels scholar.

D. Senior, *The Gospel of Matthew*, Abingdon New Testament Commentary, Abingdon Press, 1997. Written by an experienced Roman Catholic scholar, intended to help interested lay people.

Longer commentaries on Matthew

D.A. Carson, *Expositor's Bible Commentary*, Volume 8, edited by F.E. Gaebelein, Zondervan, 1984. Lots of explanation of difficult points, but concerned also to present Matthew's message clearly and directly.

W.D. Davies and D.C. Allison, *The Gospel According to St Matthew*, International Critical Commentary (on the Greek text; 3 volumes), T&T Clark, 1988, 1991 and 1997. The biggest and most detailed commentary in English. Magnificent—learned, detailed, lucid and reverent. But difficult to get full value unless you know some Greek.

R.H. Gundry, *Matthew: A Commentary on His Handbook for a Mixed Church under Persecution*, Eerdmans, revised edition 1994. A very careful examination of the differences between Matthew and Mark, linked to ideas about Matthew's situation.

D.A. Hagner, *Matthew*, Word Biblical Commentary (2 volumes), Word Books, 1993 and 1995. Very thoroughly researched and clearly written.

Other books on Matthew

R.T. France, *Matthew—Evangelist & Teacher*, Paternoster, 1989.

W. Harrington, *Matthew: Sage Theologian*, Columba Press, 1998.

U. Luz, *The Theology of the Gospel of Matthew*, Cambridge University Press, 1995.

J.K. Riches, *Matthew*, New Testament Guide, Sheffield Academic Press, 1996.

D. Senior, *What Are They Saying About Matthew?* Paulist Press, 1996.

Any of the above would be a good introduction to Matthew's Gospel. The books by Harrington, Riches and Senior are particularly accessible for non-specialists. France and Luz are a little fuller.

G.N. Stanton (ed.), *The Interpretation of Matthew*, SPCK, 2nd edition 1995. This is a selection of important academic articles on Matthew from across the 20th century, with an introduction by the editor, who is himself a leading Matthew scholar.

I have been greatly helped in dealing with the divorce passage in Matthew 19 by D. Instone-Brewer, *Divorce and Remarriage in the Bible,* Eerdmans, 2001; also by G. Theissen, *The Gospels in Context*, T&T Clark, 1992, on Matthew 11.

Where credit is due

Finally I acknowledge my personal debt to some major German commentaries, by H. Frankemölle, U. Luz, A. Sand and W. Wiefel.

PALESTINE *in the* TIME *of* JESUS

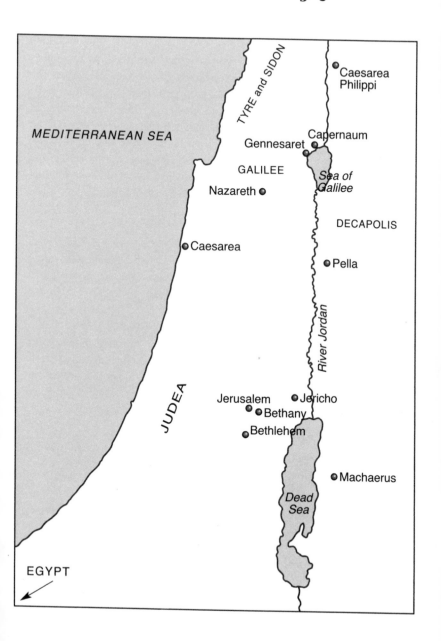

1   MATTHEW 1:1–17

LINES *of* INTRODUCTION

The scenery on a stage helps you to enjoy the play. Action makes more sense, a story carries more impact, if you can see where the events are set. The scenery can sharpen your hearing and tune your mind to the author's intentions and concerns. These opening verses of Matthew's Gospel lay out the scenery. Matthew presents Jesus against the background of the Old Testament. There were clues, longings, promises, running through the Old Testament, that had come to life in Jesus. The very first verse of the Gospel names some of them: 'Jesus the Messiah, son of David, son of Abraham'.

Son of Abraham

Abraham was the great forefather of the Jewish people. Jesus was born a Jew, spent most of his life among Jewish people, and rarely travelled outside Jewish territory. He thought, taught, argued and prayed in a Jewish way. We understand Jesus properly only if we understand him as a Jew.

Yet God had called Abraham for a wider purpose: 'in you all the families of the earth shall be blessed' (Genesis 12:3). Abraham is an international figure. The promise to Abraham is that Israel's God will do great things for the whole world. From this small people, a blessing will flow outward to the nations. To call Jesus 'son of Abraham' means that he is heir to this promise. He has blessing to share with the world.

Messiah, son of David

Jesus is also called 'son of David'. David was remembered as Israel's most successful king, who made the nation peaceful and prosperous. But that had been long ago. The Jews had grown hungry for a new David, a leader to make them great again and give them fresh hope. So the title 'son of David' is not just about ancestry. It is a job description. Through Jesus the kingly power of God will be made known in Israel. That is why he was called 'Messiah'. The word means 'anointed', a person marked out by God for a special task. In Greek— the language Matthew wrote—the word for 'anointed' is our word 'Christ'. Jesus Christ was God's anointed leader, a new David, the shepherd king who would show the loving rule of God.

Undulating path

The long genealogy (vv. 2–16) is divided into three sections of four-teen names each (v. 17). At the very start is Abraham (vv. 2, 17). The next marker in the sequence, ending the first main section, is the name of 'David the king' (vv. 6, 17). Then the second major landmark is the 'deportation to Babylon' (vv. 11, 12, 17), when many thou-sands of Jews were led across the desert to exile.

This is a roll of honour. It reflects the whole Old Testament story of Israel's long journey of faith and the patient goodness of God. Yet it is no whitewash. David and the exile are the milestones on the road, marking triumph and tragedy, fortune and failure. Jesus came to a nation with a patchy record. He stepped into real human history, the mixture of grief and glory that the world still experiences today.

Mothers with a message

The genealogy is mainly a list of fathers. Only five mothers are men-tioned. Four have unusual stories to tell. Tamar (v. 3) acted the part of a prostitute to claim the protection of the family into which she had married (Genesis 38). Rahab (v. 5) was a prostitute in Jericho who helped two Jewish spies (Joshua 2). Ruth (v. 5) was a foreigner who came into Israel's line through a complex story of bereavement and famine. 'The wife of Uriah' (v. 6) was Bathsheba, whose husband David murdered to conceal his adultery with her (2 Samuel 11); yet she later became the mother of King Solomon. These are not ideal Jewish mothers. Possibly all were Gentiles. Their circumstances and their conduct were unusual, and even irregular. Yet they underline the element of grace, that God can take human life as it is—often untidy, sometimes perverse and odd—and fill it with the rich promise of his love. They hint too that the fifth mother, Mary (v. 16), will also give birth amid unexpected circumstances. So Jesus comes out of Israel, for the world. He is born to be king, yet from a turbulent and tangled heritage. He is Mary's son and God's Messiah, a figure of perplexity, and a child of promise.

PRAYER

We praise you, God of Israel and our God, for the long reach and far horizon of your purpose, and for the breadth and generosity of your love. Through Jesus Christ our Lord. Amen.

2   MATTHEW 1:18–25

CHILD *of* GOD

The long line of ancestry has run from Abraham down to Joseph. Yet the genealogy ends with a novel and intriguing turn of phrase: instead of the repeated 'was father of', the last link in the chain is that Joseph was 'husband of Mary, of whom Jesus was born' (1:16). We discover the reason for that wording in this next passage, in verses 18–25.

Joseph was not the father of Jesus, at least not biologically. No human father was involved in Jesus' conception: he was 'born of the Virgin Mary'. The life in him came directly from God. Matthew—and indeed Joseph himself—knew perfectly well that this is not the normal order of things; that's why Joseph wanted to break the engagement when he first heard of Mary's pregnancy (vv. 18–19).

Father-in-law

Matthew tells this section of the Gospel from Joseph's point of view. He is said to be 'a righteous man' (v. 19), anxious to avoid a marriage that seemed compromised from the start, yet unwilling to make more trouble than necessary about calling the plans off. A dream helped to settle his fears (v. 20), so that he, a 'son of David', married Mary and gave his name and his family line to her child (vv. 24–25). Legally he became the father of Jesus. He protected mother and child through the hazards ahead (2:13–25). He taught Jesus his own trade (13:55; compare Mark 6:3). He seems to have died before Jesus launched into public ministry, but, so far as we can tell, his work was lovingly and faithfully done.

In a name

The child's name, Jesus, is a loaded word (v. 21). In Hebrew it is written Joshua, and means 'God to the rescue'. There had been an earlier Joshua who led the people of Israel, centuries before, into the land God had promised them. So Jesus too would make hopes become real. He would be God to the rescue. He would offer the Jewish people a new era, filled with freedom and forgiveness.

As the prophets foretold

A quotation from Isaiah helps to explain the virgin birth (vv. 22–23, from Isaiah 7:14); it had been predicted this way, we hear, seven centuries earlier. Yet no one—so far as we can tell—had taken the Isaiah text in quite that way until Jesus came. Isaiah seemed to be speaking of a young woman, perhaps a girl on the threshold of marriage, who would soon be pregnant with her first child. Then Matthew heard a fuller meaning in those ancient words, as a description of the birth of Jesus. He found fresh life in an old prophecy; but he also took up the hopes that had always been seen in it.

For this text from Isaiah 7 is about a prince, a royal leader for Israel. To connect these words to Jesus is to mark him out as a kingly figure, a new David. But he was more than a king. Isaiah's prophecy spoke of Emmanuel, which is Hebrew for 'God is with us'. In Jesus the creative power and love of God took human flesh, personally and directly. Through Jesus, in a unique and immediate way, God comes to be with his people.

Worth taking seriously

For many people, even some church people, the whole idea of Jesus' virgin birth seems a fantasy. But the evidence should not be sneezed at. Two positive points may be made.

Firstly, the Jewish people read Isaiah for centuries without expecting a virgin birth. Matthew turned to Isaiah, not primarily because he spotted ideas in the text that others had missed, but because it fitted the facts he had to tell. The scripture did not teach him his story; it resonated with what he already knew.

Secondly, Matthew and Luke tell the Christmas story in very different ways in their two Gospels. Yet at the heart of it all they match, and confirm one another's material, as two very different witnesses to the same event: that Jesus was 'conceived by the Holy Spirit and born of the Virgin Mary'.

So Jesus, son of the Jewish people, carried in his humanity the life and presence of Israel's God. The hopes of the prophetic scriptures took flesh in him. Joseph and Mary's love nurtured the Son of God.

PRAYER

Lord Jesus Christ, we praise you that you lived the life of God in our human flesh, truly one of us, yet not merely one of us.

WORSHIP *from* AFAR

Matthew's first chapter has told of a Jewish king, born of Jewish descent, according to the promises of Jewish scriptures. That raises an intriguing question. Has Israel not got a king already? If so, what will the old king and the new have to do with each other?

The Gospel begins to answer that question by telling us (v. 1) that 'in the time of King Herod... Jesus was born in Bethlehem of Judea'. Herod was a notoriously ruthless king, with grand ambitions and a paranoid fear of any possible rival. The reader expects an ugly clash. Yet this clash comes about in an unexpected way, as light and worship stream into the story from two quite new directions.

Travelling light

The word 'magi' means possessors of mysterious wisdom or hidden knowledge. They are 'wise men', not 'kings', and the text does not mention how many they were, only that they gave three gifts. Here they represent the wealth and wisdom of the Gentile world, the deep yearning and generous worship of the nations beyond Israel, coming to greet God's royal Messiah.

As the magi represent the praise of the Gentiles, the leading of the star suggests that even creation worships. The lights of heaven rise to greet the birth of the Christ, to hail the coming of God's creative love in human flesh. The nations and the skies are moved to worship. How will Israel and her king respond?

We two kings

Herod hears of the child's birth from the magi (v. 2), and apparently wishes to worship too (v. 8). But his deeper reaction is hostile and fearful. He is disturbed and troubled, he gathers his religious leaders for advice, and his plans for action are discreet and devious. Threat, foreboding and danger are in the air, and no one (except the magi, v. 12) does anything to thwart or divert the king. Gentiles can see the reality of Christ's birth, yet Israel seems curiously unaware, while her leader tries to destroy him.

For those who know the gospel story, there are uncomfortable similarities with the events of the Passion. Jesus is called 'king of the Jews'

(v. 2; 27:37). Israel's leaders gather against him (v. 4; 27:1). There are secret plots (v. 7; 26:4, 14–16). The end of the Gospel is foreshadowed in its beginning. Yet even now the wrath of men does not achieve all it plans. God is in control (v. 12), and Jesus' life is secure in his hands.

Threads of prophecy

Much of Matthew's Gospel is like woven cloth. As the lines of the story lead forward, across them run strands from scripture. The narrative is dense with echoes of and allusions to Old Testament themes.

The direct quotation in verse 6, from Micah 5:2, presents Jesus as a new David, born at Bethlehem to be shepherd king for God's people—and that royal theme will be important right through Matthew. Yet surely in this chapter we hear also an echo of Isaiah 60, which speaks of light rising in Israel and Gentiles gathering with gifts: a new era has come, an age of light and hope. Psalm 72 tells of Israel's ideal king, to whom the nations will bring worship and gifts. Numbers 24:17 prophesies the coming of a messianic figure, as the rising of a new star.

Matthew (who knew the Hebrew scriptures better than we do) would have been well aware of these echoes and of the hints they conveyed. His tapestry is rich and whole precisely because of this intersecting weave. He shows us meaning in the story by the light of the scriptures.

But is it all i-magi-nation?

So how could these events have actually happened? For myself, I am intrigued by some Iranian traditions which seem to match this story from the other end of the journey; impressed by some recent and serious astronomical enquiry into the nature of a planetary conjunction in 7BC and of a comet in 5BC; and inclined to think that improbable events become a little more probable when God's Son is born.

But I realize that this account of a wandering star and visiting foreign academics strikes some modern people as far-fetched and incredible. If that is your view, don't overlook the points of Matthew's story: that the coming of Jesus is important enough for nations and creation to honour him, for tyrant thrones to tremble, and for all the glories of scripture to be recalled.

FOR THOUGHT

'The hinge of all history hangs on the door of a Bethlehem stable.'

Anon

THREAT & PRESERVATION

This sombre story displays the shadowy side of human power. Herod shows with awful clarity that kings of his ilk fall far short of God's ideal. Israel needs a new kind of ruler. So Jesus is preserved, kept safe from the anger and harshness of the Herod kings, so that the true rule of God might one day be seen and known in him.

Directed by dreams

Joseph is portrayed in these chapters as a dreamer (1:20; 2:13, 19, 22). God helped him turn his fears into action by shaping and speaking through his dreams. This may be another echo of the Old Testament. There was another Joseph, long before (Genesis 37—50), whose dreams helped to preserve the Jewish people in hard times. Matthew may be hinting that the story of Jesus breathes new life into that episode. Jesus lives out and sums up the history of his people, as he too is kept safe in Egypt.

Leader to liberty

That first period in Egypt, more than a thousand years before, ended with the Exodus. Moses, the leader and lawgiver chosen by God, brought the Jewish people across the desert to the promised land. In these chapters of Matthew, the parallels between Jesus' story and that of Moses come thick and fast. Both were threatened at birth by an evil king (2:12–15; Exodus 2) and came out of Egypt to Palestine (2:21; Exodus 12—13). Both passed through water (3:13–17; Exodus 14) and spent time in the desert (4:1–11; Exodus 16—17). To climax this set of parallels, both taught Israel from a mountain top (Matthew 5; Exodus 20). The links are not all precise. Jesus is not exactly a new Moses. Yet he is destined to be a new leader, a lawgiver and liberator for all in Israel who will follow him. Ancient hopes and dreams will take fresh form. There will be a new journey to freedom.

Fulfilment formula

Three times in this section Matthew includes a scripture quotation, underlining the varied ways in which his story of Jesus 'fulfils' the Old Testament.

Verse 15 is taken from Hosea 11:1, which recalls Israel's special relationship with God, as a child guided by a loving Father. Jesus gives fresh vitality and meaning to that relationship: God's love focuses on him with a special intimacy, yet through him many others are able to call God 'Father'.

Verse 18 is from Jeremiah 31:15, remembering the distress of the Jewish exile in Babylon, six centuries before Jesus. The misery inflicted then by a foreign army has come again through Herod. While kings like Herod rule, the agony of exile is still present and the people still need release.

The snippet at the end of verse 23 is a mystery. Nothing in the Old Testament reads quite like this, and we do not know which text Matthew had in mind. However, Isaiah 11:1 is a strong possibility— a passage about a coming ruler, a 'branch' from David's line. The Hebrew for branch is 'nezer', a resonance with the name 'Nazareth'. When Jesus goes there, this reflects his royal potential.

Innocents of Bethlehem

The killing of the children of Bethlehem was a dreadful atrocity for which there are no quick or comforting explanations. They had done nothing to deserve it. The era into which Jesus was born was as bitter and brutal as our own. Innocent people got hurt; justice was not always honoured; rulers could be ruthless and proud. That reality remains, and the suffering continues. Yet when the adult Jesus deliberately faced the harshness, in his own crucifixion, he showed that even wrath and violence cannot overcome or extinguish the love of God.

Destination Galilee

Herod died in 4BC, and the worst of his sons, Archelaus, inherited Judea, the area around Jerusalem and Bethlehem. Galilee, in the north, was a calmer place. Here Jesus grew up and began his ministry.

FOR REFLECTION

Wherever we see refugees, violent rule and untimely death, we are in touch with the gospel story. We can pray, and we may be able to offer practical help. If we serve Jesus, these things concern us.

5

STREAM *of* RENEWAL

The story leaps forward. Matthew does not tell us how far, although it is clear from other Gospels that Jesus was about thirty years old when he started his public ministry.

Voice in the wilderness

John comes suddenly on to the scene. The story has not mentioned him until now. He comes as a man with a message. We have heard of Jesus the king. Now John proclaims the kingdom, the rule and realm of God. It is near, he says, and so people must respond, urgently and deliberately (v. 2). Lives must be made new, commitments be reviewed, patterns of behaviour changed, quarrels mended, neighbours loved, hearts set right with the ways of God.

The Gospel describes John (v. 3) with words drawn from Isaiah 40:3. This Old Testament passage told of the ending of Israel's exile; it was a word of comfort and freedom, of rejoicing and hope. God would travel ahead of his people and lead them into a fuller experience of his goodness and grace. This is John's message too. He echoes the summons of Isaiah. He speaks as a roadmaker, preparing the way, calling the Jewish people to the path where they will discover in new ways the leadership and love of God.

Town and country

John lives rough (v. 4). He is an outsider, whose dress and diet label him as a figure on the fringe of society. He resembles the Old Testament prophet Elijah (1 Kings 17; 2 Kings 1:8), who also appears in the desert, lives a rough and remote life, and yet shakes the whole land with the force of his message.

For John gathers a crowd. His fame spreads and people from the towns of Palestine flock to him. His message of fresh beginnings, of lives turned into new directions, of water that washes away the past and rinses clean for God, proved highly attractive. Many in Israel brought their desires and aspirations to live a better and more godly life down to the Jordan, and plunged into the current of John's renewal movement.

Yet John remains a man on the edge. There is no obvious link between his activity and the worship and sacrifice practised at the Jerusalem Temple. It almost seems that he is deliberately critical and subversive about what is available there. He offers prayer, preaching and signs of God's grace, far away from the main centre and recognized leaders of Israel's religion. There will surely be a collision when the two parties meet.

Troubler of Israel

We shall have to say more about the Sadducees and Pharisees at 16:1 and 5:20 respectively. They correspond roughly to the 'chief priests and scribes' of 2:4. Here John greets them sharply and aggressively, as threats and potential traitors to the renewal for which he strives (vv. 7–12). As he speaks, three fresh aspects of his message come into view.

- **John divides the nation.** His challenge splits Israel into two. Birth rights are not enough: there must be deeds to match. There is an uncomfortable separation in view.

- **John expects judgment.** His language is urgent and dramatic. He senses that through his preaching and in his own time the searching judgment of God is at work.

- **John looks for someone greater to come.** He believes that God will do a greater work than he has done, that the Holy Spirit will flow in Israel, mightier than all his preaching and baptism. There is a 'stronger one' coming who will make God's people clean and whole. Both the renewing and the divisive aspects of John's ministry will be carried forward with fresh power and fuller purpose.

Preparing the way

So Matthew presents John as the herald and forerunner for Jesus. He announces the kingdom (v. 2) in the very same words that Jesus will use (4:17). He prepares the way (v. 3) that the Lord will take. He tells of a 'stronger one' to come, through whom the Holy Spirit will refresh and stir Israel's life. The stage is set for the stronger one to appear.

PRAYER

God, let me be a roadmaker for Jesus, living and speaking so that hearts will open to his life and power.

6 MATTHEW 3:13–17

IMMERSED *into* NEW RESPONSIBILITY

When the adult Jesus steps into the gospel story, he comes first to ask for baptism (v. 13). He comes from Galilee, where he has grown up, to ally himself with the movement of renewal and hope that John has launched. The values and vision that John has been preaching will be the launching pad for his own ministry.

We have been led to look for a strong man of the Spirit, but Jesus does not make a dramatic entrance. He does not stride powerfully across the earth; he approaches humbly. The Spirit will come upon Jesus through his baptism. He will indeed be strong. Yet, as elsewhere in his ministry, his strength comes through apparent weakness, and his service touches others through his gentleness and humility.

The right way round

As Jesus approaches John, there is a brief conversation between them; only Matthew of the four Gospels mentions this exchange. John raises a question: he tries to prevent what Jesus is doing. 'Why should you need to receive baptism?' he asks (v. 14). Surely that is for sinners (3:6). Things should be the other way round: Jesus should baptize John.

Jesus replies that this is the way to 'fulfil all righteousness' (v. 15). Accepting baptism is the right thing for him to do. Matthew's Gospel portrays Jesus as constantly concerned for what is right. Here at the start it is important that he identify with the people he comes to serve, that he show his solidarity with them and immerse himself in their hopes and needs.

In baptism Jesus embarks deliberately on a long and hard path of righteousness. He commits himself, willingly and obediently, to God's mission for the sake of his people. In this way he will bring about 'all righteousness', for others as well as himself, as he carries forward the just and loving purpose of God.

Vision and voice

Matthew describes only very briefly what Jesus sees and hears at his baptism, but the words are filled with meaning and promise.

The Spirit comes upon him. John has already spoken of the

'stronger one' baptizing with the Spirit. Now Jesus receives the Spirit, not as an exclusive personal possession, but so that he may share the Spirit's life with those he serves, that he may cleanse and flood other people's lives with God's goodness.

The picture of the Spirit descending as a dove, as Jesus rises from the water, hints at the creation story in Genesis 1:2. The Spirit of God hovered over the face of the waters, bringing life out of the depths. Now the Spirit hovers again, breathing fresh life into the world through Jesus. A new work of creation is happening. Through the coming ministry of Jesus, the world will be renewed from within.

The voice from above, 'This is my Son, the beloved, in whom I am well pleased' (v. 17), echoes the Old Testament, casting Jesus—it seems—in three important roles. The first echo, 'my Son', is from Psalm 2:7, where God greets Israel's anointed king. 'In whom I am well pleased' recalls Isaiah 42:1, and portrays Jesus as God's Servant, the same servant figure who is graphically described in Isaiah 53 as suffering to make others whole. Finally, 'the beloved one' takes the reader to Genesis 22, and shows Jesus in the part of Isaac, the child of promise who is taken to sacrificial death.

Counting the cost

Three times, then, the text shows Jesus as the apple of God's eye, giving God pleasure and serving God's purpose. Yet in two of these motifs we see the awful cost of his ministry. He will be a suffering Messiah, a sacrificed Son, a Servant King.

How fully did Jesus see all this as he looked forward to his work for God? We cannot know for sure, but some points are very clear. Jesus found through his baptism a deeper assurance of his Father's presence and power. It gave him a calm confidence, a vocation to mission and service. Perhaps he also heard a warning that what he would achieve for God would not be easily gained; it would come at a cost. For it seems that he had begun to understand the costly path ahead, when he tested his vocation in the desert—as the next portion of the Gospel shows.

PRAYER

Lord Jesus Christ, may our baptism in your name
assure us of God's love and beckon us without fear
to follow your path of service.

PROBED & PROVEN

The spiritual 'high' of baptism does not last. The Holy Spirit leads Jesus into the desert for a time of testing (v. 1). The scene is strange, for the Spirit urges Jesus forward, and the evil one waits to tempt him. From one point of view this is a period of proving, as Jesus clarifies in his own mind the way in which his vocation and service must develop. From another angle this is a vulnerable moment, a time when Jesus' ministry could be skewed and distorted before it starts.

This spell of withdrawal, of rural isolation from the normal routines and contacts of human life, may seem to offer the stillness of calm retreat. But the desert is a rough, hard place—a battleground. Here Jesus might be driven back from following God's way; or it could be a place of advance, of consolidation and assurance in his Father's calling and love. From our Christian perspective it seems impossible that Jesus could have succumbed and fallen. But if we think too quickly along these lines, we miss the sharpness, the reality and the attraction of the choices he had to face.

Naming the opposition

Jesus' mysterious opponent is named in three different ways. 'Devil' (v. 1) and 'Satan' (v. 10) are really the same word. One is Greek, the other Hebrew. Both mean 'opponent', 'slanderer' or 'accuser'—the person who stands opposite you in a courtroom, challenges your integrity and tries to destroy your good name. This period in the wilderness challenges the integrity of Jesus' relationship with God, and threatens his good name and title as God's Servant Son.

The third word is 'tempter' (v. 3)—one who tries, tests and probes the quality of his target. Ultimately that probing becomes a proving: it reveals and confirms the quality and commitment that are in Jesus.

If you really are who you say you are...

There are three temptations in Matthew's account. Each of them explores—and undermines—the relationship that Jesus has with his Father. The baptism brought a word of assurance, 'This is my Son' (3:17). The tempter turns that assurance into a question, 'If you are the Son of God' (vv. 3, 6).

The first temptation asks Jesus to use his relationship with God to meet his own needs, and satisfy his hunger (vv. 2–4). Jesus replies that obeying God's word is even more basic for life than bodily food. Following God's commands will nourish him as fully as he needs (John 4:34). The Spirit has not been given him for his own comfort, but to bring mercy and love to others.

The second trial invites Jesus to prove God's love with a stunt that would be spectacular but entirely useless (vv. 5–6). If he leapt off the Temple tower and landed without injury, then he would know—and so might others—that God was looking after him. Jesus responds that God is not to be dealt with in that way. It is not our business to check on his love, except by following his will and way.

The third test suggests that Jesus mix his commitment to God with some hard-headed realism (vv. 8–9). If he wants influence over people and nations, let him honour the devil, who rules them. Jesus does not pause to question the limits, nature and intention of that rule. He speaks about the heart of his commitment, that God alone is worthy of worship, loyalty and service. Jesus has no right or desire to dilute or compromise that claim.

Signposts from scripture

In all three temptations Jesus quotes the Old Testament to justify his resistance. All three texts come from Deuteronomy (8:3; 6:16; 6:13), from chapters that look back on Israel's exodus journey as a period of testing by God. Jesus is tried as Israel was tried. The values and priorities that God taught her then will shape and direct his life—not for himself alone, but for his people. He enters into Israel's history, that he may lead her to God's destiny. He becomes as she was, that she may know the nearness to God that he enjoys.

Yet scripture can be misused, and then it can mislead. The devil quotes scripture too (v. 6; from Psalm 91:11–12). A text without a context is a pretext. Put another way, if our use of a verse or passage leads us away from the main tenor and emphasis of the Bible, it is probably doing us more harm than good.

FOR THOUGHT AND PRAYER

'Tested as we are, yet without sin' (Hebrews 4:15). Temptations, even those that make us feel ashamed and afraid, are situations that Jesus understands and can help us to handle.

8

MAKING WAVES

The end of the beginning

These verses bring the overture of the Gospel to an end. John is arrested (v. 12)—we do not hear why—and Jesus withdraws to Galilee, possibly to avoid danger himself. He bases himself twenty miles from Nazareth, at Capernaum, a fishing town on the northern shore of the Sea of Galilee. His active ministry is poised to begin.

At this point Matthew inserts another fulfilment quotation, to emphasize that Jesus' arrival in Galilee is a coming of light, hope and gladness. Isaiah 9, from where verses 15–16 are drawn, looks forward to a prince of David's line whose rule will give Israel security and joy. Thus the royal theme, which was so prominent in the birth stories, is underlined once again as Jesus begins his work. The kingdom of God is indeed at hand.

The region is called 'Galilee of the Gentiles' (v. 15; from Isaiah 9:1); indeed the area had been racially mixed in Old Testament times. In Jesus' day it was predominantly Jewish, but was surrounded by a number of Gentile communities. So although Jesus worked mostly among Jewish people (see 10:5–6), Matthew's choice of Old Testament text suggests that the effects of this activity will ripple out much more widely (28:18–20).

Kingdom come

'From that time Jesus began…' (v. 17). A new phase of the Gospel is under way. Many people think that Matthew divides his Gospel into two main sections, one of mission and the other of passion, using this sentence and the one like it at 16:21. (For more detail, see the section 'Matthew's plan' in the Introduction, pp. 13–15.)

'Jesus began to proclaim…'. He repeats the message John had proclaimed (see 3:2). Times are changing. God is at work. People should amend their lives, so as to be ready and to join in. But there is more here than the continuation of John's ministry. There will be a different emphasis to what Jesus does. A powerful and gentle mercy will be at work through him. His words and deeds will display the loving rule of God. Jesus will reach needs and griefs that John did not—as the verses ahead will show.

Networking for God

The first followers of Jesus accept a sketchy job description: 'Follow me, and I will make you fish for people' (v. 19). They come with very little prior warning (John 1:37–42 indicates some earlier contact; even so, this encounter by the seashore is still rather abrupt). They join an enterprise with no premises, no pension scheme and no obvious business plan. Even the uncertainties and dangers of the fishing trade look better than this.

There must have been something magnetic about Jesus. From any perspective he was a charismatic and compelling personality, able to inspire and influence others. He chooses disciples—the word means 'learners'—who will watch what he does and eventually do it themselves (10:1–5). They will be the core of his renewal movement, the community within a community, the heart of Israel's new life, the inner family with whom he will be at home. Jesus did not want to work alone. He wanted others to learn from him and live the life of the kingdom with him.

These encounters at the lakeside remind us that the Christian life often gives a person new directions and new tasks. That still applies today: we do not choose how much of ourselves to give to Christ. There is a serious note in his call that is sometimes urgent, demanding and quite unexpected.

Circuit of mercy

So Jesus goes around Galilee, telling the kingdom and showing its power. Verses 23–25 are only a summary. The chapters ahead give more detail, of his teaching in chapters 5—7, and of his varied healings in chapters 8—9. But the impression is already clear and powerful. He has taken time to be ready. He is marked out by God and anointed with the Spirit (3:16–17). He has understood his vocation and carefully distanced himself from the temptations of preservation, presumption and power (4:1–11). Now his time has come. Light shines in Galilee (vv. 15–16), bright, warm and strong.

FOR THOUGHT AND PRAYER

Jesus is still the light of the minds that know him, the life of the souls that love him, and the strength of the wills that serve him.

9

HONOURS LIST (1)

Hillside preacher

Jesus has been mobbed by an excited and expectant throng (4:25). Now he begins to share his own expectations, the vision for human community, relationships, lifestyle and attitudes that excites him, the way that he wants his followers to live. He climbs to a place where he can be heard, and people come to sit around him (v. 1).

The Sermon on the Mount, as we now call it, runs through chapters 5, 6 and 7. It is one of five major blocks of teaching in Matthew, with its beginning and its end point (7:28—8:1) clearly indicated.

Most of the material in these chapters appears in Luke too: quite a lot comes in the shorter 'Sermon on the Plain' (Luke 6:17–49), but other snippets are spread throughout Luke. So no one knows for sure whether the whole sermon was delivered on a single occasion, or whether Matthew is responsible for gathering it together. Certainly it has an inspiring, searching (and daunting) vision for human living. And if the present order of the material owes something to Matthew, the heart of the vision surely comes from Jesus. This is the teaching on lifestyle that he wanted his friends to follow.

Family rule

Two themes run all the way through the sermon.

- It speaks of God as Father, a figure of love and care, who knows, notices and guides his children. This idea comes many times (5:9, 16, 45, 48; 6:1, 4, 6, 9, 14, 18, 32; 7:11).

- It is about the kingdom of God, God's loving rule. We have heard (4:17, 23) that Jesus came preaching the kingdom. This sermon fills out the detail: here is what it means to enter, experience and enjoy God's good and holy reign. The kingdom is mentioned many times over (5:3, 10, 19–20; 6:10, 33; 7:21).

The 'when' of the kingdom is not at all straightforward. Jesus often talks as if the kingdom is ahead, a distant destination to aim and strive for (5:20). Yet the sermon is itself actually about kingdom living, life that reflects God's character and concerns here and now (5:48). So this kingdom is both now and not yet, here and not fully here, arrived and still on its way. The kingdom is like seed—already filled with life, but still to show its full potential.

Hallowing the humble

The sermon begins with blessing—as if Jesus looks around him and rejoices in the people he sees. These are the ones on whom God's favour rests. They should be joyful, for God is at work among them and within them. They are not great in themselves, but they are people whose lives are open for the blessing of God.

The eight 'beatitudes' (the word is Latin for 'blessings') come in verses 3–10, one per verse. Verses 11–12 repeat at greater length the point made in verse 10, and conclude the whole section. The point of the beatitudes is not to select eight different groups of people and to offer eight different reasons why God should bless them. It is a broad-brush sketch of the followers of Jesus, a pen-picture of the kind of people whose lives reflect the kingdom of God and who enjoy the blessings of that kingdom.

The picture offers an unusual view of human living. These are not the regular patterns of behaviour that make for power, progress and popularity. Something deeper than mere worldly fortune is involved. This is Christian character and conduct, the sort of outlook and behaviour that God honours, the kind of human life in which the joy and goodness of God will be at home.

Tip of the iceberg

Most of the blessings look ahead: 'they *will* be comforted… they *will* inherit…' (vv. 4, 5). The blessing is now, but the perspective is future. These people are favoured by God, but they do not yet see the full glory of his love. God has much more to show and to give them. 'Theirs is the kingdom of heaven' (vv. 3, 10), but the full reality of the kingdom is only beginning to be seen.

FOR THOUGHT AND PRAYER

'Through our lives and by our prayers, your kingdom come.'

Iona Community

HONOURS LIST (2)

Old, yet ever new

The beatitudes are striking, but not entirely new. Jesus regularly used Old Testament teaching, sometimes giving it a thrust or angle of his own. So verse 5 reflects Psalm 37:11, for example, and verse 8 reflects Psalm 24:3–4. There is an important link to Isaiah 61, which speaks of good news to the poor and broken-hearted (61:1) and comfort to mourners (61:2); they will be filled beyond their dreams (61:6), and God will turn their shame into rejoicing (61:7). In a similar way Matthew's beatitudes tell of blessing to the poor in spirit (v. 3), comfort to mourners (v. 4), the hungry being filled (v. 6), and people who were scorned bursting out in joy (vv. 11–12). The same issues and hopes are present in Isaiah and in Matthew. Interestingly, Isaiah 61 is the scripture that Jesus read in the Nazareth synagogue, at the start of his ministry, as his 'mission statement'. Only Luke (4:16–21) records that episode, but here we see how Jesus' first teaching in Matthew's Gospel, from the same period of his life, draws on the same material.

Mission of hope

So the beatitudes outline Jesus' mission in Israel. He came as herald of God, moved by God's Spirit, to bring good news to the distressed, hope in place of sorrow, a future of promise in place of a difficult and bitter past. He came to people whose lives had been hard, and he wanted to give them a keener and deeper awareness of God's healing love. He sensed that God was stirring in him, that new hopes and prospects were dawning through what he did. He called this 'the kingdom of God'. The blessings Jesus offered were for people who would receive and respond, who brought nothing but their weakness and their hopes, people with whom he could share the love and renewing power of God. These people were indeed blessed. God would use them to spread his grace, and would show them his glory.

Poor, yet making many rich

So what do these blessings say about the Christian life? Who are the people for whom they speak? What is the profile sketched out by Jesus? We work through the beatitudes, verse by verse.

Blessing comes to the poor in spirit (v. 3). They have no inflated opinion of themselves, their achievements or their worth, but look to God as their strength and hope.

Blessed people are able to grieve (v. 4). They are hurt, not only by their own misfortune, but by others' wounds too. They will sorrow for God to be better known in their land.

Kingdom living is not pushy (v. 5). It doesn't rush to grasp and grab at every opening, but takes its turn in the confidence that—though sometimes slow—God is always sure.

Godly people care deeply about what is right, for others as well as for themselves (v. 6). They feel hollow and dry when people are wronged.

Compassion—to notice, help, and support a person in need—is a regular mark of the kingdom (v. 7).

God rejoices in a pure heart, whose motives are genuine, with no hidden deceit or dishonesty (v. 8).

It is blessed to spread peace, bring divided people together, defuse anger and help others to be calm (v. 9).

Finally, true Christian living can lead to persecution (vv. 10–12). Goodness of this kind is not normal; it comes from close association with Jesus. That sometimes bothers other people and makes them resentful. There may be little the Christian can do but to bear the burden and rejoice in the Lord.

Now and then

Life in ancient Palestine was very hard. Following the beatitudes was not easy then, any more than now. But people who take Christ's beatitudes seriously are still liable to find his blessing, in ways that may surprise them. We shall think more about how we follow this teaching as we read Matthew 7:13–29 (pp. 60–61).

FOR THOUGHT AND PRAYER

Can you remember when you last heard or said, 'God bless you'? Those words really mean, 'May God make you a person whose life is ripe for blessing, the kind of person described in the beatitudes.'

TASTE & SEE

Blessed people make a difference. When lives are lived as Jesus teaches, the world is a better place. Other people notice, and feel the benefit. Jesus described this influence in two ways—salt and light.

Spread around

Salt helps food to taste good; it stops meat going rotten. So Christians bring out the best in other people; they help to keep the world wholesome. Yet if they lose the taste of Christ, they're completely useless (v. 13). Perhaps that's a sermon you've heard many times; it reflects common experience and it seems to fit the text. Jesus intended his followers to nourish the world, to sharpen the rich flavours of creation. They would not only be good people themselves; they would help to bring out the wholeness and vitality God had put in others.

Salt losing saltiness seems odd to us. Our table salt cannot lose its saltiness: it's pure, so it's salty all through. But in Jesus' time salt was dug from the ground around desert lakes, and the mixture contained various other crystals too. If the salt got washed out, the residue was indeed fit for nothing except to be used as gravel.

Good salt, however, makes food healthier and tastier. Of course, salt only works if it gets around. It has to circulate. So Christians work best as salt for the world if they are involved in it—if they look on daily work as part of their Christian service, if they spend time with neighbours and relatives as well as with church friends, if they have time to be normal as well as to be religious.

Christians should be 'salt, not honey' (Helmut Thielicke). There is an honest tang about wholesome Christian integrity: salt is clean rather than cosy, whereas honey coats everything, however sour and rough the flavour, with the same artificial film of sweetness, which can leave a sickly taste behind. Agreeing to everything, trying to be all things to all people, can strain us beyond credibility. Being ourselves, where we are and as we are, is what Jesus asks of us.

Light programme

Light is a common theme in the Bible. In the beginning God said, 'Let there be light' (Genesis 1:3). God himself is light (Psalm 27:1;

67:1). The Old Testament spoke of Jerusalem as a light for the whole world. Glory would shine out to beckon the nations, and they would come in peace to worship the God of Israel (Isaiah 2:1–4; Isaiah 60).

Jesus echoed this hope when he spoke of 'a city built on a hill' (v. 14). Jerusalem stood on a ridge: the Jews 'went up' to it year by year on pilgrimage. The life of the Jewish people was meant to be a visual aid for the world, a lighthouse to gather many peoples to God.

Now Jesus puts this responsibility before his followers. He wants them to be radiant with God's goodness. He kindles afresh within Israel the hope of what Israel might be.

Borrowed light

So when Christians read the teaching of Jesus today, we enter into a world of hope that was first Jewish. Jesus invited his hearers to take up the role and heritage God had for Israel. He, above all people, made that heritage real: it focused on him in a unique way. Then, through him, it has spread wider, as millions of Gentiles (non-Jews, including me and possibly you) have come to faith in Jesus. We have joined—as adopted brothers and sisters, as light-bearers for God—the ancient family of faith that started with the Jews.

The situation is complex, of course. Many Jewish people have not joined the Jesus movement. That is one reason why Matthew wrote his Gospel, to show how this movement, which started among the Jews, both spread beyond Judaism and missed a lot of people inside. That is still the situation today. What, then, becomes of the prophecy about light spreading out from Israel? Two answers:

- The prophecy is being fulfilled. The spread of faith in Jesus has drawn many from around the world to worship Israel's God. So we can call Jesus 'the light of the world' (John 8:12; 9:5).

- Yet the task is still going on. There is still plenty of darkness. Jesus still invites his followers to be light for the world, to be luminous with the light we borrow from him. Our actions—our 'good works' (v. 16)—should help other people to see what God is like. Light (like salt) often works best when it works gently and gradually.

PRAYER

May the light of Christ shine for us and through us, gently and clearly, even when we are not aware of it.

RIGHT NOW

Fuller meaning

These verses help us to understand the six paragraphs ahead, to the end of chapter 5. In all six of them Jesus mentions something that 'was said to the people of old' and then offers a fresh approach of his own. The key idea in all of this is the word 'fulfil' (v. 17).

Matthew has already written of Jesus 'fulfilling' Old Testament prophecies (1:23; 4:15 and so on). The life of Jesus brought a new perspective to some prophetic texts. He gave their original meaning a new lease of life; he acted them out in a new way. The old meaning of a prophecy—kingship, for example—was not rubbed out, but Jesus took the text beyond its old meaning to something greater and fuller.

In the Sermon on the Mount, the same thing happens to Israel's ancient law. 'I have come not to abolish, but to fulfil,' says Jesus (v. 17). He takes the commands of the Jewish law and uses them to point to something beyond. He is concerned for the deeper intentions of God that lie behind the law. His teaching does not ignore the old law, but gives it a new dignity and importance.

Still in place

So these verses help Matthew's readers to understand the link between their Christian faith and the Jewish way of life in which many of them had grown up. Christians have not discarded the Jewish law. It is powerful and permanent (v. 18). Christians should not speak as if the law can simply be ignored. It is important to follow the standards it teaches (v. 19). However, the way in which Jesus outlines those standards is fresh and controversial. That is the point of verse 20—but first a word about the two Jewish groups mentioned there, the scribes and the Pharisees.

Legal eagles

The Pharisees were a group of pious Jewish lay people who lived in many of the towns and villages of Palestine. They placed great emphasis on observing the Jewish law, carefully and devotedly, and they tried to encourage others to do the same. They were known for their attention to detail. Scribes were scholars of the Jewish law who knew it well, who spent time and effort in understanding what it meant and explaining how it should be followed. Obviously scribes and Pharisees had important concerns in common, and there would surely be many who belonged to both groups.

These groups clashed with Jesus because he seemed careless about some issues that mattered to them. He claimed that God was working through him, yet he apparently ignored important legal concerns. He broke some of the rules. Scribes and Pharisees—some of them, at least—could not believe that God would honour such a maverick, and they complained about Jesus and to him. We shall read often, throughout the Gospel, of arguments and angry words.

(The sections of the Introduction entitled 'Matthew and Judaism' and 'Matthew's Church', pp. 15–17, explore this issue more fully.)

Righter than right

Jesus has told his followers to value the Jewish law and observe the standards it teaches (vv. 18–19). Now he says that to enter the kingdom, they must do better than the scribes and Pharisees (v. 20).

The scribes and Pharisees could not be beaten in matters of detail; they were the experts. However, the approach Jesus takes is not one of greater detail, but of greater depth. His teaching will be different in style to the finely tuned law codes of the Pharisees and scribes. He will go behind the law, to the intention of God. He will look inside the law, to the attitudes of the human heart. He will reach around the law, and gather it into a double love command, for God and neighbour.

Yet as Jesus does this, the people who follow a traditional approach —scribes and Pharisees—will feel that he speaks against the law. They will think that he scorns and devalues it because he does not handle it in their way. So, as we move to the paragraphs ahead, which outline the 'better righteousness' Jesus expects of his followers, the reader is forewarned: firstly, to realize that Jesus is not departing from the law, but deepening it; secondly, that there will be clashes between these two kinds of teaching, which take such different approaches to deciding what is right.

FOR THOUGHT AND PRAYER

Is there any part of your life where you are committed to God in detail, but need to discover a greater depth in your service and love?

13 MATTHEW 5:21-26, 33-37

FRESH PERSPECTIVES

The six paragraphs in 5:21–48 are known as the 'Six Antitheses'. In each of them Jesus takes an idea or command from the Old Testament and looks at the issue in a new way. 'You have heard that it was said... but I say to you...' is his typical introduction. This approach was not usual in Judaism of the day. Teachers of the law tended to approach the scriptures by using the teaching of their predecessors. The sense of authority in Jesus' words is rather different.

The ingredients of murder

This first antithesis (vv. 21–26) begins with the command not to kill, the sixth of the Ten Commandments from Exodus 20.

Jesus does not look on murder as a rare and unique wrong, a sin like no other. It is the extreme case of a much more common failing. When we nurse and cherish resentment and anger, when we speak with scorn and contempt of a neighbour, when we think of another person as mere low-life, not deserving of common courtesy—this, says Jesus, is the stuff of which murder is made. This kind of attitude can occasionally, and sadly, lead to the taking of life. Whether in an individual heart or in the prejudice and collective memory of a community, this outlook lowers our boundaries of self-control. It blinds us to our proper responsibility for mutual concern and protection. If we live like this, we bring ourselves under the judgment of God.

So Jesus speaks about the importance of settling quarrels. When we worship—and especially when we take communion—we should put our lives under audit. If we are nursing grudges or contributing to feuds and disputes, we may not be properly ready for meeting with God (vv. 23–24). If we learn to settle angry disagreements sooner rather than later, we limit the damage they cause, in time and in eternity (vv. 25–26).

Direct speech

The second and third antitheses belong together, so it is convenient to study the fourth antithesis here (vv. 33–37). This is about truth, the relationship between what we say and what we do. The introductory line (v. 33) summarizes various texts in the Jewish law

(Leviticus 19:12; Deuteronomy 23:21–23). Vows to God are important and should be kept.

Jesus extends that demand to every promise we make and every undertaking we give. Oaths may seem to make some of our truth-telling solemn and important, but the result is that other things we say get devalued. Never think, says Jesus, that God is not involved. Everything we see and touch involves God. It is simpler to tell the truth without needing the support of an oath—to mean what we say and to do what we say. It is wrong to complicate our speech more than this.

Courts of the Lord?

A few years ago I had to testify in court on behalf of the church. The Clerk of Court approached me hesitantly, Bible in hand: 'Will you take the oath?' Should a Christian do this?

Obviously a Christian should be committed to honest speech at all times. Some Christians think that this regular commitment is enough even in court, and they testify without taking an oath. Others reckon the oath a useful way of showing the court—and reminding themselves—that they intend to speak the truth, plainly and directly.

The point of Jesus' teaching is that we are 'on oath' all the time. So far as truthfulness and sincerity are concerned, all Christian speech is 'on the record'. If we learn that habit in regular daily life, it will be likely to sustain us in any crises and dilemmas we meet, where truthfulness seems an awkward and unattractive choice. People who are trustworthy make a difference: others start trusting and copying them.

Inside view

So Jesus is shifting the emphasis in the ancient law. When he speaks of murder, he goes inside the law to the motives and attitudes that shape the action. When he talks about truth, he uses the ancient command as a signpost that points beyond truthful oaths to a simple and total habit of truthful speech.

FOR THOUGHT AND PRAYER

God of truth and love, give me a truthful tongue and a healing heart. Teach me the habit of honesty and the art of reconciliation. In the name of Jesus Christ. Amen.

14 MATTHEW 5:27–32

An HONOURABLE ESTATE

The second and third antitheses belong together. Both concern relations between men and women. Respect, protection, loyalty and self-discipline should shape the way we treat one another.

One thing leads to another

The command not to commit adultery is the seventh of the Ten Commandments (Exodus 20:14). The approach Jesus takes is very similar to his teaching about the murder command. He goes behind the action itself to the attitude and motivation. Adultery comes, says Jesus, not as a bolt from the blue, but as one of a chain of events. One thing leads to another. For a man to look at a woman 'desiring or imagining a sexual relationship with her' (D. Hagner) is often the first link in the chain. Jesus calls that inner intention—selfish, demeaning and impatient as it is—'adultery in the heart'.

Jesus speaks about strategies of avoidance. Temptations sometimes come without prior warning, but we do not have to make them welcome. The strong language of verses 29–30 means, 'Avoid situations that will lead you into serious sin.' It is better to make sacrifices in our routine or lifestyle than to shipwreck our character and faith—quite apart from the other people who might get hurt.

Responsible relationships

Women of Jesus' time were at a disadvantage, socially and legally, liable to be the weaker party in a situation of pressure, and suspect in a situation of scandal. Jesus tells men to respect women, to allow a woman the integrity of her own person and personality, and to take proper responsibility for their own conduct as men.

Of course society has changed since Jesus' time, and in many settings men and women mix easily and equally. Responsibility for right relationships must be taken on both sides. That is not to say that women must be more responsible and men may be less so; we all owe one another the security that comes from full and fair respect.

To have and to hold

Jesus begins in verse 31 with a command from Deuteronomy 24:1–4.

In Old Testament society, where men had most of the power, this law offered some limited protection to a divorced woman. There had to be a reason for the divorce, she had to be given a legal document, and the husband could not reclaim her later. Jesus again goes inside the law, to its aim and purpose, which were to protect the marriage bond and particularly to protect the wife. He tells men to honour their marriage vows, to accept the responsibility and permanence of their commitment.

This approach offered better security to the woman than was sometimes the way in Judaism. As long as she remained faithful, she could not be thrown aside for a trivial reason, or for a younger or prettier candidate. This created more scope for marriage to be a partnership of dignity and trust.

(The phrase 'except... unchastity' is unique to Matthew's Gospel. See comment on Matthew 19:9, page 159.)

Hurts and dreams

Marriage has become a very fragile institution in our time. Plenty of people, including many Christians, have to pick up the pieces of their own (and their children's) self-confidence when a home divides. Perhaps our pastoral responsibility for one another includes the following issues.

- Taking our own vows seriously. Being patient when problem spells arise. Seeking help if (or better before) real damage occurs.

- Being gentle with friends who limp away from collapsed marriages. We cannot know how difficult it was, nor how hard they tried to hold it together. They need friends to listen rather than judge.

- Offering careful marriage preparation to young adults.

- Helping teenagers to realize that sex is meant to be respected as well as enjoyed. It was designed to happen within lifelong committed relationship.

- Learning to forgive one another (and ourselves) as deeply as God forgives us.

PRAYER

May God, in whom are purity, pleasure and peace, help us to love and cherish the people he gives us.

15

COPING *with* HOSTILITY

Striking out

The command about eyes and teeth, from Exodus 21:24, concerns compensation for personal injury. This apparently rough law aimed to limit the amount of revenge that was exacted, to prevent vengeance turning into vendetta. Apparently, by the time of Jesus people often paid compensation in cash.

The change Jesus makes is to move from measured and limited retaliation to non-retaliation. He tells his followers not to seek revenge for physical injury, for seizure of property, or for loss of time and dignity. The Christian does not insist on personal rights or struggle to avenge every wound. We are prepared to be hurt and exploited, rather than to hurt and exploit others.

The illustrations—of a demeaning insult, a poor man being humiliated in court, a soldier's demand—give the impression of a society where might is right, where harsh men rule and good people get hurt. Jesus says, 'Don't join in. Show a different way.'

How literally should Christians take these commands today? Should a Christian contest an unjust redundancy, or resist a mugging? Probably we should, if the struggle is going to do any good, and if we can see it through without behaving just like our opponents. The issue Jesus highlights is that when we think of our rights, our protection and our dues, we may become bitter, aggressive and vindictive, and repay aggression in its own coin—tit for tat, like for like, eye for eye, tooth for tooth. Sometimes there is no middle way: the only Christian way is the path of non-resistance.

Just like God

The Old Testament does not actually say 'and hate your enemy' (v. 43), although neighbour love always seems easier when we can limit its reach to include chiefly people of our own sort. This paragraph in Matthew stretches the command to include everybody— even, indeed especially, the people who make life hard for us. Pray for them, do them a good turn, treat them decently, surprise them with the love of Christ. There are two motives.

The first is to be like God (vv. 45, 48). God sends good weather to just and unjust people alike. The rain and the sunshine fall on every garden in town, not only on the land that belongs to righteous people. Followers of Jesus should be complete and open in their care, just as God is.

The second motive is to be different (vv. 46–47). There is nothing unusual about loving our friends and greeting those who are good to us. Everybody does that. Christians will be salt and light in the world only if they show a better way, if they extend their love and care to the people they do not like.

Loving enemies can be difficult; some enemies do not want our love. Then we have to be content with 'praying for our persecutors' (v. 44). But if we want genuine chances to meet old enemies with kindness and friendship, we shall probably be able to find them.

Peaceful protest?

A man I regard highly was a conscientious objector during the Second World War. He is one of a very large company of Christians, across the world, who apply this teaching of Jesus to public issues and believe that a Christian should decline to share in military action. Another Christian friend, of deep and generous faith, reckoned it his duty to serve in military uniform during that same war, but became quickly involved in Christian efforts at reconciliation and friendship when the war ended.

There is no agreed solution of this issue. We live in a fallen world. Many people think that the best way to uphold justice and protect the weak is to resist aggression and to fight where necessary. Christians who think like this may still be gentle and calm in their personal relationships. They may also try to exert an influence for good, when decisions are taken about how and where to use force.

Others feel that armed force always causes more trouble than it solves, and that Jesus' teaching should be received and obeyed, simply and directly, in every sphere of life.

The language of being 'perfect' (v. 48) sets a high, indeed an impossible, standard. Yet we need to aim high if we are to bear suffering with the grace of Christ, and to meet hate with love in his name.

FOR THOUGHT AND PRAYER

*Where could you start handling disagreements and disputes
in a different, and more Christlike, way?*

COVER YOUR FAITH

This section has three short paragraphs. Each is arranged in a similar way, and each has a similar message: there should be modesty in the way we practise our faith.

Better righteousness

Verse 1 is a heading for the whole section: 'Beware of practising your piety before others.' Matthew's Greek word for 'piety' is 'righteousness', the same word used in 5:20. The antitheses of 5:21–48 were about right relationships; these verses are about right religious observance.

Religion that we make obvious to other people is liable to get overlooked by God. God prefers that there be privacy in our service. We should not use our piety to seek respect or honour from other people, but should be content to serve and honour God for his own sake—to give service simply because it is worth giving, rather than because anyone will notice.

This principle affects three areas of religious life: charitable and religious giving (vv. 2–4); prayer (vv. 5–6); and fasting (vv. 16–18).

Private account

'Do not let your left hand know what your right hand is doing' (v. 3). This is the knack of giving so that only the recipient finds out what has been given, and even the recipient may not know where it came from. There is privacy and secrecy in our giving, and contentment in knowing that the money is being well used. God shares the secret with us, and will honour the gift in his own way.

Prayer cell

Prayer should be private too (vv. 5–6). Jesus is not opposing the idea of meeting for prayer. This is about individual prayer. The point is that it should be truly individual, between the believer and God. Prayer is not a spectator sport. If we need to pray alone, we should find a place where we can be alone. God will be there, seeing clearly what we do, and will recognize and reward the faith and intentions we bring.

(The pattern of prayer Jesus gives, the words we call the Lord's Prayer, are in 6:7–15: see next reading.)

Fast track

Jews in the time of Jesus fasted at certain main festivals. Some Pharisees (see Luke 18:12) adopted a weekly pattern of fasts to express their devotion. Jesus does not condemn this. Indeed, he seems to assume that his followers will fast, but he urges them to fast inconspicuously. There should be nothing in their appearance or behaviour to advertise what they are doing (vv. 16–18).

Fasting is not (so far as I can see) much discussed in Christian circles these days. Perhaps we all fast on the quiet, in obedience to Matthew 6. Or has the Church largely lost sight of this tradition, and forgotten that we might be able to deepen our love for God through voluntary self-discipline?

Faith in acting

All three paragraphs urge Christians not to be like 'hypocrites'. The word meant a stage actor, whose real self was concealed, who pretended to be someone different. To give, pray and fast chiefly in order to be noticed is a piece of hypocrisy. It looks as if it's being done for God, but the real target is human praise.

The best and truest reward of real piety is that it receives what it wants. People who give want the money to be well used for God; those who pray want their prayers to be part of God's good purpose; believers who fast want that sacrifice to bear fruit in godly living. These results often come about in ways that only God fully knows, which we shall not discover this side of eternity.

Shining lights

So how does secret religion square with lights that shine so that others may see (5:16)? The shining is righteous action, 'good works' (5:16), whereas 6:1–18 is about righteous observance. The seeds of prayer and faith that we sow, we should hide. The fruit that we bear, other people will notice anyway.

PRAYER

Lord Jesus Christ, hallow our desires and shape our habits, so that we may serve chiefly out of love for you.

When You Pray...

The Lord and the prayer

This is the Church's model prayer, pattern for all our Christian praying from the earliest times until now. This prayer comes from Jesus. The mix of ideas—the Fatherhood of God, the coming of the kingdom, the emphasis on forgiveness—matches the message of Jesus as we find it elsewhere in the Gospels. Here, in the form of a prayer, are the issues and concerns that mattered most deeply to him.

Some prayers use grand and stirring language. This prayer has depth and glory through its brief and direct way of approaching God. There is nothing casual or irreverent here, but there is nothing elaborate either. This clear, compact yet profoundly worshipful style of prayer is typical of Jesus, who knew God deeply and intimately, and could speak of faith plainly and simply.

The disciples and the prayer

This is a prayer for disciples. Jesus has spoken to his friends as 'children of their Father in heaven' (5:9, 45, 48). This prayer begins from within that family circle, and says 'Our Father'. The prayer is plural—'we, us, our'. This prayer represents a group—the Church—that serves God together. There is a strong reminder that we, as disciples, should reflect God's forgiveness in our own forgiving (vv. 14–15). Only a community committed to good relationships can do that.

Heaven and earth

'Our Father in heaven' is the prayer's point of entry. It comes into God's presence in confidence, as one of the family, yet knowing that God sees and rules a larger family and a wider world than ours. To draw near to God is to enter a broad panorama of grace and love, and to see our own concerns against that greater background.

After meeting God as 'our Father in heaven', the prayer yearns for heaven to touch earth, and for earth to be like heaven. The Christian prays that God's name would be hallowed, God's kingdom come and God's will be done, on earth as truly as in heaven. May God's praise, power and purpose be known among us. Yet even while we pray, our own daily worship hallows God's name, our faith rejoices tó serve him, and our obedience seeks to follow his will. Today's service is part of the dawning of God's kingdom on earth.

Today and tomorrow

More than that, today's requests are part of the Church's longing for that kingdom. The second half of the prayer concerns everyday struggles. Yet it sees the claims and pressures of every new day—our need for provision, pardon and power—against the grand horizon of the kingdom's coming.

- Bread is a regular physical need, but also a signpost and foretaste of the great family banquet in God's nearer presence, the kingdom company for which the Church hopes and prays.

- Forgiveness concerns the current account of sins we accumulate day by day, but also looks ahead to God's great and final judgment, when all the richness of God's forgiving love will be tasted, deep and full.

- Temptation is a daily reality, and the Christian prays not to succumb. (Realistically that should often be a prayer to be spared the battle.) Yet even everyday temptation is part of the great tussle between good and evil, whose final outcome is in the hands of God.

Hopeful and practical

So this is a hopeful prayer. It is also a practical prayer, seeing the daily horizon, the struggle to get to tomorrow. The two perspectives fuse—today and eternity, daily concerns and kingdom hopes. The prayer brings them together. We hope now, and we serve the world ahead; we live now, and we long for what we cannot yet see. Hope and practicality, confidence and obedience, faith and service, shape our praying and our being—until we see God face to face.

(You may have missed the 'kingdom, power and glory'. This line is not in the oldest manuscripts, and was not in Matthew's original wording. It got added later, as the prayer was used in the churches.)

FOR THOUGHT AND PRAYER

Pray the Lord's Prayer, in the words you know best. Pause to reflect on each line. If you take a long time on any line, then stop. Let that be your prayer for today. Come back to the rest another time.

18 MATTHEW 6:19–34

LONG-TERM INVESTMENT

Matthew 6:1–18 was about piety; these verses are about property. One theme remains the same—an invitation to trust God. In 6:1–18, can we trust God enough to pray, give and fast secretly? Then, here, can we trust God enough to use our money in ways that serve the kingdom?

Making a pile

Instinctively we stack up resources against a rainy day. It is practical, and also biblical: be like an ant, work hard for winter (Proverbs 6:6–8). Jesus does not say, 'Do not work.' He does say, 'Do not accumulate for its own sake. Do not invest in the wrong place.' Anything stored on earth is fragile—liable to damp, decay and declining markets. Heaven is a better place to invest. Treasure there is secure, not subject to the ravages of bugs and burglars.

For we tend to invest our emotional energy in the place where our material resources are stored. We give ourselves to the causes to which we are already committed (v. 21). Only people who invest in God's kingdom are likely to get really involved in God's kingdom.

So how does one invest in heaven? The answer appears to be, 'Follow the teaching of the Sermon on the Mount—even if it costs us financially or materially.' What is given or lost for Jesus' sake, in situations where the path of Christian duty is plain but costly, is not really lost: it is securely invested.

What you see is what you give

People in Jesus' time did not think of the eye as a window, but as a lamp, radiating light from inside the body. If your lamp, says Jesus, is generous in outlook—if your eye lights cheerfully, sincerely and kindly on opportunities for giving and sharing—then there is bright and generous light within (v. 22). If, on the other hand, the eye is mean and tight in its outlook, that suggests a dull and narrow-sighted personality. So our vision, our ability to spot occasions for kindness and generosity, is a sign of our inner self.

Silver service

Obviously no servant can take orders from two bosses. Wires get hopelessly crossed. In the end, the servant has to choose which master should take priority (v. 24).

So there is no effective way to serve the constant call of mammon (the word means 'wealth') and the way of God. They regularly lead in different directions. Mammon is only concerned with the level of our bank account; God always has other things in mind. There is only one sensible way to handle the situation: decide which one to follow, and stick with that decision.

Worried, of Galilee

All these challenges would concern many who heard Jesus. 'What if I take him seriously?' they would say. 'How will I survive? How will my basic needs be met?' Jesus explains himself in three ways.

- First, he looks at nature (vv. 26, 28–30). Birds find food and the grass is clothed with colourful flowers. They do not worry, but God provides for them. So neither need you worry. God cares for you even more than for them.

- Second, Jesus reflects for a moment on worry (v. 27). Anxiety by itself never achieves anything. Experience can teach us that.

- Third, Jesus asks his friends to consider what is really important. Life is more than food and clothing (v. 25). To forget this is a faith-less outlook. God, who controls the great issues of life, can surely provide for his children's everyday needs (v. 32).

The main thing

So the passage leaves the reader with one major concern (v. 33)—to seek God's kingdom, to come into its way of working, and to follow its pattern of right living. Jesus has not given an exact plan for the Christian use of money. He has encouraged his followers to use their money with heaven in mind, to put God first in material matters, confident that God will honour those who honour him. The last verse (v. 34) is more than homespun wisdom. The point is not just that tomorrow is another day. Tomorrow is God's day, a day to taste God's faithfulness, love and care. That is our reason not to worry.

PRAYER

Lord, show us ways of investing in your kingdom that will help us to invest our hearts there too.

NEIGHBOURS & GOD

The theme running through these verses is relationships with people around us and with God.

Clarity begins at home

We are often ready to form opinions on the people we deal with. 'Be careful' is the warning here. Of course Jesus expected people to use their common sense: there is a place for discernment, for dealing wisely and appropriately with the different people we meet (7:6, 15–20). But we need to deal humbly and patiently too. Critical gossip, comment that demeans and destroys, interference without love, and opinion without knowledge—all of this is ruled out.

Jesus' story about specks and logs (vv. 3–5) sounds like a memory of the carpenter's shop: eyes sting and stream as the dust flies around. The story applies, of course, to judging: we have to deal with our own failings first. Clarity begins at home: the one person whose faults we can tackle is ourself. Maybe later, our experience will leave us in a position to offer help to others (v. 5). But the main point is to avoid judgments we are not in a position to make. In particular we should avoid trying to do God's job for him. True assessment of a person's faith and worth is a judgment only God can make.

Pearls in the pigsty

Verse 6 probably concerns people who are hostile and antagonistic to us and our faith and simply want us to get out of their hair. In that sort of situation, we should go. We shall not convince them of the worth and wisdom of the gospel; they will just discredit and despise us. There is a time to break contact—and give God a chance to approach these people in a different way at another time.

Child benefit

Christians deal not only with neighbours and with our own failings. We have a bond with God and access to God in prayer. Ask, seek, knock. Keep in the habit; keep contact; for God answers when people call and gives good things when his children ask (vv. 7–11).

The line of argument in verses 9–11 is very similar to that in 6:26

and 6:28–30. The aim is to reassure followers of Jesus who are troubled or pressured. The atmosphere is pastoral, comforting, encouraging, showing how the disciple's relationship with God gives help and strength for earthly trials. Jesus appeals to ordinary experience (birds and flowers in 6:26–30, family relationships here), then raises his hearers' sights beyond the ordinary to God. 'How much more' will God care for, answer and provide for those who trust him as Father (6:26, 30; 7:11).

The Sermon on the Mount put many strenuous demands before the followers of Jesus, both in Jesus' own time and among Matthew's first readers, and it continues to challenge everyone who reads the Gospel today. Yet it is not simply a list of instructions, God's wish-list for human behaviour. It is much more intimate than that.

This is family talk, for people who are learning to trust God as Father with the same hope and confidence that Jesus himself had. This is for people who love and serve as sons and daughters, who are able to live in the assurance that they are guarded and supported by the love of God.

This is also kingdom teaching, about heaven's power touching earth. There is a new world dawning. Followers of Jesus are invited to look at the kingdom from the inside, to taste its joys even now, to live with faith and to trust without fear. They are indeed blessed (5:3–12).

Good as gold

The formula, 'Do to others as you would have them do to you' (v. 12) has been called the Golden Rule. Ideas like this are found in many religions and philosophies. It is basic to human understanding, that this is how life ought to be.

We hear that this sentence sums up the commands of the Old Testament: 'for this is the law and the prophets'. It also seems to summarize Jesus' sermon, so that the sermon is an outline of how to follow the Golden Rule. This simple rule—so short and so profound, so basic to how life ought to be—would be realized in full measure if only people would follow the Sermon on the Mount.

PRAYER

Lord God, show us how to shift the barriers to our own vision, encourage us to knock confidently on your door, and so teach us to treat other people as we would like to be treated.

TAKING IT SERIOUSLY

The final half-chapter of the sermon is mostly emphasis, with four graphic reminders that the teaching of the sermon is vital. This is the stuff of life, the way to live life, the way to find life.

Routes and fruits

There are two routes through life (vv. 13–14). The route outlined in the sermon is tough, arduous and unpopular, but it leads to life. Jesus never pretended that his teaching was easy. Yet he often spoke about life: we become most truly and deeply human, we find the wholesome and enduring life that God gives, when we commit ourselves to the pattern of living that Jesus taught.

Verses 15–20 present the Church with an acid test for any new movement or leader that emerges: what fruits are being produced? Is there anything solid, dependable and wholesome to show for this? That may not be immediately obvious, of course: even good fruit takes time to ripen.

Fine words and foundations

Before we move on to miracles and healings in chapters 8 and 9, verses 21–23 remind the Church that mighty works cannot be the core of our Christian living. Without the bread and butter of daily righteousness, even our best achievements for Christ count for little.

There is one major difference between the two builders in verses 24–27: both hear Christ's words, but only one acts upon them. To hear and not to do is to build an insecure life: eventually the storms of misfortune or persecution or final judgment will leave us empty and ruined. However, a life built on habitual obedience is built solidly, with good hopes of withstanding the pressures ahead.

Strange authority

So these four paragraphs are like nails, fixing the teaching of Jesus' sermon firmly to our minds, giving us reasons for returning again and again to this material, to measure our lives against its wisdom.

Yet the sermon can stick in the memory by itself. Many of its phrases have come into our regular speech: salt of the earth (5:13);

light under a bushel (5:15); blow your own trumpet (6:2); turn the other cheek (5:39); wolf in sheep's clothing (7:15). No wonder that Jesus' hearers found him a teacher of unusual power and authority.

Here and now

There are still questions about interpretation for today. 'Did Jesus mean all this literally?' people ask. Or is there an element of graphic exaggeration in some of his teaching? Is he provoking people to think, by overstating his case? Perhaps Jesus was deliberately teaching a high ideal, so that people would realize how much they needed God's mercy.

Another view is that Jesus meant this only for unusually devoted individuals; you could not expect most people to live like this. So while many Christians may observe some of the sermon in private life, you could not extend these principles to the conduct of public affairs.

How do we respond ourselves? We need to keep several things in mind:

- This is teaching for disciples of Jesus. We read it as his followers. What we do with Jesus' teaching is not a matter of theory alone, but should be worked out in our relationship with Jesus himself.

- This is teaching for the whole Church. We are all involved in working out how to follow. I long to see Christians take time to help each other discover how to obey Christ in a changing world. Some of this we shall only do well if we do it together.

- This is teaching for Christian contribution in society. It is good news for the world, a sign of God's love and of hope, when people seek to live in this way. That is what it means to be salt. For the salt to do its job, we must be in touch with the life our neighbours lead, but prepared to be different if necessary.

- This teaching is part of the gospel. Only the good news of Christ crucified and risen will make it at all possible for us to obey from the heart. Often his teaching will seem out of our reach, but it should not be out of our mind. When we turn to the cross for forgiveness, that forgiveness should send us back to the Sermon on the Mount. The world is still meant to see Christ's pattern of life in us.

PRAYER

Christ be our light, that we may shine for you.

21

For a WHOLE PEOPLE

Mercy moving through

We have read in 4:23–25 of Jesus going around Galilee, telling the kingdom and showing its power. Chapters 5—7 have given detail of that kingdom teaching. Now, through chapters 8 and 9, come a series of miracles, showing in different ways how Jesus expressed the power and mercy of God. Jesus was applauded for the authority of his teaching (7:29). Now we shall see that same authority in his deeds.

These two chapters have nine miracle stories altogether. To run the whole sequence without a break would be splendid in its effect, but almost overpowering, like a fast-moving firework show that leaves you exhilarated but breathless. So it is helpful that Matthew presents the nine incidents in three separate groups, with three stories in each. The groups are 8:1–15; 8:23—9:8; and 9:18–33. In the gap after each of the groups there are short sections that help the reader to digest the material. These include summaries of what has happened and scripture quotations to show the meaning of the events.

Following and fuming

Each of these intervals also has a short episode involving Jesus and his disciples. Jesus has already called disciples (4:18–22), and the teaching of the Sermon on the Mount was intended for them. But we have more to learn about them. Who will be called next? What sort of person might be suitable? What else will Jesus teach them? Is there a special task he has in mind for them? These two chapters develop the theme of discipleship.

They also warn us of coming conflict. The incidents in chapters 8 and 9 spread mercy far and wide. Jesus meets many sorts of misfortune, many desperate and disappointed people, with the hope and wholeness of God. Yet the reactions of those who watch are sometimes quite unpleasant. By the end of the series (9:33–34), people have become very polarized: the crowds are excited and enthusiastic while the Pharisees are sour and sceptical. So these chapters give the impression of clouds gathering on the horizon. The sun may be shining now, but there is a storm brewing in the distance.

Restoring touch

The condition called 'leprosy' in the Bible probably included a number of different skin diseases. These may have varied quite a lot in their physical severity. But the physical symptoms were not the only problem. For leprosy led to social isolation, exclusion from a lot of normal community life, for fear the disease would be passed on. A leper was treated as an unclean outsider.

Jesus touches the man (v. 3). His hand reaches across the gulf between clean and unclean, not with the risk that he will contract uncleanness himself, but to pass on his own cleanness, the wholeness and purity of the kingdom of God. This is a physical healing, but also a social healing. Jesus refuses to treat the man as an outsider. He treats him as an insider and he brings him inside.

Jesus wants to heal the man (v. 3). There is nothing accidental about what he is doing. God's creation is bruised and broken, and Jesus acts to restore it. Jesus sends the man to the local priest (v. 4). Priests acted as public health officers in Israel. They had to inspect and certify suspected cases of leprosy, and when a sufferer recovered it was the priest's duty to check and confirm the recovery (Leviticus 14). Certain animal sacrifices would then be offered, to mark the person's return to normal society. So Jesus tells the man not to broadcast his news himself, but to have his cure checked in the proper manner. He should offer the due sacrifice to let his neighbours know what has happened. So Jesus is working within the requirements of the law. He respects the leaders of Judaism. Will they respect him?

All-round wholeness

This first miracle shows what a complex and diverse thing healing is. Body, mind, emotions, faith, relationships—all are bound up together, and when any one is damaged the others are liable to suffer too. That means that healing of any sort always has a knock-on effect. It produces a fuller wholeness than it seemed to be aiming for. So the Church's pastoral care has a greater potential for healing and wholeness than we often realize.

PRAYER

May we love God, and receive God's love,
with our heart, soul, mind and strength.

FAITH *from* AFAR

Hope of healing

Capernaum had been Jesus' base for his travels around Galilee (4:13), so he was well known there. The centurion was probably not a Roman legionary; he belonged to the security force kept by Herod Antipas, the ruler of Galilee. He was a Gentile. The sick person was either his son or his servant (v. 6)—the word Matthew uses can mean either. The parallel story in Luke (7:1–10) suggests it was a servant, while a similar story in John (4:46–54) features a son. Whatever the relationship, this tough and travelled soldier is disturbed by the boy's illness and comes to seek help.

Not in the race

Jesus seems willing to come (v. 7). It is difficult to know whether this was a direct offer, or a question: 'Shall I come and heal him, then?' At any rate, the remark touched a tender spot. It was not regular practice for Jews and Gentiles to mix socially, and the centurion knows that it would be odd to have a Jewish preacher in his home. But he does not think it necessary for Jesus to come. Jesus can heal with a word, from a distance: 'Only say the word, and he will be healed' (v. 8).

Holy orders

The centurion explains why he is so confident (v. 9). He can recognize authority in Jesus. He himself has the authority to instruct his soldiers and his servants, and they do what he tells them. But he realizes that he is a man *under* authority. His authority comes from higher up in the army. He is who he is because of the power that operates through him. Now he sees the same sort of authority in Jesus, authority that comes from higher up and gives real power to command. If only Jesus would say the word, distance would not be a problem: the healing would surely take place.

Beyond expectation

Jesus is amazed (v. 10). This is not the sort of faith he is used to. Not even Jews have worked him out as plainly as this. No one, but no one, has seen as clearly as this centurion has that God's power is working in Jesus and that mighty works are flowing because God is in charge.

So this Gentile, this man of faith from outside the people of faith, becomes a sign of the breadth of God's grace. This is just the first instalment of a great movement of God. The promise to Abraham, that all the families on earth would be blessed through him (Genesis 12:3), seems suddenly alive. When the kingdom comes in all its fullness, it will be a grand international banquet with guests from all round the world (v. 11).

Then, sadly, the darker side of that future comes into view (v. 12). As Gentiles flock into the kingdom, as the world gathers to the gospel of Jesus, many Jews will turn away and never come back. For them the rise of the Christian Church will be an offence; its attraction to Gentiles will compound that offence. By Matthew's time the trend will be obvious, that a gulf is forming between Gentiles who are drawn to the gospel from afar and the many Jews who are missing out.

Faith that works

Finally this is a story of faith. This man from outside Israel, who preferred that Jesus stay outside his house, saw the inside of God's purpose with astonishing clarity. He saw the authority in Jesus and he trusted that authority to work for him. That is faith: seeing that God is at work in Jesus, and asking Jesus to touch our lives with his love. That is enough. 'According to your faith be it done for you' (v. 13).

Outside chance

Both miracles so far have been about outsiders: the leper was outside normal society, and the soldier was outside Israel. Jesus finds people, and finds faith in people, who are not at the centre of things. So when we get pushed to the edge, excluded or caused to feel unworthy by what is happening around us, we are not out of range of Jesus' love. We may still pray and we may expect answers.

PRAYER

Lord, I am not worthy to receive you. But only say the word and I shall be whole.

LIFTING *the* BURDEN

Mother's day

The first snippet of this passage (vv. 14–15) has just enough detail to make it a story. It has characters, a sequence of actions and a plot. The healing is simply told, in six movements. Three are actions of Jesus: he came, he saw, he touched. Then three things happen in response: the fever left, she got up, she served. Yet we can read between the lines of this report and sense the anxiety caused by the fever. There is a buzz as Jesus arrives, and the hope that he can do something to help; then relief spreads as the life of the home returns calmly and gradually to normal.

If the previous two healings were of outsiders, this is very much an inside job. Jesus is among the people who know him best. Simon Peter's house at Capernaum seems to have been Jesus' retreat now that he had moved away from his own home town. Though unmarried himself, Jesus understood family life and shared in it. Yet he had also placed heavy demands on this family: calling Peter away to discipleship would have strained relationships and possibly caused some financial difficulty.

Jesus was not easy company; you never knew what he would plan next. But this is a moment when the healing love of Jesus touches a home that has given him much. Surely in church families, when the demands of Christian service ask much of us, we may also ask Jesus to be present at times of crisis and fear, helping us to handle the burden, carrying it with us and lifting its weight.

Servant signs

Matthew has completed the first group of three miracle stories, and there is an interval before the next group begins in 8:23. The evening encounter (v. 16) was probably at Capernaum (compare Mark 1:21–34), and the scene contributes to Matthew's story in two ways. First, it stresses that the healings Matthew reports are only a sample from a much wider range of activity. Second, it leads into a scripture quotation from Isaiah 53:4, which Matthew introduces with another fulfilment formula (as at 2:15).

Isaiah 53 is a famous Old Testament chapter. It describes a figure it calls the 'Servant', who will suffer for others, who will be hurt and broken to make other people whole. So—as Jesus takes away the burdens of others—Matthew's quotation links his healing ministry to the Servant passage in Isaiah. This connection hints that the work of Jesus will be costly. His love for Israel will not be cheaply delivered. The opposition that will emerge in these chapters will eventually exact a heavy price from Jesus himself.

Pictures of wholeness

This use of Isaiah 53 also helps to show the purpose of the miracles themselves, for the Servant passage is at the heart of a journey to freedom. Throughout chapters 40 to 66 of Isaiah, the story is of Israel coming out of exile, back home to God. Her release comes through suffering, through the pain and humiliation of the strange figure called the Servant. He seems to represent Israel's own struggles, and also to represent God's love to her.

So as Jesus wears the mantle of the Servant, that is a sign of freedom coming, of a people brought back to themselves and to God. His healings are important for their own sake, as deeds of love and care for people of faith and need. Yet as part of Jesus' servant ministry, the healings point to something greater and fuller still. They are visual aids, signs of a nation made whole.

Blind people in Israel will see, and Israel herself will see God more clearly. Lame people will walk, and Israel will walk more confidently and surely with God. Lepers will be drawn back into society, and Israel—who has lived long with the bitter memory of exile, who has felt discarded by her neighbours and even by God—will be gathered again into the joy of the kingdom.

In the home where Jesus lodged, a woman has been healed. Surely the nation where he belongs is also offered his hand, full with the healing and wholeness of the love of God.

FOR THOUGHT AND PRAYER

The Church continues the servant work of Jesus, helping people to find their way home to God. That is sometimes costly work. Pray for patience, courage and love, as you serve in the footsteps of Jesus.

OPEN AGENDA

To boldly go

We are still in the interval before the second group of miracle stories. The scene is beside the Sea of Galilee. This freshwater lake, about twelve miles by eight, marked the border of the land of Galilee. Around the western edge, both on the lakeside and in the hills and valleys that led back from the shore, was the land where Jesus belonged, where most of the Gospel is set. On the eastern bank was the territory of the Decapolis, more Greek than Jewish. So when Jesus takes a boat to cross the lake (v. 18), he is not only avoiding the crowds, but is also heading into strange country (8:28). For some Galileans, whose lives had been sheltered and local, the far shore would be a world away. Following Jesus suddenly feels challenging and uncertain. Discipleship will not be a comfortable cruise but a voyage into the unknown.

Ready, steady... maybe

These two short encounters with potential disciples contrast with the earlier calling of Peter and his friends (4:18–22). On that earlier occasion Jesus had taken the initiative, and the response was swift and sure. They left their nets and followed. Even if the new disciples had private fears, they were willing to go.

Here the pattern is reversed. When Jesus speaks he seems to warn rather than invite, to push the enquirers back rather than beckon them forward. He probes their inhibitions and reservations, testing whether they are really ready to follow.

To the scribe (v. 19), whose religious commitment has revolved around books, a man who has laboured to learn the Hebrew scriptures and has loved that work, Jesus sets the demands of the open road. Can he cope with sleeping rough, not knowing quite what each day will bring? Or would he prefer a regular seat in the library? We do not know what his answer was.

Throwing a lifeline

On the face of it, verse 22 is an outrageous saying. Was Jesus really telling the man to miss his father's funeral? Burial of parents was a sacred duty, part of honouring one's father and mother. What possible reason could there be for not taking part? On the other hand, if the father had just died—and in such a hot climate the funeral would be the same day—it is odd that the young man had time to seek Jesus out. So both sides of this brief encounter are difficult to understand.

Obviously Jesus wanted to stress the urgency of his own mission, and the young man was inclined to hesitate. Beyond that we do not know quite what was going on. It is just possible that the father was not dead, so that the young man is saying, 'I'll come later, when I'm my own master.'

Whatever the precise circumstances, Jesus realizes that a person who is held too tightly by family ties will never get away. There will always be some excuse. Jesus himself has had to make the break out of Nazareth. So Jesus' word, 'Leave the dead to bury the dead', is a challenge. If the family have shown no interest in Jesus, it is time for the young man to face that fact. He is discovering God's kingdom, he is coming alive in a new way, and they are not. Hanging around for one more family event will not solve anything. He must either stay or go. If he is serious about discipleship, he must follow Jesus when the chance presents itself.

In the looking-glass

Jesus' call to commitment can be a mirror in which we see ourselves. Jesus confronts the bookish scribe with the uncertainties of an outdoor life. He presses a conscientious son to face the question of whether he could ever bear to leave home.

If you or I consider some new kind of Christian service, Jesus' question might be, 'Which aspect of this are you going to find hardest to handle?' The answer to that question might show whether or not we are cut out for the task. Along the way it could show us our own commitment: what we can handle is not just what we can do, but what we are willing to put up with.

PRAYER

Teach me, O Lord, to serve thee as thou deservest: to give and not to count the cost, to fight and not to heed the wounds, to toil and not to seek for rest, to labour and not to ask for any reward, save that of knowing that I do thy will.

Ignatius Loyola

Tossed *by* Storms

Here are two storms: one on open water, the other—equally wild—in the recesses of human personality. Jesus has healed physical diseases (8:1–15). Now he brings peace to a rough sea and to troubled minds.

Raging sea

Jesus, who has nowhere settled to lay his head (8:20), has the inner peace to sleep anywhere (v. 24). Meanwhile the disciples are alarmed and afraid. Some of them fish this water: they know its moods; their fear is informed by experience. This boat is on the point of capsizing with the loss of all on board. Then Jesus rises. He asks about their faith, and he calms the sea.

This story is about faith. 'Little faith' (v. 26) is faith that has embarked on the voyage of discipleship but is not properly aware of Jesus' power. It is fearful faith (as in 6:30). Matthew's readers would have pictured themselves in the disciples' situation. The tossing of the boat would remind them of the Church's trials, its doubts, struggles and persecutions. But even in trials, Jesus is 'with you always' (28:20). The Church is often a people of 'little faith', but never a people alone.

'What sort of person is this?' (v. 27). This is someone who can cross stormy waters and bring order and peace, who can quell raging seas, who can bring his community through danger to the further shore. In Jesus, the God of creation (Genesis 1:2), of Exodus (Exodus 14) and of Israel's praise (Psalm 107:29) is at work.

Storms within

The two sad people in verse 28 live on the burial ground. Death is around them, and something has died inside them—the peace and balance to live a happy human life. They challenge Jesus, calling him God's Son (v. 29)—as if their troubled minds can recognize the approach of God's goodness, and fear to tangle with him. For his work is premature: he brings God's healing love to a troubled world as an advance instalment of the wholeness of the kingdom. He brings the power of Israel's God to this Gentile land, before the Church's

Gentile mission is properly begun. In every sense he is ahead of time (v. 29).

The pigs seem odd (vv. 30–32). No other gospel incident has anything like this. For a Jew, pigs expressed the impurity of the Gentile world; these were unclean animals, forbidden for Jews to keep or eat. Yet even they cannot contain the disturbing forces released from the two people. The flight of the pigs suggests that Jesus is fighting a greater evil than anything regulated by the Jewish purity system. He has larger concerns than laws can measure.

Finally Jesus is asked to leave (vv. 33–34). He is viewed as a strange and dangerous magician. Goodness can be uncomfortable if it brings hope and joy to people we prefer to avoid.

For clear minds

A lot of human disorders in scripture are described as caused by demons (for example, 8:16, 28, 31, 33). Two responses to this are common among church people. Some feel very aware of a world of evil forces around them, and identify very easily with these biblical stories. Other folk are sceptical, and dislike reading of 'demon possession'; they feel that such ailments would be diagnosed by clinical psychiatry nowadays. I come somewhere between these two viewpoints.

To the first group mentioned, I make several brief points. Good and evil were polarized around the ministry of Jesus. His own spiritual power enabled him to discern and address human disorder very acutely and effectively. None of us is as sharply aware of spiritual forces as he was. Only Christians with considerable pastoral experience, well informed by responsible psychology, should claim discernment in such matters. Discretion, training and accountability are vital; most of us will not seek deep involvement.

None the less, whatever language we use to describe them, 'the mystery of evil and the web of malevolent causation behind it remain' (D. Hagner). We may surely pray for the power and love of Jesus to penetrate the mystery of psychological disorder, as readily as we pray for friends with physical illness. Mental health, like physical health, is a spiritual issue—by which I mean that it matters to God.

FOR THOUGHT AND PRAYER

Pray for anyone you know who lives with storms, for whom distress is a bleak horizon, for whom peace of mind would be another world.

26   MATTHEW 9:1–8

WALKING FREE

Four themes are woven together in this story: physical healing, forgiveness, opposition and authority.

First movement

This is first of all a healing story about a man who could not walk, about faith (of the friends who brought him and perhaps of the sick man too), and about the thrill of heading for home—on his feet! 'Stand up, take up your bed and go,' says Jesus, and the invalid actually walks away. It seems straightforward, direct and powerful. Yet this impressive storyline is almost totally overshadowed by other concerns.

Which is easier?

Sin is the root problem in human living; there will be no final wholeness, no full view of God's kingdom, unless sin's work is undone. But there is no simple link between a person's sin and any illness or misfortune that person might suffer. It is not that straightforward. Some people around Jesus spoke as if the link were obvious (John 9:2–3), but Jesus never supported that idea.

So why does Jesus talk about forgiveness, when people expect him to heal (v. 2)? We do not know. There may have been some personal reason why this man needed to hear those words: this is a town Jesus knows (v. 1), and he may know these people. But no such reason is mentioned. We have to connect to Matthew's message in other ways.

Forgiveness was always going to be important in Matthew's Gospel. Jesus came to save his people from their sins (1:21). Forgiveness is a sign of the kingdom (6:10, 12). So as Jesus travels through Galilee showing the kingdom by mighty deeds, we expect him to bring forgiveness.

'Is it easier,' Jesus asks, 'to speak a word of forgiveness or a word of healing?' (v. 5). Obviously forgiveness is easily spoken, whereas healing requires action. So Jesus heals the man—the more difficult task—to prove that he is entitled to offer forgiveness. He shows he can forgive, by showing that he can heal. But which is really easier—to heal a limb, or to draw the poison of the world's sin on the cross? Which was the more difficult for Jesus in Galilee? Healing had made him many friends. Forgiveness started to make him enemies. In the long run, forgiveness will become the bigger issue.

Heart dis-ease

For the first time Jesus has to confront some of Israel's religious teachers. These scribes seem to have had their opinions written on their faces. Their hearts were uneasy. Blasphemy (v. 3) means insulting God. It was an insult to God, they thought, for Jesus to forgive sins. That was God's job, and no one else should try to claim it.

On this occasion the opposition peters out, and the encounter finishes without serious trouble. Once the lame man walks, Jesus has shown his credibility. The sceptics will be back before long, but for the moment they are silent. The story ends with loud praise to God for the authority that is in Jesus.

Authority from God

We have seen Jesus' authority already—in teaching (7:29), in healing (8:9), and now in forgiveness (9:6, 8). Jesus offers on earth the pardon that only God can truly give. He forgives as 'Son of Man' (v. 6).

'Son of Man' is a riddle. Perhaps Jesus meant it to be. It could be a roundabout way of saying 'I'. That fits Matthew 8:20, for example. However, there is a figure in Daniel 7:13–14 called the Son of Man, a human figure who rises to receive great authority from God. He rules with God and for God. Some Jews in the time of Jesus were starting to connect this figure in Daniel with their hopes for a Messiah.

When Jesus said 'Son of Man' in Matthew 9:6, some people might have heard only 'I'. But since he is talking about authority, I reckon that Jesus had Daniel at the back of his mind. He was hinting, for those with ears to hear, that Daniel 7 helped him to see his own mission: he shared, in a unique way, the authority and kingly rule of God.

Fullness and freedom

The theme of authority is important throughout Matthew. So is forgiveness: Christians need to receive and share it. We often learn most about Jesus' authority through forgiving and being forgiven.

PRAYER

*Lord, release me, where I need it, to enjoy being forgiven,
and to forgive truly and finally.*

PARTY SPIRIT

This is the second interval in Matthew 8 and 9, the buffer zone before the next group of miracle stories begins in 9:18. The material here is mainly about the purpose of Jesus' activity.

Duty free

The call of Matthew the tax collector is very similar to the earlier call of the fishermen (4:18–22), and a contrast to the last two encounters with hopeful disciples (8:19–22). There was a frontier near Capernaum, dividing the Galilee of Herod Antipas from his brother Philip's territory in north-east Palestine. A tax office there could levy dues on goods that were moving through. But Matthew himself moves out. He just leaves, simply, decisively and instantly, and follows Jesus.

Many people have asked if Matthew the tax collector is the Matthew behind the Gospel. That is certainly possible. It could have been the tax collector's civil service mind that produced the orderly, arranged feel of Matthew's Gospel. Another possibility is that this Matthew was the source of much material for the Gospel. He remembered Jesus' words and deeds and handed his memories on. But he may not have compiled and written the Gospel in the form we now have. For more detail, see the section 'Who was Matthew?' in the Introduction (p. 15).

Responding to an invitation

Shared meals were important occasions in the time of Jesus. People who ate together felt they belonged together. Pharisees used meals to meet with like-minded friends, to express their devotion to God through the careful observance of food and purity laws. It seemed odd to them that Jesus ate with 'tax collectors and sinners' (v. 11).

Taxation is never popular, particularly when the system allows the collector to keep a slice of the takings. Taxation in Palestine was doubly suspect because it involved dealing with Gentiles and Gentile money, and it supported a system which was ultimately under Gentile control. Tax collectors were despised. So it seemed odd when Jesus, a religious man, visited Matthew's house for dinner. This was a company of rather irreligious Jews, different in their outlook from the zeal and care of Pharisaic faith. What business has Jesus got, eating with them? What could they have in common?

Jesus' answer has three punchlines. 'These people need me,' he says. 'Sick people need a doctor; others don't.' Secondly he quotes scripture, from Hosea 6:6. There are times for showing the favour and mercy of God in ways that do not follow strict legal expectations. You can keep the rules and miss the point, if you're not careful. Finally Jesus talks about his own target audience. He comes to people who need the forgiveness of God and know it—not to those who think they don't.

Feasting and fasting

John the Baptist is in prison (4:12), and his followers are concerned that Jesus' friends have not copied John's earnest discipline (v. 14). They seem more at home in the dining-room than the desert, and ignore the regular fasts that mean so much to some Jews (see comment on 6:16–18, p. 53).

Jesus uses the Old Testament idea that God's love for Israel is like a bridegroom's for his bride. The kingdom ministry of Jesus is like a wedding feast. It marks the arrival of God's love in a new and intimate way. Fasting would be out of place: you should eat when you are celebrating. But the sunlight also casts a shadow: the bridegroom will be taken away, and that will be a time for gloom and grief. The Gospel is beginning to show us the suffering ahead.

The two sayings in verses 16 and 17 shed light on the incident in 9:1–8, as well as on today's portion. Jesus brings something genuinely new to Israel, and must not be pushed into old ways. The kingdom requires patterns of conduct and friendship that are flexible enough to contain its potent new wine. The righteousness of the scribes and the Pharisees cannot hold it.

In our church life today, we still need ways of meeting that celebrate the generosity and promise of the gospel, events that bring people of different backgrounds cheerfully together, occasions that remind us all that we are welcomed and loved—even though we don't deserve it.

PRAYER

Lord Jesus Christ, you are the unseen guest at every meal we take.
May we eat and meet in the gladness of your love.

DAUGHTERS *of* FAITH

Here is one miracle story nested within another, like layers of a Russian doll. We are only able to see the whole of the outer layer when we have read through the inner layer and picked up the outer story again. This sandwich pattern is found a number of times in Mark's Gospel, with these two incidents (Mark 5:21–43) and in several other places. If Matthew is using Mark, then he has shortened this passage from 23 verses to nine. That is typical of much of Matthew's work. The stories are told briefly and crisply, the essential points are well made, but much of Mark's graphic detail is missing.

Urgent summons

After the challenges from scribes and Pharisees (9:3, 11), it is remark-able that a leader of the local synagogue (for that is what 'ruler' will mean here) should come to Jesus so freely and humbly. His daughter has just died, but surely—he believes—something can still be done for her (v. 18). So the story moves quickly from introduction through request to response. There is a sense of urgency. As Jesus and his friends follow the man home, the reader's mind runs ahead of them: what will happen when they get there?

Healing touch

Suddenly and abruptly the story breaks. There is another encounter, and Jesus pauses (v. 22). The woman's ailment would have made her ritually unclean, and that surely explains some of the fear and appre-hension that led her to touch Jesus from the back. She may have often been treated as a marginal and dirty figure in society, and learned not to risk another insult or rebuff. Yet there is an urgent con-fidence that drives her to seek Jesus' help. She touches the corner of his garment from the back: that will be enough. And it was.

In the house

Funerals happened quickly in Palestine (they still do). Music was playing and a weeping crowd had gathered by the time Jesus got there (v. 23). When he said that the child was only asleep, they could not take him seriously. However, he was not denying the reality of the situation but looking beyond it. God could do more than they could see. Privately, calmly, he raised the girl to life.

Words of hope

These two stories are filled with faith. The ruler's enquiry at the beginning, 'But come... and she will live' (v. 18), sets the tone, and Jesus' word to the woman as he leaves her and moves on, 'Your faith has made you well' (v. 22), confirms the mood. These two people recognize that God is powerfully at work through Jesus, and have the confidence to act on that belief. This is the faith the centurion expressed (8:8–13). It is the faith the disciples found hard to grasp— they had 'little faith' (8:26). The same faith is here, not 'little', but big enough to reach out confidently towards Jesus.

The woman was healed. But the word also means 'save'. '"If I touch his cloak I shall be saved" ... "Your faith has saved you." And from that moment she was saved' (vv. 21–22). Matthew's readers would have heard the double meaning. There was certainly physical healing, but the words resonated with the promise of a greater and more permanent salvation. 'Believe and be saved'—this they understood for themselves. Years after the earthly life of Jesus, they could still experience his salvation. They could have faith, by trusting in the gospel of Jesus. They could enjoy the sure love of God that lasts for ever, to death and beyond.

Life out of death

There are only a few accounts in the Gospels of people being brought back from death to life. Apart from this incident, there are two (Luke 7:11–16; John 11:1–44). These three people would all die again. Yet their resurrections give advance notice of the great resurrection, the decisive breach that Jesus would himself make in the boundary wall of life. When we read that Jairus' daughter 'rose' (v. 25), we start to glimpse that hope. Jesus will rise, and in him the faithful dead will find their eternal life. They will be saved through their faith in him. Death will truly be 'sleep' and there will be glad waking beyond.

PRAYER

Lord Jesus Christ, give us faith in the power of your love
and hope in the victory of your resurrection,
that we may live in trust and die in peace.

COMPLETING *the* CIRCLE

Seeing the king

The blind men shout from a distance, calling Jesus 'Son of David'. This is new. Matthew connects Jesus and David at the very beginning (1:1), but no one in the story has called Jesus by this title until now. The title hails Jesus as Israel's Messiah. He is their promised anointed leader, who will usher in an age of hope, and his healings are signs of that hope appearing. Strangely, Jesus does nothing until he is in the house. There the blind men approach him again, and he heals them. As we saw before, faith is a vital factor (v. 29). The privacy of the house provides opportunity for Jesus to speak with the men, to probe the faith behind their excited shouting. But there may be another reason for his seeking privacy.

'Son of David' was a dangerous slogan. Palestine had rulers already, and they would scarcely welcome a rival king. Jesus was not a violent revolutionary, and did not wish to be seen as one, either by eager nationalists or by the current political powers. So he speaks with the two men out of public view, and urges them to keep quiet (v. 30). If they want to call him David's son, they should not shout about it. In the end they were too exuberant to be silent—but their enthusiasm may have created some danger for Jesus.

Fresh sounds

A mute man receives the gift of speech (vv. 32–33). The incident is described very briefly indeed. The sounds and voices that rise from the encounter are reactions, the opinions that Jesus has provoked among bystanders. In this last of the miracle stories, the contrast is very marked indeed.

Some rejoice in the freshness and promise of what Jesus does, in the hope and new dawn they find in his coming. Others, who cannot connect him with their own religious patterns and practice, react very differently: 'He must be in league with evil, fighting the devil with his own weapons.' Jesus will counter this accusation later (12:22–30). For the moment the Gospel moves on, leaving the reader aware of a widening and potentially damaging gulf.

Rounding off

Finally the circle closes. Verse 35 echoes 4:23, and brings this circuit of Galilee, these chapters of teaching and healing, to a close. Several themes have come into view.

- The number and variety of the miracles show God's mercy and power at work in Jesus. Often it is weak, helpless or marginalized people who find help. God is not limited by human status.

- The various sorts of healing fit Old Testament expectations and hopes, as Matthew's story will indicate before long (11:2–6). The work Jesus does shows that he is God's true Messiah.

- Many of the individual stories have a message for the Church that reads them, in Matthew's day and in ours—about faith, salvation, resurrection, peace, and so on. They are 'transparent', as one writer puts it: you start seeing your own experience through them.

- There has been sharpening controversy in these chapters. Jesus is not an easy figure to grasp or control. His mercy does not fit traditional patterns, and some people cannot understand that.

- Discipleship has been a recurrent theme. The disciples have often been in the background, but never far away. Chapter 10 will show us more of their work.

Some people today wonder what to make of these miracle stories. It all seems so irregular, as if it cuts against nature. But for Matthew these incidents point to the wholeness of nature: the creator is restoring his handiwork and ending the dominance of illness and suffering. These healings speak of mercy in a world that is too often hindered and blinkered by misfortune. There is a smell of the future about them. They hint at the final purposes of God, and link all that to the coming of Jesus, in whom God was truly 'with us' in flesh and in love. They invite us to discover more of the loving power of Jesus in our own lives.

PRAYER

Lord, show me how to bring your restoring love to broken places,
in my own life and around me.

30 MATTHEW 9:36—10:4

WORKERS *for the* HARVEST

A new phase of mission

The second main block of teaching in Matthew, sometimes called the 'Mission Charge', fills the next chapter. Jesus is preparing his twelve apostles to go out on mission. They have followed him, listened to his words and watched his deeds. Now he sends them out to make God's kingdom known by word and deed, just as he has done. So another horizon opens—the Church's mission.

Matthew's first readers know that Jesus' own career as missionary has ended, long before their time. He is still with his people (28:20), but no longer present in the flesh. His mission has now become their mission. So this passage in the Gospel, showing the disciples taking up the task from Jesus, will be unusually 'transparent' for Matthew's Church. They will see themselves in it. They will expect their own experiences to be illuminated by this material.

Today's section is a transition in the Gospel, leading into chapter 10, opening the way for the instruction Jesus will give to the Twelve.

Shepherd concern

Jesus looks at the crowds, as he did when he began the Sermon on the Mount (5:1). On that earlier occasion he spoke of blessing. This time he sees a people straying (v. 36). Surely many of them are still open and ready for the blessing of God, but Jesus is grieved: they seem to have no direction, no strong spiritual leadership and care. They are a people 'harassed and helpless'.

Several Old Testament passages speak of sheep without a shepherd. Most (for example, Ezekiel 34:5 or Zechariah 10:2) reflect situations where Israel's spiritual leaders have not given the guidance they should. That matches the picture we are beginning to see in Matthew, where there is a deep gulf in outlook between Jesus and the scribes and Pharisees. If they are at the helm, Jesus feels that the people will never receive his kingdom message.

So Jesus makes other plans. The picture changes, from wandering sheep to ripened crops (v. 37). Elsewhere in Matthew the image of harvest is used for God's last judgment, with the solemn picture of wheat and weeds being separated from one another (13:24–30). But the picture of a harvest seems to be used very positively in this verse. There is good fruit to gather, and rewarding work to be done. Now we meet the people who will do it.

Authority to serve

We met several of these men earlier, when they were called. Jesus may well have started to form an inner circle among his followers some time before this. That could fit the impression given in Matthew 10:1. Now he commissions them for a new kind of work.

The number twelve is heavy with meaning. Israel had twelve tribes, descended from twelve patriarchs, the fathers of the nation. Now Jesus appoints a new leadership patterned after the old tradition, a new core for Israel, promising a revival of her life from within. The twelve are sent out as shepherds, for a responsible ministry of care and guidance. By what right and strength will they do this? The two key words are 'apostles' and 'authority'.

The authority of Jesus was an important theme in the last few chapters (7:29; 8:8–13; 9:6–8). He has spoken and acted with authority. Now he passes it on, authority to heal and overcome evil. We are not told precisely how he passes it on—other than by the words of commission throughout chapter 10. Certainly the authority seems to work (Mark 6:12–13, 30). The twelve will preach and heal as he has done (10:7–8).

Only in verse 2, after receiving authority, are the Twelve called 'apostles'. The idea has a Jewish background. It means a messenger of a special kind. An apostle is an agent, commissioned and trusted by a senior and more powerful person, sent to carry out the master's business. This requires wisdom, responsibility and initiative, and also loyalty to the master's policy and wishes.

The mission of the Church continues the mission of Jesus. The basis on which the Twelve were sent remains the basis for all our Christian work, for our pastoral care, our mission and our leadership. We work for the Lord and are committed to following his purpose, ahead of our own preferences.

PRAYER

Lord God, let your Church be truly apostolic, obedient to your sending, faithful in your service.

NEWS CAST

The 'fishing for people' (4:19) is about to begin. The apostles of Jesus are going out as messengers of the kingdom of God. These verses give them instruction about what to do.

Broadcast

This is a mission to Jewish people. Jesus himself has worked mostly among Jews in Galilee, and his disciples should stick to Jewish communities. Israel are the lost sheep (v. 6) for whom Jesus grieves (9:36). The time for wider international mission will come, but is not yet.

Matthew's Gospel reminds his own Church—and us—that Christianity comes from a Jewish stock. Jesus came in fulfilment of Israel's ancient hopes, bringing fresh energy and vision to a long tradition. The Church celebrates a gospel that was given to Israel first, a message that is faithful to Israel's history and heritage. (See the section 'Matthew and Judaism' in the Introduction, pp. 15–16.)

So the disciples are to preach the kingdom and show its presence, as Jesus has done. Signs will support the preaching, and preaching will explain the signs. God is stirring in Israel. This message of God's kingdom fits the Jewish audience that Jesus has in view. The idea of God as king was an old and honoured belief among Jews. Jesus was speaking in language they could grasp—and was bringing the reality of the kingdom within reach.

Supporting cast

The missionaries are not to take a lot of equipment. This will be a simple venture, unsophisticated in style. They should not trouble themselves with money, either by taking any with them (v. 9) or by accepting payment for what they do (v. 8). 'Labourers deserve their food' (v. 10) and they should expect to get food and lodging on the road—but without money changing hands in either direction. They are not to act as beggars, but should accept hospitality in the communities they visit.

When they arrive in a place (v. 11), they should seek out a known sympathizer, someone who is already inclined to support the work of

Jesus, and lodge with that person until they leave town and move on. In Jewish society, with its tradition of close national solidarity, a request for lodging would not be strange. Even so, the kingdom message would divide people. Some homes and villages would not be welcoming.

Cast out?

The style of the mission is straightforward. The preachers should go from house to house, and greet people as they go, bringing a word of peace to each place (v. 12). We should think of houses as grouped, often around open yards, with extended families gathering from work in farms or crafts. Many a place would prove 'worthy', and welcome the news of God's kingdom. Others, however, would have no interest or pleasure in what they heard: the greeting of 'peace' would find no place in which to rest, and would leave with the one who gave it.

A shadow side to the good news comes into view here. The kingdom is an urgent message. It is near. You cannot ignore God's reign, and you cannot remain the same once you have heard and seen it. Places that turn away will be the worse for that decision. The cities of Sodom and Gomorrah were notorious Old Testament examples of disobedience and judgment (Genesis 19:24–28), but even they never heard this word of the kingdom (v. 15). What a catastrophe it would be, to be really near and then to resist and reject the good news!

Cast of thousands

So what of the Church's mission today? Matthew 10 fits a society with a solid faith tradition, where there is fresh and important news to bring. The message must be shared. It is immediate, alive, urgent, a movement of God not to be missed.

If we find mission heavy going, that is partly because there is less of a faith tradition into which we can speak: our Western society is becoming very secular. It may also be because we overlook the sheer life and vigour of the gospel, the passion that fired the first Christians and that sparked the spread of their faith. Their style was simple but the grace and mercy in their message were rich and full.

PRAYER

Lord, please give us a love for the communities around us, and the ability to make the kingdom known by word and action.

SHEEP *among* WOLVES

The Church's mission will not be all smooth progress and sunny days. There will be opposition and rejection, and some of it will be harsh and painful. Today's verses give warning of dangers ahead.

Serpents and doves

Verse 16 is like a headline across the coming section, sketching the attitude the apostles must adopt if they are to survive and serve when the going gets tough.

In 9:36 the 'sheep' were the nation of Israel, seen as a wandering and wounded flock. In this verse the disciples are sheep, and the point is that sheep are vulnerable. When they are in open country and unprotected, they cannot defend themselves. The disciples will meet threats and even violence. Some of the people they encounter will be 'wolves'—brutal, deceitful, malicious.

There is no sure way of preventing other people's wolfishness. Sheep have to keep their eyes open and their minds clear; they must be 'wise as serpents'. But they should keep their integrity too; they must not be wolves themselves. They need to be above reproach, people whose conduct is honest, true and fair. They must be prudent and pure, shrewd and straight. They have to live the good news if they are to tell it.

Governors and kings

The next verses speak of arrest and harassment, first by the religious authorities of a local synagogue, then before the civil judgment of Jewish kings and Roman governors. 'Be careful,' says Jesus (v. 17). Do not invite danger. But if serious trouble does come, the advice he gives is 'not to think beforehand what you will say', but to depend on God's Spirit for words when the time comes (vv. 19–20). Even a court appearance can be an occasion for witness.

These few verses seem also to look across to a broader horizon, to the Church's mission among the nations. Christians who heard them, even in Matthew's time, would find their own trials mirrored here. Two thousand years on, persecution of Christians remains a live issue. Brothers and sisters in various lands value this passage, with its promise of the Spirit's help, very highly indeed. They deserve our prayers.

Brothers and fathers

It takes a rare toughness to cope with the force of the legal and judicial system when your only crime is faith. It is surely even more hurtful to face hatred in the family. But when a person changes faith and leaves an old family tradition behind, that may be seen as betrayal. Relatives feel personally degraded and insulted, and strong reactions can result (v. 21). There will be times, says Jesus, when all the world seems against you (v. 22). It is still worth hanging on: there is a finish line, and salvation beyond it.

Unfinished business

The first half of verse 23 is quite clear: when one community reacts strongly against the gospel, move to the next. There is a job to be done, and it is right to get on with it. But the second half is very difficult to interpret.

One understanding might be that however long the world endures, the Church's mission will never be finished. It is like painting the Forth Bridge: you just keep going. Mission to Israel still remains an unfinished task, just like mission to the rest of the world.

However, we may see more of the original meaning of the saying if we connect the 'coming of the Son of Man' to the destruction of Jerusalem in AD70 (see also comments on 24:29–35, p. 202). That event catastrophically disrupted Israel's life, and ended an era of Christian evangelism within Israel. So while there was still time, the task of preaching the kingdom to Jews was an urgent one.

Still biting

A minister I know remembers the sermon text at his ordination: 'I am sending you out like lambs into the midst of wolves' (Luke 10:3). Looking back on his home mission work, serving in the name of the church but outside the walls of the church, he says it was a well-chosen text. There can be real discomfort in speaking, living and being recognized as Christian. Both wisdom and innocence are still required of us.

PRAYER

Pray for Christians—possibly including yourself—whose faith causes them pressure, hurt and hardship.

GETTING PERSPECTIVE

The apostles' mission will be dangerous. They will be hated, hurt and harassed, for Jesus' sake. Can they cope? Have they strength to bear the burdens, stamina to go the distance, and nerve to face the opposition? These verses offer encouragement for the task, with a blend of challenge and comfort.

Do not be afraid

The middle section, verses 26–31, is chiefly comfort. The words 'Do not be afraid' (vv. 26, 28, 31) recur like the chorus of a song. Jesus gives his followers three reasons to keep fears in their place.

Open secret (vv. 26–27): When Christians get discouraged, we may lose sight of God's purpose and forget what a grand message the gospel is. These verses are about the power of God's truth. The message of the kingdom is not going to remain a secret. One day the whole world will know that God is king. It is a mighty privilege to start spreading that message already, to let people know the way things really are. This is the truth that fills heaven and renews the earth. It is worth sharing without fear.

Body and soul (v. 28): This verse is about God's judgment. He holds the future and controls human destiny. Final power never lies with persecutors. Judgment is in God's hands, and he weighs a person's whole life, for good or ill. Even if persecution ends in death, it cannot kill the soul. Christians should revere God—that is the right kind of fear. But we do not need to fear people who oppose and obstruct God's work; their power is very limited.

Parting shot (vv. 29–31): These verses describe God's clear-sighted love that notices sparrows falling in the street and can count the hairs on our head. Now, says Jesus, understand the depth and detail of God's care. You matter more than sparrows. God is concerned for far more than your hairstyle. Nothing can happen to you, to take you outside his love.

These are Jesus' reasons for not being afraid. God guards the future: his truth and judgment will prevail. God guards the present: his care and love are sure. Let Christians proclaim God's truth, respect his judgment, and trust his love.

The one we follow

Now we come to the challenging material. This urges the disciples to take their relationship to Jesus seriously, and not to be afraid of admitting that they follow him.

Teacher and pupil (vv. 24–25): Jesus himself attracted opposition in his ministry. 'He casts out demons by the prince of demons,' people said (9:34, RSV), and they linked him with Beelzebul, the ruler of the world of evil. We shall hear this accusation again, and Jesus will make a vigorous response to it (12:22–30). For the moment he reminds his friends that they are serving his cause, copying his activity, and working under his leadership. They should not be alarmed or surprised to be treated as he was.

Earth and heaven (vv. 32–33): Verses 24–25 said that if the apostles serve Jesus, their relationship with other people will be just like his. Verses 32–33 say that their relationship with God will be like his too. For he will speak to God about them and call them his friends (v. 32). If, on the other hand, they do not admit to being his followers— and so avoid the risks of discipleship—they will miss out on the bond that he has with God (v. 33). Christianity is a personal relationship, not only with Jesus but with God too. You cannot have one without the other.

Calm and courage

I personally have not faced opposition as severe as this chapter describes. But I know that Christian witness is still a difficult task in almost every part of the world. It needs courage to let our own relationship with Jesus be known to others. Certainly there is a time and a place for discretion (7:6; 10:16–17: 'be careful'). There are also times when we should acknowledge clearly whose we are and whom we serve. God's kingdom is still worth telling, and God's love can still be trusted. If Jesus is real to us, we need not be afraid to say so.

PRAYER

Lord Jesus Christ, let my life make you known, through my silence and my speech, in ways that will help others to believe in you.

POURING COLD WATER

This last part of the Mission Charge could dampen the zeal of many an aspiring Christian and, indeed, of more seasoned believers. It asks about loyalty and about commitment, but speaks also of costly discipleship and the abundant love of God.

Families at war

The first part of the passage picks up from verses 32–33, which were about acknowledging Jesus in front of other people. The language of verse 34 is stark, to stress the point. Jesus did indeed come to bring peace, but the peace of the kingdom can be costly. The call of Jesus can split families when some want to follow and others resist. Jesus quotes the Old Testament (vv. 35–36; from Micah 7:6) and describes the division that faith can bring to some families as the cut of a sword through human flesh. The person who is always inhibited by family opinions and pressures will never take the kingdom seriously enough (v. 37). There is no easy peace in the service of Jesus.

Commitment for life

Verse 38 continues the rhythm of verse 37, but gives an alarming new twist to the warnings. Taking up the cross is a picture of death—grisly, humiliating, ugly and painful death. To take up the cross is to commit oneself to that path, to turn aside from the route of personal pleasure and interest, into the way of humble, self-denying and demanding service. The way of the cross has no comfortable guarantees.

Taking up the cross is a description of Christian commitment. It is not about personal problems—'the crosses we bear'—although personal distress is an important biblical theme elsewhere. This is about a deliberate choice to follow a crucified man, whatever the cost, because he deserves our loyalty and love. The surprise of the gospel is that in giving ourselves, we receive ourselves (v. 39). Christ asks nothing that he cannot repay—as the next verses confirm.

Doors open for God

The idea of the apostles as Jesus' envoys, which we met at 10:1–4, explains verse 40. They come in his name, under his instructions, on his business. To offer them help and hospitality is like offering it to him. And as the apostles are Jesus' envoys, he is God's envoy. He represents God, advances God's kingdom, and acts in God's love and power. Helping someone who does Jesus' work is like helping God.

So people who support the work of the missionaries will indeed be rewarded. To offer lodging, or even the refreshment of cold water, to people engaged on Jesus' work is a gift to God, and a gift that God will cheerfully repay. Those who spread the good news of the kingdom may feel very vulnerable. In 10:16 they are called 'sheep among wolves'; in 10:42 they are 'little ones'. But all their ways and all their days are under the eye and the love of God.

Mission improbable?

Much of this chapter seems far away from our life, our era and our church situation. This teaching comes from a time when the new wine of the kingdom was heady and hot. Even then it was intended primarily for roving missionaries. What, then, can we make of it? How do you translate it into your age and place? Two points in response.

First, Christianity involves commitment and we should not pretend, to ourselves or to new Christians, that it is easy. The faith will slip like water through our fingers if we start thinking it is a soft gospel. It can sometimes be very tough indeed. Material like Matthew 10 both challenges our complacency and offers real comfort to Christians who face particular pressure and opposition just now.

Second, this material speaks about the sort of situation where Christian witness may be painful. Whoever we are and wherever we live, that pain could affect and involve us. Even where the Church is comfortable now, the cost of Christian witness in any society or era is not really under our control. Matthew 10 is a resource to keep against the day when the heat is turned up. None of us should say, 'It will never be like that here.'

FOR THOUGHT AND PRAYER

*'It is not foolish to give what you cannot keep
to gain what you cannot lose.'*

Jim Elliott, American, missionary martyr in Ecuador in 1956

35

MATTHEW 11:1–6

SIGN LANGUAGE

The next couple of chapters show a rising tide of opposition to Jesus. Many people did not understand what he was doing and some did not like it. Within these chapters Jesus speaks a number of times about seeing properly. What he is doing is clear enough, for those who have eyes to see (11:4, 25; 13:10–17). He is showing the work and life of God. Today's passage invites people to look.

Words from a sentence

John the Baptist's own preaching had got him into trouble and into prison. This happened when John criticized King Herod Antipas for dumping his first wife and marrying his sister-in-law (Luke 3:19–20). John was doubtless a stern and sharp critic, and the king decided to shut him up. So John lay in prison. His horizons were narrow, but his hopes remained. He had spoken of one who would come after him (3:11–12). Now he wanted to know what to make of the rumours he had heard about Jesus (vv. 2–3). Was Jesus the coming one, or was there something more to look forward to?

We simply do not know what was in John's mind, and what particular concerns were behind his question. Had he expected a sterner messiah, with more judgment and less mercy than he found in Jesus? Had he hoped for something more sudden than the mission tour of Galilee that Jesus had undertaken? Had prison so demoralized him that he needed to be assured and encouraged? Or did he just want to know more about what he could not see? We cannot be sure.

Seeing is believing

Jesus does not give a direct answer to John's question, but his meaning seems straightforward enough. Watch what's happening (v. 4). Look at the healing, the newness, the wholeness that is coming to battered and troubled folk. That should be sign enough that Jesus represents the active mercy of God. But this answer has another level of meaning coded within it.

For the signs to which Jesus draws attention are mentioned in scripture, in Isaiah's prophecy. Isaiah 35 speaks about Israel coming home, and rejoices in the hope of blind people seeing, the deaf hearing, the lame leaping, and the dumb speaking. Isaiah 61 (which also influenced the beatitudes of 5:3–12) looks forward to the work of God's anointed: God's Spirit rests on him; he will bring good news to the poor. Now Jesus turns hopes into happenings, and invites people to see not only the signs but also the scriptures, not only the healings but the hopes as well, not only the marvels but the meaning too. This is a time of renewal. Ancient promises are coming to fulfilment. This is a movement that will bring Israel back to God. Jesus is the Messiah on whom God's Spirit rests.

So this short exchange, at the start of Matthew 11, reflects the long sequence of miracles from chapters 8 and 9 and underlines the point made there, for example at 8:17 and 27. This is messianic activity, fulfilling hopes and dreams from long ago. Healings are good in themselves, but these events do not stand on their own. They have a place within the pattern of God's purpose. They carry a message about the one who does them.

Signs and blunders

'Blessed is anyone who takes no offence at me,' says Jesus (v. 6). He has already faced jealous criticism (9:34), and others too would miss the point of what he was doing. Some would take offence. There would be people unable—or unwilling, or unprepared—to recognize what they saw in Jesus, groups who would act and react against him. So Jesus ends his answer to John by hinting that there is conflict coming. He will not be a comfortable or easy presence in Israel. In his way he will be as divisive a figure as John has been, both a healer and an irritant within Israel's life. There will be choices to make. The blessing that he brings will come only to those who want it.

Answering back

Two thousand years on, Jesus still attracts questions. Christians tell his story and live his life, as our way of answering the questions people bring. Many still discover him as the answer to their deepest hopes. And some still take offence.

PRAYER

Lord Jesus Christ, help us to know you as a figure of liberty and wholeness. Help us to live by your love, so that others may discover your healing power.

MORE *than a* PROPHET

The question in yesterday's passage was, 'What does John think of Jesus?' Today's section turns the question round: 'What does Jesus think of John?' The answer is that Jesus thinks very highly of him. He respects John for the quality of his work, and also for the vital role that John had in preparing for his own ministry. John was a prophet, a spokesman for God, and a very good one too. He was also a sign that times were changing and a new phase in God's purposes was dawning.

Reeds and robes

Of course people did not go to the wilderness to admire the vegetation (v. 7); they went to hear John. And John was not dressed in soft royal robes (v. 8). All that is obvious. But there may be another layer, a hint of satire in the words of Jesus. For the reed-man is Herod. There is a reed on some of Herod's coins, a symbol of his territories in the Jordan valley and beside the Sea of Galilee. It may be that the coinage gave Herod a nickname as a flexible fellow, a man easily swayed. He switched his capital city from Sepphoris to Tiberias; he exchanged one wife for another; he could trim and twist his loyalties to the gusts of political fortune. There was no inner firmness in the man.

But John is different. He was straight and consistent in his ministry, firm in his faith and conviction, committed to God even though it cost him dearly. He is different in every way from the king who holds him in prison. He has no wealth or rich clothing, but his trust in God gives him an inner toughness. This man was worth travelling to the desert to see and hear. He is a real and worthy prophet. But he is something more.

Voice from the boundary

When Jesus speaks of John as 'more than a prophet', he thinks of John's role in the coming of God's kingdom. Promises have come to fulfilment through John's ministry. So as Jesus describes John, he looks first backward and then forward, to the ancient prophets and to the coming kingdom.

'The law and the prophets spoke their message until John came' (v. 13). The Old Testament was a long era of promise, a period when God dealt with Israel in love and care, yet an age that looked forward to fuller and more intimate knowledge of God. Jesus uses words from the last Old Testament prophet, Malachi, to explain John's role. John was a messenger, making way for the coming of God (v. 10; from Malachi 3:1). He was a figure like Elijah, turning the nation to God's ways and preparing them to meet God's holy presence (v. 14; from Malachi 4:5).

So John stood at the hinge between Old Testament and New, the latest of the prophets and the herald of the kingdom. No one did a more important or better piece of work for God than John the Baptist (v. 11). He ushered the kingdom in. He was its announcer and forerunner. Yet once the kingdom comes, John's work is completely overshadowed. A fuller grace is at work than he knew. Something much bigger is happening (v. 11).

Verse 12 is difficult. It probably means, 'The kingdom of heaven presses strongly forward, and people press forward to grasp it.' John has launched something forceful that has a vigour and energy of its own, through the love and power of God at work in Jesus. Many people respond with enthusiasm and commitment, although others will be cautious and sceptical (11:16–19).

Tuning in

There are hints in this chapter about seeing properly. In verse 15 the metaphor changes to hearing. 'Listen,' says Jesus. Understand that John's whole ministry is pointing to something much bigger than himself. God is present, in Jesus.

God still stirs, in our times. As times change, God may work in new ways. Christians should listen, to be sensitive to what God is doing. But all the work of God in every age is an echo of his greatest work—the coming of Jesus. There we see God's kingly rule and fatherly care. There we see the hope of the gospel and the generous love of the Lord who brought it among us.

PRAYER

Lord Jesus Christ, let me speak for you and listen to you, that my days may be a time of your grace.

37

MISSING GENERATION

Blind spot

'What you see is what you get' is a slogan of our times. But we do not always live that way. Sometimes we see very clearly, but are unwilling to 'get' what we see. We decline to take real notice of the things we observe because they could lead us to conclusions and commitments we prefer to avoid.

Jesus met precisely that sort of response. His deeds were 'the deeds of the Messiah' (11:2), but still he said, 'Blessed is anyone who takes no offence at me' (11:6). John's preaching was powerful and important (11:7–14), but still the invitation has to come, 'Let anyone with ears listen!' (11:15). For some people were offended by what they saw, and some were determined not to hear. So verses 16–24 are about excuses, evasiveness and resistance.

No time to dance

Have you ever tried to play with children when they are bored and cannot lift themselves out of it? Whatever you try falls flat. That's the picture here (vv. 16–17). Someone is trying to start a tune, and nothing catches on. The children do not want to dance, but they do not want to sing a sad song either. Nothing will suit them, neither foot-tapping rhythms nor the slow strains of a folk lament. The children are bored and nothing will stir them.

That, says Jesus, is how some people greet God's messengers. For the preachers had different styles. John followed a simple lifestyle, without beer or banquets, and people said, 'What a dull, unbalanced fellow. He must be possessed by something odd' (v. 18). Then Jesus came, living a very different life, welcoming friendship and hospitality, and the same people shook their heads: 'Just look at the company he keeps. What an undisciplined character!' (v. 19).

Excuses are easy to find at first, but eventually they wear thin. Grumbling at everything is a childish attitude. That is no way to approach a serious issue like faith. Yet, in the end, God's wisdom will show itself, plainly and truly, by its effects (v. 19). Jesus and John have achieved much for God, and that is what really matters.

Urban priorities

The 'cities' were major population centres in Galilee, but were not very big by our standards—more like market towns. They had their share of sceptical and suspicious people. So when Jesus visited, and people gathered for healing (8:16), many of the townsfolk did not turn a hair.

Jesus grieves over the cities that reject his message (vv. 20–24). He compares them with rebellious towns of Old Testament times. Tyre had been intoxicated with her own wealth (Ezekiel 26—28). Sodom was a lawless place (Genesis 19). But they never had a chance to see the signs of the gospel or to welcome the arrival of God's kingdom. Their evil was of a lesser kind, so even they would fare better in God's judgment than towns which shut their eyes to Jesus himself. The places that were first to hear would be last in God's reckoning, if they took no notice of what they heard.

These verses repeat the point made at 10:15. Jesus expected his ministry to bring a time of crisis and judgment to Israel. His message was challenging rather than cosy. He warned people to be ready, to respond, to be on the right side. He wanted people to 'repent' (4:17; 11:20–21), to follow the path of kingdom loyalty and lifestyle. God's kingdom would be durable, and those who found it would have nothing to fear. But those who missed out on the kingdom, who saw nothing because the lenses of their minds were closed, would realize one day how hollow their excuses really were.

Excuse me

The Christian message often encounters excuses—from outsiders who resist getting drawn in; and from Christians, when we are content with a shallow and superficial faith. Only God can really deal with the human heart and help a person to get beyond excuses to commitment. But all of us have a responsibility here: to be honest with God about our own attitude, and to live credible Christian lives, so that neighbours find in us reasons to believe in Jesus, not excuses to avoid him.

PRAYER

Lord Jesus Christ, help me to grow away from poor excuses, into the richness of faith.

The GENTLE YOKE *of* JESUS

Here is the other side of the coin. The previous passage was full of gloom and warning. Now come warmth and invitation. Jesus has attracted opposition and misunderstanding, but he has also found people who want to follow, and he welcomes them into the love and friendship of God. Like so much in Matthew's Gospel, these verses are 'transparent': they have a proper place in the gospel story, but they also leap beyond the story and beckon the reader. 'You come to Jesus as well,' they seem to say. 'Discover the pattern of life he offers his friends. Enjoy the security and peace that come through trusting him.'

Jesus appears here as a uniquely important figure, the only person who truly knows God, and the one who brings others to God. Yet he is also a humble man: he is gentle and lowly; he offers an easy yoke to his followers; children understand his truth. That paradox runs right through Matthew and, indeed, through all the Gospels. It is the mystery of Jesus himself: he was humble yet mighty, accessible to little people yet himself a person of greatness and majesty.

Through the eyes of a child

The Old Testament suggests that learned and clever people can miss the mark in their dealings with God, but that God's law is a lamp to humble folk (Isaiah 29:14; Psalm 19:7). That same thing may happen when people encounter Jesus. He knows God like a son knows a father. The people who respond to him he calls 'little children', and he gathers them into his own special relationship with God. Others have turned away—sophisticated and sure of themselves, yet not really open to the kingdom.

The picture of children playing was used in verses 16–17: bored and weary children can be difficult company. But here in verse 25 children are a pattern to copy. For children are often trusting and straightforward, firm in their loyalty, and receptive to love. Their minds are not cluttered by prejudice, cleverness and pride. These are the sort of people—those who can be humble, open and child-like—who will discover the secrets of the kingdom of God. This teaching is very like the beatitudes (5:3–12). The poor in spirit and pure in heart are truly blessed. They find it easiest to follow Jesus, and they get to know him most deeply.

Rest for the weary

Jesus offers relief to tired people, and rest to the troubled and weary. Here is a pattern of life that is bearable and wholesome; here is the promise of refreshment and renewed strength. But in Jesus' own time these words carried other resonances and hopes. They echo the invitation wisdom gives, in Proverbs 1—3, to come and enjoy the life of God. So Jesus speaks as God's wisdom, the creative power of God in human flesh.

Jesus offers an 'easy yoke' (v. 30). A yoke was not always easy to bear. It was part of the harness of a working animal, and meant load and toil. In some Old Testament texts the word refers to Israel's experience of heavy-handed foreign rule. Jews also used the word 'yoke' to describe the discipline of the Jewish law—which could be applied in burdensome ways. But Jesus speaks of an alternative 'yoke', the loving rule of God that will not chafe and destroy. The 'yoke' of Jesus, his teaching of the law, is bearable rather than oppressive. He interprets the law in different ways from the Pharisees (for example, 12:1–14).

So Jesus speaks of a pattern of life, of discipleship, that is indeed a 'yoke'. It is a path of service, involving commitment, discipline and hard work. But it is not a hurtful or unnatural yoke. It is lined with mercy. It is shaped by the loving wisdom of God, not by human anger. It fits especially well on the child-like in heart.

These words in verses 28–30 are used in some churches as an invitation to communion. Although communion was not the setting where they were first spoken, they suit the occasion well. For communion is not a stopping place; it is a refreshment station on our journey of discipleship. The yoke of Jesus is for the rhythm and routine of Christian living, that we may follow without fear and serve without strain.

FOR THOUGHT AND PRAYER

Can you still come to communion like a child, receptive and trustful, expecting God to refresh and teach you, ready to be surprised by God's grace and love?

AGAINST *the* GRAIN

Chapter 12 is full of arguments. The first two stories, in verses 1–14, concern the Jewish sabbath. The Jews kept one day each week as a holy day for God. There were rules to ensure that you observed the sabbath properly, and—as often happens with systems of laws— some of the rules had become quite detailed.

Eyeing the ears

A few raw grains of wheat would scarcely fill the stomach. They might just take the edge off midday hunger. This was not a real meal. Nor was it theft. Jews were permitted to pluck a few ears from a neighbour's field (Deuteronomy 23:25). But even this counted as work, so far as the Pharisees were concerned. Harvesting corn, and threshing it to separate grain from husk, were disallowed on the sabbath (Exodus 20:10; 34:21). The behaviour of Jesus' disciples aroused comment and indignation. If he was a religious teacher, it was odd that his followers did not conduct themselves in a careful and law-abiding way. They seemed not to bother about obedience in the way that Pharisees did. What can Jesus say to justify his friends' conduct?

Prophet, priest and king

The answer Jesus gives is surprising. He does not say (as we might have done), 'It's only a very small matter. This is not real work. It's the spirit of the law that counts.' He does not discuss (as the Pharisees might have expected) detailed interpretation of ancient laws. He makes a bigger point. He talks about his own ministry, what he is doing as God's Messiah, and the new age of opportunity that he has brought. He uses Old Testament examples to make the point.

Jesus refers first (vv. 3–4) to an incident from 1 Samuel 21:1–6. David was running for his life, and he and his men were tired and hungry. They were given holy bread by the priests, bread that had been dedicated to God for use in worship. Now Jesus is a new David, another king-to-be in Israel. He also has a vital mission to carry out, that overshadows the normal sensitivities of religious and ceremonial law. Let no one stand in his way.

Jesus' second point (vv. 5–6) refers to the regular practice of Jewish priests. There were sacrifices and offerings to be made on the sabbath (for example, see Numbers 28:9–10), and the priests had to ensure that all was done properly. They needed to work on the sabbath. The Temple, the place where heaven touches earth and Israel meets with God, warranted a break with the normal sabbath pattern. Yet Jesus is greater than the Temple. The kingdom of heaven touches earth in his ministry. People meet the mercy and power of God in what he does. The normal restrictions and patterns of everyday law need not all apply to him. Something more important is happening.

Thirdly (v. 7), Jesus cites a text from the prophets, from Hosea 6:6. Mercy matters more than sacrifice. The active compassion that God shows in Jesus takes precedence over the laws that shape holy days. Jesus brings the ancient prophet's hope to life. Indeed he fulfils the whole direction of the prophetic scriptures (5:17). He brings a new era of messianic intention and action.

Lord's day

The short controversy ends with a flourish. 'The Son of Man is lord of the sabbath' (v. 8). Jesus is in charge. His purpose, his activity, his mission, are important enough to make the sabbath holy. He does not need the protection of detailed laws to secure his holiness. The days he lives and the deeds he does are holy in themselves. Whatever serves his cause surely hallows the sabbath.

Trading places

The Christian Sunday is not the same as the Jewish sabbath—although it conserves much from that older tradition. So how should we use it, and what should be done to protect it? Shops are now free to open in England on Sundays, but for fewer hours than on other days. Many Christians view even this as a dubious liberty, a threat to healthy patterns of community and family life.

This passage in Matthew suggests that one question above all should shape a Christian's use of Sunday: does my use of Sunday enhance and advance the work of Jesus and the spread of his mercy, love and good news?

PRAYER

Lord Jesus Christ, help me to keep every day as holy as I can, by living in ways that please and honour you, whatever I am doing.

JUST HEALING

This second sabbath incident revolves around the healing of a withered hand. But we hear little about the person who is healed. Nothing is said about faith or salvation. Those points have been well made through chapters 8 and 9, and now Matthew's story has moved on. This chapter emphasizes the opposition that emerges and the way that Jesus responds to it.

The dead hand

Healing counted as work. Indeed it can be hard work—ask any doctor! So Jewish law did not allow healing on the sabbath, unless there was a danger to life. Here is Jesus in the synagogue, the local centre of scriptural and legal knowledge, and some people challenge him (v. 10). Is he going to heal? Is this allowed?

Jesus is quick to explain himself. The answer he gives is less complicated than in the previous incident. There is no recourse to the Old Testament, no complex piling up of points. He makes one single comparison. If a sheep falls into a ditch on the sabbath, the farmer will drag it out as soon as possible. Concern for the animal's health, for the distress and waste that delay could cause, will lead to prompt action. Surely, says Jesus (v. 12), a person is a more deserving case than a sheep. We ought to relieve suffering. There is no point in delay and every reason to act immediately. So it is lawful to heal on the sabbath.

Jewish rabbis of the time discussed how much help should be given to a stranded animal on the sabbath. But Jesus is not really intervening in that debate. He is more direct. This is what people do, he argues. They act quickly to avoid serious harm. Jesus is equally straightforward in his healing. He is concerned for human need and pain, and acts wherever he can make a difference. If law fails to see that, then it is a dead hand, choking life and hindering the work of love.

The incident ends with a little conference among the Pharisees about how to get rid of Jesus (v. 14). For the first time in Matthew, the possibility of the cross comes into view. A withered hand has indeed been restored, but we are beginning to see a widening rift within Israel, that will not be healed.

Gentle for the Gentiles

Jesus retreated once before, in order to avoid sharp opposition (4:12). He does not seek controversy, nor excess publicity (v. 16; compare 8:4; 9:30). For the moment, he wants time and opportunity to extend his ministry among receptive people.

Matthew quotes the Old Testament in verses 18–21, the longest quotation anywhere in the Gospel. It comes from Isaiah 42, a chapter which has already figured in a smaller way at 3:17 (see comment there, p. 33) and will echo again in the transfiguration story at 17:5. Matthew has a particular reason for putting these verses here, for we have just read of a threat to Jesus' life. But God's purpose will not fail. Jesus will accomplish his task. Graciously, steadily, persistently and successfully, he will carry God's work through to its destination. So these verses from Isaiah offer a wide-angle view of the course of Matthew's Gospel, where it is leading and how it will get there.

Jesus is the Servant of God. God's Spirit rests upon him (v. 18) from his baptism (3:16–17). He will not court controversy; his messianic style will not be aggressive and arrogant (v. 19; compare v. 15). He will be sensitive in his dealing with vulnerable, hurting and discouraged people (v. 20; compare 11:29). And in all that he does, there will be a wider horizon. He will spread the mercy and justice of God to Gentile nations, and give them reason to hope and rejoice (vv. 18, 21; compare 8:11).

This quote gives Matthew's readers a moment of insight into what is going on behind the scenes of the story. The controversies will continue. Jesus will not avoid them. He will eventually suffer and die. But the lamp of the gospel will not be snuffed out. The deliberate gentleness of Jesus may seem oddly unmessianic to some. Yet his ministry will restore withered and broken lives to wholeness and launch a message to take to the world. Out of the tragedy of his cross will come resurrection and international mission (28:18–20).

FOR THOUGHT AND PRAYER

Can gentleness ever be a successful strategy in a world where so many people are sharp—in mind, tongue and deed? These verses suggest that it can. But it may be a costly path to follow. Review your relationships and dealings with people: is there anywhere where you should be gentler than you have been?

41 MATTHEW 12:22–30

CROOKED THINKING

The scripture quotation in 12:18–21 sets the stage for this next incident. The main point of the Isaiah text is that Jesus is filled with God's Spirit and doing God's work. Now, immediately afterwards, people ask about whose power really drives him. Is it God's, or someone else's?

Matthew's story has been leading this way for a while. In 9:27 and 9:34 we read of two very different views about Jesus: is he Son of David, or agent of the devil? Again in 10:25 Jesus spoke of being tarred with the title 'Beelzebul', the prince of demons. So this very direct clash is not unexpected. We are ready for Jesus to respond.

Talk of the devil

Matthew does not describe the miracle in much detail (v. 22). The point of this incident is to show how trouble and controversy arise and how Jesus explains himself. The healing leads, apparently very quickly, to clear sight and ready speech for the individual concerned. But can the people around see properly for themselves? What have they got to say? Have they really noticed what and who is at work among them?

The crowds are enthusiastic—they sense messianic activity (see comment on 9:27, p. 78)—whereas the Pharisaic voices strike a discordant note. They cannot believe that Jesus is inspired by God. They see him as a maverick, a lone ranger. He sits light to their laws, so they cannot take him seriously. If there is superhuman power in his life, it must be a devilish power.

Power points

Jesus shows that his accusers' thinking is topsy-turvy. Their logic does not make sense. His response has five stages: two arguments (vv. 25–26, 27); two conclusions (vv. 28, 29); and a challenge (v. 30).

- **No inside job (vv. 25–26):** Jesus cannot be inspired by the devil in his mission of healing, because he is actually attacking the devil's territory. He is loosening the grip of evil on human lives. Evil power would surely not work against itself. Any kingdom or community that fights itself will quickly dissolve and collapse. Satan's kingdom could not go on standing if it were battling against its own successes.

- **Fair play (v. 27):** Some other Jewish writings of this era also mention exorcism. There were people who could do this—although it appears that Jesus was unusually prolific, that others did not exorcise on the same scale as he did. So Jesus asks his accusers if they would recognize other exorcisms as God's work. If they would, why do they challenge him? They should be more consistent.

- **Whose kingdom? (v. 28):** This first conclusion takes up from the previous point. The number, variety and power of Jesus' signs come from a very intimate relationship with God. He is inspired by God's Holy Spirit, as a sign of God's kingdom, an indication that the loving rule of God is at work in him.

- **Right of entry (v. 29):** This second conclusion moves on from the first. The Spirit of God gives Jesus power over evil. The only way a burglar can ransack a house is by first tying up the householder and securing a clear entry to the property. So, implies Jesus, the reason he makes inroads into the realm of evil and releases people from suffering and fear is that he has already overcome the devil. In his temptations (4:1–11) Jesus proved himself stronger than the powers of evil, and claimed the right to serve as God's Spirit-filled Son.

So Jesus is the man in control. He is not possessed by any evil power. But he himself has the right to push back the boundaries of evil, to release people held in its clutches and to spread the clean and holy power of God's kingdom.

No soft options

Finally Jesus poses a hard choice (v. 30). This group of hearers has come close enough to recognize what is going on in his ministry. Now they should decide. If they will not support what Jesus is doing, they are actually turning against him and making his work more difficult.

FOR THOUGHT AND PRAYER

The cause of Jesus is a power struggle, for the victory of gentleness and wholeness over the damaging harshness of suffering and evil. Do not be afraid to take sides.

OPPOSING MATTERS

Limits of forgiveness

Verses 31 and 32 are hard to understand. The great Christian thinker Augustine reckoned them the most difficult in the Bible, and many readers since have been puzzled and disturbed by this awkward saying. We shall try to make sense of the words, by connecting them to the storyline in Matthew.

This passage continues the theme of yesterday's portion. Pharisees have accused Jesus of acting as an agent of the devil (12:24), and he has not only defended himself but has challenged them. It is time for them to make their minds up about him. If they are unwilling to recognize the Holy Spirit's work in him, then they are standing in the way of God's kingdom (12:30).

The hard saying in verses 31–32 takes up from there. People may start by criticizing Jesus thoughtlessly, without understanding what they do. But once they understand that God's Holy Spirit is at work in him, and then deliberately oppose this work—'thoughtfully, wilfully and self-consciously rejecting the work of the Spirit, even though there can be no other explanation of Jesus' exorcisms' (D.A. Carson) —they are turning their backs on the mercy of God. When people sense that the powers of God's kingdom are at work, and then shut their hearts against that work, they 'undercut the very possibility of experiencing God's salvation' (D. Hagner). They have seen what God's love looks like, and decided it is not for them. There is no way home from this sort of position, other than retreat.

The inner life

Our outer appearance and actions can sometimes reveal a great deal about our inner self. A nurse or doctor will 'hear' the movement of a person's heart by taking a pulse. We can read the tiredness in a friend's mind when we see a drawn face or dull eyes. In exactly the same way, we learn a great deal about a person's inner feelings and attitudes by listening to what they say. What is inside becomes visible on the outside. Good trees bear good fruit; if you do not get decent fruit, then you must have a poor-quality tree (v. 33). What is in the heart comes out of the mouth (v. 34). A good person's heart is like a treasure chest of good things, where it is easy to select kind, fair and true words to speak (v. 35), whereas the people who speak harshly about Jesus are actually saying more about themselves than about him. Jesus invites them to look inside and reflect on what they find.

Counting words

Verses 36 and 37 link together the two paragraphs above. God judges our words, our casual, everyday, instinctive speech—because the words show what is inside us. People of integrity and love, where the goodness of God is active within, will show that inner self to God— in a thousand ordinary ways. God will see the reflection of his own love, and will welcome what he sees. But the person who speaks deliberately and maliciously against Jesus, and persists in that opposition, is showing God a heart that wants nothing to do with the kingdom. They should not be surprised to find that their words count against them.

Do not be afraid

This passage has sometimes given rise to serious pastoral problems. Verses 31 and 32, and their parallels in Mark 3:28–29 and Luke 12:10, have caused perplexity and distress to some sensitive Christians, who look back fearfully across their own lives in case they have committed sins God cannot forgive.

The wisest pastors deal gently with such worried souls. For their very fear and sorrow come from belief in Jesus. They realize how important he is, and they do not want to reject or spurn his love. If they ever did reject him, they have not persisted in that course, but have found a way back to a different and more positive attitude. Theirs may have been a temporary sin, but it is not the 'eternal sin' of which we read in Mark 3:29. It was well written of such a troubled person, 'If you repent, then you have the Spirit' (Ulrich Zwingli); the very fact that you are seriously concerned shows that this is not your problem.

PRAYER

Lord God, when I am careless or cruel in my dealings, remind me that you see and hear what I do; and when I feel the weight of my own sin, assure me of the openness and depth of your forgiveness.

MOMENT *of* OPPORTUNITY

Asking the impossible

Jesus has performed many healings and exorcisms. Why ask for another sign? (v. 38). Had these people not seen enough of his activity already? What difference would one more incident make?

The point seems to be that they have seen, but have not been receptive to what they saw. The controversy began at 12:24—'he casts out demons by the prince of demons'. Jesus' opponents are suspicious of his exorcisms. So they ask if he could perform a different sign to show quite clearly that God is with him, a sign which will not allow any other interpretation or leave any room for doubt.

Of course, signs are not like that. Strange or unusual deeds can usually be understood in more than one way. We interpret the signs we see according to the ideas and prejudices of our hearts (12:34). So Jesus did not perform signs simply to impress people or to prove himself. Signs do not prove God. They invite faith and show grace, but only to those who are ready to believe and receive.

'For God all things are possible' (19:26). But we come near to asking the impossible if we ask God to show us something convincing, when we do not actually want to be convinced. When I hear people today say, 'I'd believe if only…', I sometimes wonder if they would.

Hard to swallow

There would, however, be one great sign, to Israel and to the world. It would be a sign of life, to show how God can overcome suffering and death. It would echo the story of the prophet Jonah, who was gulped down and then vomited back up by a giant fish (Jonah 1:17; 2:10). For Jesus too would be lost from view in the tomb, and then emerge to life again (v. 40). Death would not consume or destroy him. Here would be one final majestic sign, to show the meaning of all the signs Jesus had done, to show the power and strength of his love, and to beckon people to the vitality and hope of his good news.

Yet even the resurrection requires a response. The evidence is firm enough to support Christian belief, but not enough to force people into faith. Signs show where the road is, but we still have to follow it for ourselves.

Voices from afar

The ministry of Jesus was a moment of unparalleled opportunity. There was never a better time to see the grace of God at work (vv. 41–42). So from the vantage point of eternity it would seem very odd indeed that many rejected him. In Old Testament times, the people of Nineveh listened to Jonah's preaching (Jonah 3:5). The Queen of Sheba came to hear King Solomon teach (1 Kings 10:1–3). They were Gentiles, they had no obvious reason for heeding Israel's God and they had seen nothing of Jesus, but they responded to what they heard. Yet when Jesus comes to Israel as a greater prophet than Jonah, a mightier king and a wiser and holier teacher than Solomon, he meets resistance and resentment. Surely there will be Gentile voices, from the past and from far away, to criticize the generation that refuses him.

Occupied territory

Like so many of Jesus' parables, this last story (vv. 43–45) has a second layer of meaning lurking beneath the surface. On the face of it, the story suggests that religion must be a positive thing. If we merely try to avoid sin, without energetically embracing a positive goodness, we shall be vacant territory for all sorts of other evils—pride, bitterness, resentment, meanness, selfishness. Christian commitment has to be active.

But that may not have been the original meaning of the story. Jesus reminds his opponents that their generation has experienced the cleansing and releasing power of God's Holy Spirit—in his own healings and exorcisms. But the very removal of evil creates a dangerous situation for Israel. It presents them with a sharp choice. They could welcome the work of God's Holy Spirit. Or they could slip into greater and deeper evil, if they reject and resist the grace they have seen in Jesus.

FOR THOUGHT AND PRAYER

Spiritual opportunities can be dangerous for us too. When we learn something fresh and new about Christ, we cannot make a neutral response; we cannot stand still. Ask God for wisdom and courage to take the chances you are given for growth and advance in the Christian life.

FAMILY GATHERING

Man apart

We have heard nothing about Jesus' home and family life since chapter 2. He is operating away from home, moving from place to place, and using Simon Peter's house at Capernaum as an occasional base. He has gathered some followers, but has also attracted suspicion and criticism. He already seems a vulnerable, threatened and isolated figure (see 10:25; 11:19; 12:14).

He is a man apart. Yet he is not a man alone. He is shaping a community, forming a company of people where the life of God will be known in fresh ways. It takes a visit from his natural family to show, in stark and even hurtful ways, just how much he values his followers.

Outer circle

Mary is here, but Joseph is not mentioned, and it may be that he had died by this time. There were at least four brothers, for 13:55–56 mentions James, Joseph, Simon and Judas and also some sisters. Indeed, two of the letters in the New Testament come from two of these brothers, James and Jude. But there is no indication in Matthew's story that the brothers are men of faith at this stage.

In fact, the reverse may be true. Mark says (3:20–21) that Jesus' family were concerned about his balance of mind and had come to restrain him. That detail is missing in Matthew's version, but when we meet the family 'standing outside' we realize that they do not belong to Jesus' inner group. They address him from a distance, from the edge of the crowd, while his followers are much closer.

Family likeness

The question in verse 48 must have sounded cruel and harsh to Jesus' relatives. He sees his truest family not as the people he comes from, but as those who come with him. The family likeness is not determined by DNA and genes, by the similarities of face or form that show the parent in the child. The really important family likeness concerns what people do: it is a likeness of lifestyle and habit, of commitment and action.

This family likeness comes from God. Members of the family of faith show by doing God's will that they are God's children. That is the mark of true sons and daughters (21:28–31). It was the way that Jesus lived (John 5:19), and is also his family's way.

That does not mean, though, that Christians should ignore the needs and welfare of relatives. Jesus was very critical of people who used religion as an excuse to neglect elderly parents (15:4–6), and a similar warning comes later in the New Testament (1 Timothy 5:8, 16).

Sister actions

Jesus spoke of 'brother and sister and mother' (v. 50). Judaism of that time usually stressed male leadership in religion, and women were often overlooked as people whose faith and commitment need not be taken very seriously. Jesus broke with that pattern. He respected women and the faith they showed, and he wanted them among his followers as full members of his community.

The Church as family

Some Christian churches talk much about family, in an effort to strengthen and support the parents and young children in the congregation. 'Family worship' means that services are planned and led with parents and children in mind, and many other church activities have these same households in view. That pastoral concern is important, but it can sometimes be emphasized in ways that cause hurt.

Not all Christians belong to neat or easy families. Many live alone, and not all of them by choice. If 'family' always means two parents and 2.4 children, it leaves a lot of people out. More importantly, it misses the really big point that the Church is a new, large, inclusive and very mixed and untidy family, united in Christ, committed together to doing the will of God, and knit tight in active love. That's real good news, a pattern of community life and love to enrich and shape the whole of our living—a home that is open for all to belong to and for all to enjoy.

FOR THOUGHT AND PRAYER

Pause to realize—especially if following Jesus is tough at the moment—that he counts you among his family. What can you do to treat other Christians as brothers and sisters?

45

Grains *of* Truth

Jesus often used words to draw pictures, and then employed these word-pictures to illustrate and explain his message about God's kingdom. We have already seen some of this, in 7:13–27 and 9:16–17, for example. But now the word 'parable' appears for the first time. This chapter is full of parables; but also it is a chapter about parables—what they are, how they work and what they achieve.

Beach mission

The Sea of Galilee was a mainstay of the local economy. It was full of fish, and a circle of small towns stood around it. When Jesus went out along the beach, he would find people at their work. He sat down among them, like a rabbi sitting to preach in a synagogue (as in Luke 4:20). But the sheer numbers who gathered obliged him to push out from the shore in a boat, and use it as a floating pulpit. One can imagine people fanning out around a little bay, with Jesus a few yards away on the water.

Plain and perplexing

Strictly speaking, the word 'parable' means 'comparison'—one thing put down beside another so that people can see how they match. But there was an ancient Hebrew word, *mashal*, that could mean a parable but could also refer to a much wider variety of sorts of saying. A *mashal* could be a mystery or riddle, a proverb, a story with a meaning, as well as a comparison of one thing with another.

The parables of Jesus often begin, 'The kingdom of God is like…' as in 13:24; that is obviously a comparison. But his stories also seem to reflect the mysterious aspect of the *mashal* tradition.

This story about a sower, for example (vv. 3–8), appears simple and accessible. None of the towns in Galilee was big by our standards: people lived near the land, and would understand farmers and fields very well. Yet there is a perplexing aspect to this parable too. It does not really explain what it is about. It leaves the reader—as it would have left its first hearers—with work to do. People would find themselves starting to think. Then the story would take a grip on them as they tried to puzzle it out.

Scattered success

What—on earth—is this about? Is Jesus provoking attention by sketching a picture of a careless farmer, who scatters his precious grain all over the place instead of spreading it on the best of the soil? Or is Jesus describing the mixed fortunes that regularly follow the sowing of seed? The process is rather random, and you cannot always tell which of the grains will grow.

There is a strong positive climax at the end (v. 8). The lavish fruit-fulness of the last batch of seed exceeds all normal expectations. But the story takes a long time to get there; the farmer's hopes are frustrated over and again. So does the story make its impact through the long sequence of failed sowings, or because of this eventual success? Is it really about final plenty? Or about the patchy and discouraging process that came first?

Easy listening?

Jesus was easy to listen to, but hard to hear. He was a master teacher. These parables were so ordinary that people would remember them. But the stories had an elusive quality too, like mercury, gleaming with light but constantly slipping out of your hand.

So responsible hearing required hard work. The stories had to be kept in mind, allowed to rub around the hearer's mind for a long time, like grit in an oyster, until grit became gospel and the puzzle turned into a rich pearl. 'Use your ears,' said Jesus. He meant not just physical hearing, but inner hearing too, holding on to the story until the good news of God's kingdom lodges firmly in a person's heart and life.

Dwelling place

Learning the truth of the gospel needs effort and patience. The love of Jesus is big enough to deserve that commitment. Sometimes we can only grow when we make room for his teaching to dwell in our minds and shape our lives. Then we start to hear his word in fresh and deeper ways.

PRAYER

God of mystery and majesty, help us to cherish your word in our hearts, that we may truly hear and see, and may turn afresh to you. Through Jesus Christ our Lord. Amen.

TURNING *a* BLIND EYE

This is difficult material. It appears so different from the open teaching style that Jesus often adopted. Did he really mean to prevent people understanding? This strangeness has prompted a suggestion that these words did not come from Jesus at all, but were added to the story some years later to explain why the gospel had not spread very well. But the substance of what is here fits fairly well with a number of other things Jesus said, and could very well have come from him. We consider what he might have meant, a section at a time.

Stating secrets

The followers of Jesus had begun to understand how God's kingdom was working in him. For them the parables were fresh shafts of light. A 'mystery' is hidden and impenetrable—until an interpreter comes, who can unveil it and explain it to others. Jesus' teaching had begun to open the mystery of God's work for his friends to understand and follow (vv. 10–11).

But for people who knew nothing of God's coming kingdom, parables seemed opaque and obscure (vv. 12–13). We need not think that Jesus meant people to remain in this condition. 'Seek and you will find,' he said (7:7–8). But there were those who had not found and showed little desire to seek. Indeed Jesus said that his message would be like a closed book to sophisticated and self-sufficient people (11:25–27). So his parables left people with a responsibility: either to brush the message aside or to dwell on it until its truth became clear and compelling.

Taking leave of their senses

The quotation in verses 14 and 15 comes from Isaiah 6:9–10 (part of God's call to Isaiah to be a prophet) and told how hard and resistant the Jewish people would be to his ministry. Jesus used these verses to point out that many of his own hearers would prefer not to understand. For them the message would be too threatening, too disturbing and demanding, to be worth the risk of proper hearing. Clarity would be too costly; they would rather stay in darkness and silence. But two hopes lighten the gloom.

First, there can be a difference between the words we say and the effect we mean them to have. A sports coach or musical conductor may say in apparent frustration, 'You people will never get this right', as a challenge to greater earnestness and application. The actual words are negative, but the intention is positive. So Isaiah—and Jesus too—could use words of gloom and sorrow with the positive hope that there would be a responsive remnant, people who would make the effort to grasp the message, whose hearts and minds would be open to God's word. That remnant is the second hopeful element in Isaiah's text. He calls it 'the holy seed' (Isaiah 6:13), the same image that Jesus used to describe the rich promise of God's kingdom, despite many setbacks and disappointments.

Vantage point

Even though hearers are responsible for what they do with the message, just to be allowed to hear is a gift of God (v. 16). Response is a duty, but revelation is a gift. The disciples of Jesus have a special place in history. They can see Jesus' deeds (11:4) and hear his words. They are watching the fulfilment of Israel's hopes, and this is a moment for which many in Old Testament times longed and yearned (v. 17). The disciples have not yet fully understood, but they are on the way. This is indeed a blessing, the unveiling of a mystery.

Long division

Since the end of chapter 9, Matthew's story has portrayed a mixed reception to Jesus' mission in Israel (9:34; 10:17; 11:20; 12:10). Many are unreceptive, swayed by other pressures, suspicious and sceptical of what Jesus brings. So this portion of chapter 13 has an important role. It helps the reader to interpret the advancing story, to see behind the varied attitudes of the people. The text from Isaiah in verses 14–15 is a reminder that God's word has not always been well received in the past. Yet the confident words of verses 16–17 speak of God doing a new thing. Here is—for those who will respond—a moment of fresh promise and rich harvest.

PRAYER

Thank you, God, for the privilege of hearing your good news. Help us to value it. Through Jesus Christ our Lord. Amen.

GROUNDS *for* HEARING

Because the disciples have been given a special moment of opportunity (13:16), Jesus stresses that they must listen (v. 18). The parable concerns them: it is about people who hear and what they do with the message afterwards. Indeed the interpretation of the parable begins by striking exactly that note: 'When anyone hears the word of the kingdom and...' (v. 19). So these verses offer a challenge to every reader: what are we doing with the gospel; which of the four groups in the story matches our response most closely?

Soil types

The four soils where the seed landed are typical of people and the different receptions they give the word. One person simply does not grasp what is said. Another reacts brightly for a while, but lacks the solidity to stand up to persecution and pressure. A third has too many competing concerns and ambitions, is too tightly bound to material possessions, and so finds no real room for nurturing the message until it shapes heart and life. Only the fourth hears, understands and bears fruit—in deeds and a renewed life. It is typical of Jesus (7:21–27) and a long Jewish tradition (for example, Micah 6:8) that hearing and doing belong together. Jesus' words were always intended to affect the way people lived.

Old, old story

The parable of the sower has come to us in three phases: the parable itself (13:3–9); the middle section (13:10–17) about sight and blindness; then the explanation of the parable. N.T. Wright (in *Jesus and the Victory of God*, SPCK, 1996) shows how this structure is curiously similar to an Old Testament passage from Daniel 2. That too speaks of a God who reveals mysteries (2:28–30), of a strange story, in this case a dream (2:31–36), and of its interpretation (2:37–47). The three slices are admittedly not in the same order. But the similarity is quite detailed.

In Daniel, as in Matthew, the mystery involves several phases—the earlier parts of the story ending in waste and the last phase showing the triumph of the kingdom of God. In both passages God's kingdom involves the revelation of a mystery; only some are given to understand it; it rises amid alien powers, and eventually triumphs after setback and opposition. So Jesus stands within an older Jewish tradition, telling a veiled story. Yet he now proclaims the moment when God's kingdom appears. Still there is opposition, setback and delay, but there is also the prospect of abundant fruit.

What's in a name?

We call this the 'parable of the sower', but by the end of the story the sower is almost a forgotten character. His work is done, and the emerging results are the real focus of interest. That brings us back to the question posed in the comments on 13:1–9: is this about failures or about fruitfulness, about plentiful harvest or patchy harvest? The 'parable of the soils' might be a better title, if we think the main emphasis is on the differences in the ways that people respond: they react differently just as portions of a field give different yields.

Or we might call it the 'parable of the seed', if we reckon that the chief point is the eventual harvest. One Old Testament echo suggests that the stress should be on these final results. Isaiah 55 speaks of God's word not returning to him fruitless, but producing seed and bread (55:10–11), and triumphing over thorns and briars (55:13). So in Jesus' story, the word triumphs, to produce a full and lasting crop.

But the name 'parable of the sower' should not be dismissed completely. This whole section is about Jesus himself. This is a parable about a man who teaches in parables. Jesus himself is the sower. In his ministry, God's kingdom has arrived. But it grows and advances gradually and quietly, like seed rising up to harvest.

Spring of life

Jürgen Moltmann, in *Jesus Christ for Today's World* (SCM Press, 1994), points out that the gospel parables frequently describe growth and harvest. They picture a world laden with potential, where it is always springtime and fresh promise is bursting to the surface all around. This is the kingdom of God, the spiritual environment in which we are invited to live the Christian life.

PRAYER

God of life, let us live as people of hope and expectancy, bearing fruit that will endure, rejoicing in your rich provision for us in Jesus Christ. Amen.

TANGLED GROWTH

This is the first of six parables beginning, 'The kingdom is like…' (vv. 24, 31, 33, 44, 45, 47). They expand on the story of the sower, to give a fuller insight into how God's rule grows. Like the parable of the sower, this story has an explanation attached. But the explanation is not given straight away—there is a pause before the meaning is unveiled.

Creative suspense

The interval between parable (vv. 24–30) and interpretation (vv. 36–43) achieves two purposes. First, it reminds Matthew's readers that Jesus did not give instant answers, nor explain his material to everyone. Parables were intended to stimulate thought and to lead to response. Because of their cryptic style, the parables were always potentially divisive, sharpening the interest of those who wanted to follow Jesus, puzzling any who did not. Second, the gap creates room and time for us as readers to think about the meaning of this parable for ourselves. It draws us into the story, and into the crowd who were themselves trying to understand what Jesus intended.

Weeding between the lines?

Tares are a mongrel form of wheat, with smaller leaves, suitable for chicken feed but quite unfit for human consumption. A few tares would be almost inevitable in a field of sown corn. But when a disconcertingly large quantity is discovered, the first thought is to weed them out immediately (v. 28). However, that would be risky if the roots were tangled, for then the corn would be uprooted too (v. 29). So the farmer follows another plan. He lets both crops grow together and will separate them when they are fully grown (v. 30).

Spelling it out

The explanation falls neatly into two sections. Verses 37–39 are like a little dictionary. They define the meaning of each of the words in the parable. Then verses 40–43 tell a new and parallel story, of the coming judgment of God, as the destination to which the parable points.

These verses bring out a number of themes that are important in Matthew, emphases that occur again and again: Jesus as Lord and judge of the world; judgment that divides and rewards people according to what they have done; the call to be 'righteous' (v. 43). The parable itself ended (v. 30) with an echo of the judgment preaching of John the Baptist (3:12; Luke 3:17), which Jesus had himself taken up. The explanation of the parable stresses and explains this theme. But what Matthew must have seen, and the first hearers may not, is the view from after the resurrection. The coming judge, whose power now spans the whole world, is Jesus himself.

Putting evil in its place

Following the parable of the sower, which showed a very mixed response to Jesus' kingdom preaching, this parable of the wheat and tares has offered a broader understanding of the complex mystery of good and evil. There is an 'enemy' whose malicious work is spread wide in the world. But evil has a limited span of life: in God's good time it will be finally and fully destroyed. The kingdom may seem hampered and blocked by much opposition and ungodliness, but God's eventual victory is certain and sure.

There is no call here for panic measures to separate good from evil, for there is no easy and practical way of drawing a line between them. The Church must wait. Jesus may have deliberately taken a different approach from some Jewish groups of his time. Groups such as Pharisees and Essenes were keen to form pure religious community, where all the members would be godly and righteous, and where contact with outsiders might be rather limited. Jesus was more open. He was in no hurry to put a firm and permanent boundary around his own group of followers. God knows who is serving his cause, and in due time he will judge truly and rightly.

In the meantime, Christians are called to be 'salt of the earth' (5:13), influencing its life, attracting others to Christ, and playing our part in the energetic and certain growth of the gospel—which is graphically illustrated in our next passage.

PRAYER

May God grant us the persistence to do our work, and the patience not to try to do his. For Jesus Christ's sake. Amen.

MAJESTY *in* MINIATURE

The two short parables in verses 31–33 balance the picture of the wheat and tares in verses 24–30, and together the three stories help to expound the parable of the sower. The sower spoke of a piecemeal, even apparently erratic, set of responses to the word of the kingdom, but still looked forward to an abundant final harvest. The wheat and the tares showed how good and evil must live side by side for the moment; there are serious difficulties to be endured before God's final triumph comes into view. These next two little comparisons tell of the promise and power the kingdom has within it; their focus is on the sureness and scale of the coming glory.

Growth point

The mustard seed was tiny indeed, but could grow to be a sizeable shrub, expanding far beyond its original scale. Its usefulness in the parable is not in the initial smallness alone, nor in the great destiny, but in the way that one is already stored and stirring within the other. There is a massive contrast, but also a close correspondence, between start and finish. Jesus invites his disciples to look beyond the difficulties and opposition of their own day. These small beginnings have immeasurable power within them, to lead to a glorious end.

Jesus stretches his illustration beyond its natural scope. The mustard plant was big for a vegetable, but it scarcely counted as a tree. Yet Jesus echoes an Old Testament text which describes God's coming rule as a great cedar (Ezekiel 17:22–24). He appears to be suggesting, 'Nature has no proper match for the remarkable growth of the kingdom; it will surpass all the scales and parallels available.' And by alluding yet again to the scriptures, he roots his own vision in the history of God's dealings with Israel. He is no maverick. The nation's whole tradition of faith and grace is coming to focus in him.

Lifting power

In a couple of other places (Luke 15:3–10; 18:1–14) we find a pair of parables together, one about a man and the other about a woman. Jesus was rather unusual among Jewish teachers, in welcoming women into his circle of followers and learners. His teaching reflects the work and world of women as well as of men.

The yeast parable itself (v. 33) is not an exact contrast with the mustard seed. Nothing is said directly about the smallness of the yeast. But Jesus points to the hiddenness of the rising process. You do not see how it happens, yet the effect is almost explosive. Three measures of flour amounts to more than fifty large loaves—enough for quite a crowd. Perhaps this short word-picture hints at an incident to come (see 14:15–22).

The word 'hidden' is picked up in a couple of other places in the next few lines, at verses 35 and 44. The kingdom is growing in a quiet and concealed fashion, and the cryptic language of the parables is part of that growth. But when the hidden suddenly comes into our view, we should grasp it as surely and strongly as we can, like treasure turned up in a field.

Hiding secrets

Matthew's quotation of Psalm 78:2 in verses 34–35 speaks of secret things being brought to light. It links Jesus' teaching style to scripture —as this Gospel so often stresses the fulfilment of scripture in Jesus' life and work. The parables have the capacity to reveal the kingdom. Yet even when they are brought into the light, they remain hidden; there are people who cannot grasp their truth. These parables both reveal and conceal; they explain and they exclude. So the crowds have work to do in weighing the stories in their minds. But as the Gospel moves on, it moves indoors to the privacy of 'the house' (13:36) where Jesus will teach his disciples.

Forward movement

Jesus vision of God's kingdom is dynamic. It has an inner power. It reaches, quietly and yet surely, for a splendid and spectacular future. It is obscure now, like the parables themselves. Though small amid the world's doubt and opposition, it will shine in God's good time with the greatness and grandeur of heaven.

PRAYER

Lord God, when everything around us seems to cloud and obscure your love, give us calm and confident faith, to wait and watch for the coming growth of your work. Through Jesus Christ our Lord. Amen.

TREASURE NEW & OLD

So far, the parables in this chapter have spoken of the kingdom's struggles, and of its certain growth. They trace what God is doing. Now come three short, punchy stories that urge us to join in.

Doing business with God

It must be every farmer's dream to turn up a hoard of gold coins beneath the blade of the plough (v. 44). In ancient Palestine, land that had often been fought over, there was always a chance. A former tenant might have hidden valuables in the ground before fleeing or going out to war.

Historians have puzzled over the legal background. Would it be lawful to cover treasure up and then buy the field, without telling the owner? Certainly that question could have been in Jesus' mind. Perhaps he told the parable with a twinkle in his eye, to stir people into thinking about such an odd and dubious tale. But his main point is at the end of this little story: the kingdom is so important, it is worth everything you have to make sure you secure it.

That matches exactly the parable of the pearl merchant (vv. 45–46). Again the story is about a single treasure which turns a businessman into a lover. Suddenly he can no longer simply buy and sell. Here is something so precious that he must possess it. And so he is possessed by it; he gives himself to make sure he gets it. This is not commerce; it is commitment.

Matthew has already shown his readers a couple of times that Christians must not be preoccupied by property and possessions (6:19–34; 10:9–10). These two little stories, with their line about 'selling everything', remind us that seeking and serving God's kingdom may involve material sacrifices. Commitment to Christ includes the commitment of our wealth.

Coming to the surface

A drag-net was long, and hung from floats a few feet beneath the surface of the water. It could be positioned by two boats and then hauled in by ropes to the shore. The sifting of the catch was an everyday job, but Jesus uses it as a picture of God's great day of judgment (vv. 47–48).

An explanation is given with the parable, rather like the one that followed the wheat and the tares (13:37–43). But the focus here is sharper: nothing is said about waiting; there is only one point, the final sorting out. The emphasis is on the down-side of judgment (vv. 49–50). Alongside the two little treasure parables, which stress the excitement of finding the kingdom, this strikes a solemn warning. It is vital to be 'righteous', to be like soil that welcomes the gospel seed, to grasp the kingdom when the opportunity arises and to serve it faithfully from then on.

The first time I worked carefully through Matthew, I was struck by its solemnity. This Gospel presents discipleship seriously. Every one of the five long discourses ends with a parable about judgment and reward (see also 7:13–27; 10:41–42; 18:23–35; 25:31–46). 'Don't be casual,' Matthew seems to be saying. 'Don't take the kingdom for granted. Take it seriously.'

Wealth to share

The disciples have been given privileged insights into the parable material (13:11, 36). They still need to 'hear' (13:18, 43) and to respond earnestly and actively (vv. 44–46). But their nearness to Jesus gives them a special role. They have been able to understand, and now they can share that understanding with others. They will have a teaching role in the Church to come.

So when Jesus says, 'Have you understood?' he goes on to speak of the 'scribe trained for the kingdom'—someone who knows the ancient scripture, and can use it to proclaim and explain the freshness of God's kingdom. Treasure is to be grasped (v. 44), but also shared (v. 52). The kingdom message is to be passed on, in a way that shows its firm base in God's past work.

So the disciples' task is threefold: to grasp the message of the kingdom; to live by its truth, as people whose lives will be judged; and to share its message.

FOR REFLECTION

The gospel still needs teachers whose message is up-to-date and yet is firmly grounded in ancient scripture. There is just a suspicion (see the section 'Who was Matthew?' in the Introduction, p. 15) that 13:52 is Matthew's own 'signature', his hopes and ideals for his own teaching ministry. Could it also be yours?

No Local Hero

This passage is a counterpart to 12:46–50. There Jesus gathered his new family, the followers who wanted to serve God with him. Theirs was the company where he felt he belonged, where he could find sympathy and support, whereas in today's passage he goes back to the district where he grew up. The people there—quite understandably—recall him and relate to him as a member of his old family. No wonder that this was not a very easy or happy encounter.

Moving on

Each of the five major blocks of teaching in Matthew has a very clear ending: 'When Jesus had finished…' (v. 53; compare 7:28 and 11:1, for example). Matthew lets his readers know that they are returning to the action of the Gospel. But the parable chapter has sharpened our expectations: will people understand; will they grasp the kingdom; what sort of ground will the seed fall upon?

The next couple of chapters show some very varied reactions to Jesus and his cause. Many people show faith and give praise, but there is hostility too, and the prospect that Jesus will die a martyr's death begins to come into view. By the time we meet the next concentrated instalment of teaching in chapter 18, it has become clear that there will be a painful clash ahead.

More questions than answers

Jesus moves on from the lakeside to the western hills of Galilee. It seems (although it does not say directly) that he comes to his own home village of Nazareth, and teaches during sabbath worship in the synagogue. Nazareth was a small place, off the main routes—the sort of tight rural community where people knew one another well. Jesus' old neighbours remembered his upbringing among them, and a number of his relatives still lived in the area.

There are six questions in a row in verses 54–56. These begin with amazement (v. 54) and end in disbelief, disdain and disapproval (v. 57). The people in Nazareth know plenty about Jesus. 'Where did he get all this from?' is a question they feel they should be able to answer. They cannot believe that there might be another aspect to

Jesus' life, something about him that they do not understand. The same sort of question crops up in another setting, in John 6:42.

Carpenter's house

Joseph was a skilled craftsman. The word used in verse 55 commonly means 'carpenter, woodworker', but it can also refer to a small building contractor, who made houses out of mudbrick and wood.

Jesus' brothers are named, and his sisters are mentioned, for the only time in this Gospel. These may have been younger sons and daughters of Joseph and Mary. However, many Christians throughout the Church's history have wondered about another explanation: either that these were Joseph's children by an earlier marriage, or that they were actually Jesus' cousins, children of the other Mary who appears at Matthew 27:56. None of these suggestions can really be ruled out.

A number of these relatives later believed in Jesus and took leading roles in the spread of the Christian faith after the resurrection. On this occasion, however, they offer him little support.

Fortunes of a prophet

There are other ancient sayings to roughly this effect, that an emerging public figure receives scant applause in his own backyard (v. 57). This particular proverb surfaces in all four Gospels (Mark 6:4; Luke 4:24; John 4:44), though not always in exactly the same setting. In the end, Jesus acknowledges his former neighbours' lack of faith, which has prevented him accomplishing much in Nazareth.

So the visit ends on a note of disappointment. But a more disturbing and distressing shadow is about to fall, for Jesus has described himself as a prophet, a spokesman for God. John the Baptist too is a prophet (11:9; 14:5), and we are just about to hear of John's imprisonment and death (14:3–12). It seems that a prophet's eventual fate may be a good deal worse than home-town scepticism.

PRAYER

Holy Spirit of God, teach me to see the goodness you have put in my neighbours. Give me grace to rejoice when friends show gifts I had never noticed. And when people are unimpressed by me, help me not to get angry, nor to give up what I ought to be doing. For Jesus Christ's sake. Amen.

POINTER *to the* PASSION

This is one of the few passages in the Gospel that is not directly about Jesus, one of few scenes where he is not on stage. John was a man of spiritual depth and great courage, who deserves much credit for his ministry. But in all four Gospels he is much more than a prophet (11:9). He is the forerunner whose work launches and prepares for the work of Jesus. Jesus has spoken of him with warmth and honour (11:10–19). The preaching of the two men had much in common (3:2; 4:17). So when John comes to such an ugly and undeserved end, the reader may rightly fear what will become of Jesus.

Troubled tetrarch

The 'Herod' of this passage is Herod Antipas. His father, Herod the Great, was the king who had tried to kill Jesus at birth, and had himself died a year or two later, in 4BC. Antipas ruled a third of his father's lands—Galilee, and Perea on the east bank of Jordan—under the permission and power of the Roman Empire, until AD39. He was known as 'tetrarch', which means 'ruler of a quarter', but was not allowed to use the title 'king'; that was Rome's way of reminding him who was really in charge.

When Herod heard about Jesus, the attention he was attracting and the signs he was performing, he was disturbed. He had recently executed John the Baptist, and yet here was a prophet creating just the same sort of stir as John had done. Like so many others (13:13, 54–58), Herod completely fails to understand Jesus. But before we return to Jesus, and hear of his response to Herod's interest (14:13), Matthew explains how John died.

Man in a corner

Herod had switched wives, abruptly and illegally. John criticized him for it, and Herod threw John into jail (see comment on 11:2–3, p. 90). But once John was locked up, Herod himself was trapped. He wanted to kill John and silence him for ever, but he was afraid of popular opinion (v. 5). There was a corner of his own conscience, too, that was disturbed by John and would not have been comfortable with the idea of putting him to death (Mark 6:20). Herod had no easy room for manoeuvre.

Dance of death

According to the Jewish historian Josephus, writing about AD100, John died at the desert fortress of Machaerus, high on a mountain-side east of the Dead Sea. Archaeologists digging at Machaerus have found the remains of two separate large dining-rooms, which would match the indications (clearer in Mark 6:14–29 than here) that men and women dined separately on festive occasions.

The whole affair seems sordid and demeaning. The woman Herodias comes across as a bitter and cynical opportunist. The dancing princess is simply used by the adults around her. And Herod—the host who should be in control, the man responsible for law and order—is totally spineless, cornered by 'his oaths and his guests' (v. 9) into an action that lacks any trace of justice or dignity.

But John is dead. His active ministry is over, although the memory of what he has said and done will not be easily quietened. Herod himself could not shake off the memory of that murky night (vv. 1–2), and (again from Josephus) his public image and popularity never quite recovered from this episode.

Matthew's Gospel says a good deal about the pressure and persecution that frequently come to God's prophets (5:12; 22:2–6; 23:29–39). In a few chapters' time, it makes a direct link between the death of John the forerunner and the fate that is waiting for Jesus (17:12–13). For the moment, those connections are not underlined. But Jesus would surely have realized, when he heard of John's death (v. 12), that his own work could become increasingly difficult.

FOR THOUGHT AND PRAYER

Dangers always arise when power is not linked to principle, and when people use public office for their own pride and pleasure. Criticism is sometimes a right Christian response—as it surely was when John challenged Herod Antipas.

But quick and thoughtless criticism is unlikely to be helpful. More regular, more constructive, are the commitments that Christians have to pray for our rulers, and to offer respect, support and obedience whenever we properly can. We should pray too that in every generation people of faith and integrity will come into public life, to serve God and neighbour there.

TABLE *in the* WILDERNESS

Alone with a crowd

Jesus withdraws to a lonely place. But the wording of verse 13 is not very clear. Has he just heard of John's death (14:12)? Or has he heard of Herod's concern about his own ministry (14:1–2), so that he feels the need to avoid an ugly confrontation (as at 4:12 and 12:15)?

Surely Jesus wanted to reflect and pray about the growing atmosphere of conflict and danger around his ministry. It appears (from Mark 6:45 and John 6:1) that he went to the area around Bethsaida on the north-east shore of the Sea of Galilee, just out of Antipas' territory. Jesus did not lack courage. But he did not want to provoke a needless and premature clash. He may already have realized that he would finish his work in Jerusalem (Luke 13:33).

Jesus is pursued by eager, needy people. They come for healing, but the remoteness of the place, and the time taken to get there, lead quickly to another concern: where will they get food?

Dinner in the desert

The word 'evening' (v. 15) has a pretty broad span, starting in mid-afternoon. But there would be little food available in the small, unwalled hamlets and local farmsteads. 'You give them something to eat,' seems mysterious, and even perverse. John 6:6 says that Jesus was testing the disciples, but Matthew's writing style is very compressed, and he does not dwell on this sort of detail.

The resulting expansion of food is spectacular indeed. Bread and fish were the staple foods in Galilee, and there was plenty to be shared that day. Matthew's first readers might have thought back to the Old Testament, to Moses with the manna and quails (Exodus 16; Numbers 11). But the clearest echoes in the story are of a lesser-known passage, Elisha's bread miracle in 2 Kings 4:42–44.

As well as looking back, the episode points ahead. Israel looked forward to a great banquet with God (Isaiah 25:6–9; see also Matthew 8:11), and this desert feeding would suggest to some that Jesus was ushering in those days of prosperity and hope. Some other popular leaders in this era, so-called messiahs, had also promised signs and gathered excited crowds in the desert. No wonder, then, that Jesus was hailed as a 'king' (John 6:14–15). But again he stepped aside (Matthew 14:23). God's kingdom was growing under his leadership (13:31–33), but he was not the sort of king many people wanted.

Lord's supper

The language of verses 18–19 matches Matthew's account of the Last Supper (26:20–29): 'When evening came… he took bread, blessed, broke, and gave to the disciples'. The earliest Christians told the story of this feeding in ways that showed a clear connection to the Last Supper, and so to their own sharing of bread and wine in holy communion. Jesus nourishes his Church spiritually at his table, as surely as he fed his first followers in the lonely hills of Galilee.

But the connection works the other way round too. Matthew's story suggests that Jesus is already gathering and tending the community that will become the Christian Church. He has been harried by Pharisees, cold-shouldered in Nazareth, and growled at by Herod. As many in Israel turn against him, Jesus starts to shape a new community, a people within a people, and feeds them in a way that already foreshadows the Christian eucharist.

But what really…

But what actually happened? Could Jesus really multiply bread and fish? Certainly Matthew believed it; the feeding is mentioned again (16:9), in a way that shows he thought it true. The other Gospels include it—only this miracle, apart from the resurrection, comes in all four. The numbers five and two (v. 17) have no obvious symbolic meaning—which tends to suggest that they were remembered from the event.

C.S. Lewis (in his book *Miracles*) links this feeding to our belief in God as Creator. We know that God can multiply fish in the sea and corn in the field, although we are accustomed to him doing this gradually. But when God comes in human flesh, just occasionally he shows his creative power as if it were accelerated, compressed into Jesus' ministry of care and compassion (v. 14).

PRAYER

To God who is known in creation and compassion, in humility and humanity, be praise and glory, now and always. Amen.

STEPS *of* FAITH

This passage has two messages, entwined around one another. The first concerns who Jesus is. These verses present him in a new and fresh light, and show the disciples growing in faith and understanding. The second message is pastoral, about faith and how it operates. It invites Christians to see ourselves as the disciples in the boat, or even as Peter struggling to stay afloat, and to place our trust in Jesus. For Matthew, the two messages go together: because Jesus is Lord of the storms, he is worth trusting in our own times of turbulence and fear.

The action takes place at night. If the first 'evening' (14:15) was the slight cooling of the afternoon sun (see comment on 14:15–21, pp. 126–127), this second 'evening' (v. 23) must be the deep dusk of falling night. 'Early in the morning' (v. 25) refers to the last few hours of the night, from about 3 o'clock onwards.

Presence in the storm

This is the second sea miracle in Matthew (the other being 8:23–27). When the wind blew through the steep valleys around the Sea of Galilee, the waters could get rough and rowing would be hard. Then Jesus comes, portrayed here in ways that speak simply and directly of the presence of God.

He walks on the sea, as only God can do (Job 9:8; Psalm 77:19). He greets his friends, saying, 'It is I' (v. 27): the words echo the 'I am' of God's presence in Exodus 3:14. His 'Fear not' (v. 27) recalls the assurances of Isaiah 43:1–2: 'Fear not... you are mine... when you pass through the waters I shall be with you.' This is truly Emmanuel, God with his people (1:23).

Wading for God

In the next few chapters there are several places where Peter takes the lead among the disciples (15:15; 16:16, 22; 17:4, 24; 18:21; 19:27), and most of these episodes are mentioned only in Matthew. This Gospel, in particular, shows Peter emerging from the group of disciples as spokesman, venturer, even as leader. During these chapters, which foreshadow the life of a new community called the Church, we meet the man who will become its first leader.

Here Peter emerges from the group, and quite literally goes over-board for Jesus (vv. 28–29). He comes over as impulsive, committed and enthusiastic, but also as fragile, ordinary and vulnerable. Many Christians find him an attractive character for that reason. We see something of ourselves in his undulating spiritual pilgrimage, his blend of devotion and disaster. Here Jesus calls him, 'You of little faith' (v. 31; the same word used at 8:26). Peter is not faithless, but his faith is faulty, patchy, not complete or secure.

Yet Jesus trusted Peter, and went on doing so, even after Peter's threefold denial on the night before the crucifixion. You do not need to be perfect, or have an armour-plated Christian faith, to hold office in the Church. Doubts are allowed (see 28:17). But it helps to be honest with God—and with yourself—about your failures.

Faith finding solid ground

For the disciples as a group, this experience was a moment of growth in their faith and understanding. The incident ends with, 'Truly you are the Son of God' (v. 33), which is a stronger and clearer ending than their 'What sort of man is this?' of 8:27. They do not know Jesus nearly as well as he knows them. But their eyes are starting to open.

Contagious mercy

Gennesaret is an area of flat land stretching back a few miles from the north-west shore of the Sea of Galilee (v. 34). Again Jesus encounters a throng of needy people, but the whole episode is summarized in just a couple of sentences. There is scarcely any detail, only this: Jesus appears as a pious Jew, wearing a robe with a tasselled hem (Deuteronomy 22:12), and that is what people touch to find healing (v. 36). In the crowd there may be all kinds of unclean people. But when they touch Jesus, he does not become impure too. The influence flows the other way. Jesus communicates the wholeness and mercy of God (8:3; 9:20–22), for the healing of others.

But matters of purity were important to Jews, and our next passage centres on just this issue: what makes a person truly clean?

PRAYER

Pray for any people you know who are struggling to stay afloat, who feel insecure and unsupported, that they may know the steady hand of Jesus reaching to them and holding them up.

CLEAN HANDS & *a* PURE HEART (1)

There were many debates in Judaism about interpretation of the nation's ancient law. Jesus got involved in these, in the Sermon on the Mount. He spoke about 'righteousness that exceeds that of the scribes and Pharisees' (5:20) and, in the 'Six Antitheses' (5:21–48), Matthew shows him dealing with a number of legal questions.

Since that sermon, ill-feeling has been rising. Scribes and Pharisees have become a regular irritant in Jesus' ministry (9:3, 11, 34; 12:2, 24, 38), while his popularity has made him a serious nuisance, so far as they are concerned. He strikes them as dangerously lax, teaching his followers to live an irresponsible and irreligious life (9:14; 12:2).

So this clash is no surprise. But there is a sinister feel about it. Questioners come from Jerusalem (v. 2); Jesus' reputation has evidently spread. He answers back quite aggressively at his questioners (vv. 3–9). Once before, he felt seriously threatened by Pharisaic anger, and moved out of danger (12:14–15). After this incident he will move on again (15:21).

The whole episode (15:1–20) unfolds in three scenes. The first (vv. 1–9) shows Jesus in discussion with scribes and Pharisees.

Honour your elders

Pharisees wanted to live by the biblical ideal that Israel was a 'priestly kingdom and a holy nation' (Exodus 19:6). So they tried to import some of Israel's priestly laws into daily life, so that home and table would express in a small way the holiness of the Temple. The priestly duty of handwashing before Temple service (Exodus 30:17–21) was one of these laws. To observe it at every meal was a 'tradition of the elders' (v. 2), handed down from one generation of Pharisees to another. But Jesus' disciples do not follow this pattern. 'Why not?' the visitors ask.

Jesus defends his disciples. He counter-attacks on the issue of tradition, which had been the basis for his opponents' question. 'Your tradition,' he says, 'violates a basic command of scripture' (vv. 3–6).

Jesus refers to the practice called *korban*, the making of vows. It was possible to assign property to the Temple, and call this a vow to God (Deuteronomy 23:21–23), without actually losing one's right of ownership. A tight-fisted person could adopt this device in order to protect wealth, and could avoid having to help needy neighbours or support elderly parents. So this tradition actually used a biblical law about vows to break the command to honour father and mother (Exodus 20:12).

Lips and lives

It is all too easy to say one thing and to do or desire something else. Our words may be very godly, but what we really want, and how our motives work out in action, might be rather different. That, according to Jesus, is the problem with the scribes and Pharisees. Tradition has taken over. Building on scripture, tradition has actually eclipsed and obscured the real force that is in scripture. Their words sound grand; the real character of their religion is not.

The quotation in verses 8 and 9 is from Isaiah 29:13, in a chapter which speaks of God leading Israel from blindness to sight (Isaiah 29:10, 18). Sight is an important theme in Matthew. Jesus offers people a fresh view of the presence of God, but those who persist in blindness (15:14) he regards with suspicion verging on despair.

Open table

There were some big differences between Jesus' approach to religion and that of the Pharisees. He was not committed as they were to the idea of tradition. When he taught, he did not start with the sayings of other teachers, from a generation or two earlier. His 'I tell you...' (8:11; 12:36) was much more direct. He showed a great personal authority. He reflected for himself on the Old Testament, and on the work of God in his own times and ministry.

Jesus appeared casual and careless to some of his opponents. He was not bound by other people's custom. But this freedom allowed him to be very open in personal relationships. With Jesus, meals were an occasion for showing the wide mercy and care of God (as at 9:9–17), not for expressing a strict and exclusive purity.

FOR THOUGHT AND PRAYER

May God grant us wisdom to see when our tradition diverges from truth, or destroys trust, or causes more trouble than it is worth. For Jesus Christ's sake.

CLEAN HANDS & *a* PURE HEART (2)

The discussion about purity continues. The opponents slip out of view, as Jesus turns first to the crowd (vv. 10–11), then privately to his disciples (vv. 12–20). He wants to deepen his disciples' understanding and also to give the crowds—many of them people without fixed opinions—a chance to respond to his teaching. Although Jesus' clashes with scribes and Pharisees become more painful as the Gospel goes on, the crowds remain supportive (see 21:46). Only very late in the Gospel does their attitude change.

Which matters more—input or output?

Thus far Jesus has met his opponents' question by counter-attack. In stressing tradition, he said, they stand on very shaky ground. Now he answers directly the question they raised: why don't his disciples wash as the Pharisees do? Here—very briefly, and to be expanded later—is the nub of his argument.

Food and purity laws attend to what goes into the mouth, what a person eats and drinks: only if input is pure will the person be pure as well. Jesus disagrees. True purity, he says, is not known by the mouth's input, but by its output (v. 11). Our speech shows the quality of our inner self—sometimes with the utmost clarity (12:33–37).

Blind guides

In the final phase of this long conversation, Jesus is talking with his disciples. There are two parts: the first (vv. 12–14) refers again to the scribes and Pharisees; the second (vv. 15–20) will explain at greater length the brief saying in verse 11.

'The Pharisees took offence' (v. 12)—presumably at the attitude to purity that Jesus had just stated (v. 11). He is unmoved by their anger. If they are not rooted in God's purpose, their faith will lack staying power; they will be like tares amid the wheat (13:24–30, 36–43). They objected to his healing of a blind man (12:22–24), but they are the truly blind ones. They cannot help others to find the way of God, because they cannot see it for themselves. In spiritual matters we can rarely lead other people into wisdom we have not first made our own.

Teaching to digest

Verses 15–20 clarify the little saying in verse 11. Peter calls it a 'parable' (v. 15), meaning that it is a riddle, a cryptic and perplexing statement (see comment on 13:3, pp. 110–111). So Jesus explains himself.

Food, which goes into our mouth, does not contaminate a person, because it is digested and then goes to waste. It does not become a permanent part of what we are. But what comes out of our mouth comes from the heart, and reveals our true nature. It is the heart that gives rise to all sorts of wrong actions, and these actions make for real uncleanness.

This list (v. 19) includes several of the Ten Commandments (Exodus 20). Jesus mentioned the fifth command in verse 4. Now come the sixth, seventh, eighth and ninth. All of them express the love for neighbour that Jesus regarded as such an important standard of human behaviour (7:12; 22:39).

Finally the discussion ends where it began. 'Why don't your disciples wash their hands?' (15:2). 'Because eating with unwashed hands does not make a person unclean' (v. 20). The ceremony really doesn't matter. It does not touch the roots of real uncleanness in the human heart.

Side by side

It is interesting to compare Matthew's version of this conversation with Mark's. For example, Mark includes some words of explanation (7:2–4) which Matthew's audience would not need. Matthew has some sharp words about Jesus' opponents, which might have been especially relevant to his readers and their situation (vv. 12–14). The summing up in Matthew 15:20 is not as sweeping a statement as the last few words in Mark 7:19. These differences may reflect the different groups and settings in which the two Gospels were written. But the very broad and deep similarities between the two accounts come from Jesus, from the impact he made and the teaching he gave.

FOR THOUGHT AND PRAYER

Focusing on outward conformity is a constant danger for religious people. We feel safe with regular and respectable conduct. Unusual people, who break tradition and sit lightly to custom and convention, are less likely to impress us. Ask God to help you recognize true purity of heart in the people around you. Then welcome that, whatever their personality or style.

CROSSING *the* FRONTIER

This incident is one of the most puzzling in the Gospels. Why was Jesus so slow to respond to the woman's appeal? And why, after refusing at first, did he eventually help? A number of suggestions have been made. We come to them after working through the passage itself.

Lying low

Galilee was a small province, and we have already seen Jesus moving out of range when Herod became curious (14:13). After his latest clash with scribes and Pharisees, he goes up into the high ground of north-west Galilee and crosses into lands that belong to Tyre and Sidon. These were port cities, on the coast that is now southern Lebanon, and their territory stretched a few miles inland, to the edge of the Galilean hills. We may picture Jesus pausing for a few days in a highland village, to gain peace and perspective on his work and its effect. Even there his reputation has gone ahead of him.

A woman comes for help. Mark (7:26) calls her a 'Syro-Phoenician' —she belongs to the local area. Matthew writes 'Canaanite' (v. 22), stressing that she is a Gentile; that is the issue around which the whole story will revolve. The conversation has four movements.

Four movements to mercy

'Son of David,' she says (v. 22), hailing him as the Jewish Messiah. Some Jewish traditions thought of the Messiah as a miracle-worker and healer, and she has latched on to this hope. Her daughter is desperately ill, and she needs help. But Jesus does nothing.

Then the disciples join in. 'Send her away' (v. 23). That could mean either 'Refuse her' or, possibly, 'Do what she asks.' Only then does Jesus respond. He speaks of 'the lost sheep of the house of Israel' (v. 24) as his proper mission field.

The woman is not a Jew, but she persists (v. 25). Still Jesus seems reluctant to get involved. Children's bread should not be thrown to dogs. His mission is to the children of Israel, to God's chosen family of faith (v. 26), and he seems unprepared to spread his work.

Eventually the woman breaks through. Even if Gentiles are 'dogs', a dog may come near enough to the table to gather up the crumbs that spill, and so share the same food as the family. So finally Jesus commends her 'great faith' (v. 28), and her daughter is healed.

Who's listening?

Different readers respond in different ways to this story. Some see the woman pushing Jesus to do something he had not intended to, opening his mind, and expanding his vision of what his mission could be. He had a narrow Jewish perspective (as in 10:6), and it took her persistence and stubbornness to shake him out of it. He healed her daughter, but she taught him what it meant to be God's Son—not just a Jewish Saviour, but a man for others too.

A problem in taking that view is that Jesus had already worked among Gentiles (see comments on 8:5–13, 18, 28–34, pp. 64–71). He was impressed by the centurion's faith, surpassing anything he met in Israel (8:10). And in this meeting with the Canaanite woman, it is faith that settles the matter. So another way of reading the story is to see Jesus as the person pushing the conversation to its eventual destination, testing the woman by his hesitancy, to show the quality of her faith. Does she really recognize that 'salvation is from the Jews' (John 4:22)? Is she ready to trust another nation's grace?

Ahead of her time

As you think about the passage for yourself, keep two things in mind.

First, the New Testament is clear that the gospel is for the whole world. But it comes to the world only through God's long work of preparation within Israel. Some in Israel were able to see the signs of God's dawning kingdom in Jesus. But many in the Gentile world would not recognize these as kingdom signs at all. Their time for the word would be after the cross and resurrection. Jesus came to bring light to Israel first (see comments on 5:13–16, pp. 42–43), and this woman has come to faith ahead of time. She has pressed into the kingdom from outside. She is—in more ways than one—an exceptional believer.

Second, recall that Jesus told a parable about a woman's persistent prayers (Luke 18:1–8). He admired faith that was unyielding and determined, the sort of trust that could hold up even when tested.

FOR REFLECTION

Prayer sometimes has to be persistent and determined,
to gain all that God has for us.

SIGNING OFF

The incidents earlier in this chapter have shown Jesus adopting an unconventional attitude to the Jewish law, and extending his grace beyond the fringes of Israel. He has spoken as a loyal Jew, emphasizing scripture (15:1–20) and the special place of the chosen nation (15:21–28). Yet his work will eventually strain to breaking point his relationship with the leaders of his own people. Matthew 16 will begin Jesus' long pilgrimage to Jerusalem and the cross. From then on there will be less emphasis on signs, and more on suffering. The last couple of sections of Matthew 15 conclude his ministry in Galilee.

Mountain of mercy

Mark 7:31 suggests that Jesus went to the Decapolis, Gentile land south-east of the Sea of Galilee. But this passage in Matthew is not directly parallel to Mark's, and is not specific about place. We only hear that Jesus went to a hillside near the sea, and sat down as if to teach (v. 29). Then, as people brought sick and disabled friends, he healed them. This is almost the last of Matthew's short 'healing summaries'. Others were at 4:23–25; 8:16–17; 9:35–36; 14:13–14, 34–36; two more snippets follow, at 19:2 and 21:14. This account is distinctive, for it ends on a note of glad gratitude to God (v. 31). God is at work in Jesus, and God is to be praised for Jesus.

Second sitting

This feeding (vv. 32–38) is told in a very similar way to the previous feeding of five thousand (14:13–21), although the dialogue at the start between Jesus and his disciples is not identical (vv. 32–34). The numbers involved are different too—seven loaves, four thousand people, and seven baskets picked up afterwards. Yet once we get to the feeding itself, the two accounts stay closely in step (vv. 35–38; 14:19–21). Once again there is a strong resonance with Matthew's account of the Last Supper, and so with the Church's holy communion service.

Some readers of the Bible think that these two accounts go back to a single incident, that Jesus would not have done this sort of thing more than once. But it becomes clear, in a few verses' time (16:7–12), that Matthew thinks of two separate feedings. The early Christians remembered and spoke of two feedings. And they told of these feedings in words that also recalled the Last Supper. So they remembered, when they shared bread and wine, the power and provision of their Lord.

Homecoming to God

Some careful scholars have found echoes of Israel's Old Testament hopes in these verses.

- Crowds of people come together on a hillside, like pilgrims going up to Mount Zion, in Jerusalem (Isaiah 2:2–4).

- The healings reflect the hopes of Isaiah 35:5–6, a chapter which ends with the redeemed of the Lord coming in praise to Zion.

- There may also be an echo of Isaiah 29: as God judges shallow and stubborn hearts (29:13, quoted at Matthew 15:8–9), he brings healing and hope to the needy (Isaiah 29:18).

- There is a banquet, like the promise of Isaiah 25:6–9, a feast for peoples from far and near on the mountain of God.

If these connections were in Matthew's mind, then he is hinting that an age of promise has come, and that prophecies are fulfilled. Jesus is God's great meeting point, the new gathering place for the faithful. 'Something greater than the Temple is here' (12:6). The nations will come to him, to learn of Israel's God. That hint becomes clear and compelling at the very end of Matthew's Gospel, when good news goes out to reach the world (28:18–20). In Jesus God is known, God is with us, and the world may come to God.

Going out alone

After many have been fed, Jesus leaves on his own (only at 16:5 do the disciples join him). Magadan (v. 39) is a mystery: we do not know where it was. But as the coming chapter brings warning and sorrow, we may reflect that Jesus' going alone towards suffering and death was the means by which he gathered the nations to God.

PRAYER

For the mercy of God in Jesus Christ, seen by those who knew him in flesh, shared with us who trust him in faith, be thanks and praise to Israel's God, now and evermore. Amen.

RISING OPPOSITION

Noblest foe-men

Sadducees appear, for the first time since 3:7, to question Jesus. They were a much smaller group than the Pharisees, and were based in Jerusalem. This group of a few wealthy families controlled the religious and economic life of the Temple, monopolized the succession of Jewish high priests, and wielded a good deal of judicial and political influence. By comparison with the Pharisees, they appear as rather worldly ecclesiastics; but they had a great deal more clout.

It is curious to meet Sadducees in Galilee. However, some rich Jerusalem families had big agricultural estates in northern Palestine, and indeed several gospel parables refer to such estates. So possibly some Sadducees heard of Jesus through local contacts or when visiting their property.

Colours of day

Verses 1–4 include a large 'textual variant': some of the most ancient copies of Matthew that we have omit most of verses 2 and 3. A footnote in your Bible may mention this. We really do not know whether Matthew wrote those two verses or not. (The verse numbering does not help; it was inserted long after Matthew's time.)

If we left out verses 2–3, then what remained of 16:1–4 would be very similar to 12:38–39. But one small difference here is the word 'to test him' (v. 1), which makes this interrogation seem like devilish work—for Jesus' temptation by Satan was also called a 'testing' (4:1).

If the 'missing verses', 2–3, are included in this little dialogue, then they make the point that even Jesus' opponents should have spotted what God was doing through him. They can read the sky when they have to, but cannot read the marks of the kingdom of heaven. They are perverse in asking 'a sign from heaven' (v. 1), for they ignore the signs they already have of God's activity on earth.

Crumbs of comfort

If ever a conversation starts off like ships passing in the night, with no point of contact or even of real hearing, here it is (vv. 5–12). It seems more typical of some of the misunderstandings in John's Gospel (such as 3:1–16 or 4:7–26), than of Matthew. The two halves of the conversation begin at the same time, and both mention bread, but they set off in opposite directions.

'Beware of the yeast of the Pharisees and Sadducees,' says Jesus (v. 6), meaning his opponents' influence and teaching.

Meanwhile it occurs to the disciples that they meant to bring bread and had not done so. They respond as if Jesus were asking about the supply of sandwiches (v. 7).

So Jesus calls them 'little faith people' (v. 8; as at 8:26; 14:31). Their faith is real, but it does not always connect very well with experience. They should have realized that he can supply hungry people when he has to. They have seen him do that twice. He would not need to worry about a few loaves, if his friends were in need (vv. 9–10).

'You should have understood,' says Jesus, 'that I wasn't using the word "yeast" literally.' Finally he says again, 'Beware of the yeast of the Pharisees and Sadducees' (v. 11), and this time his friends realize that he means the opponents' teaching.

Of course Jesus knew what he was doing. Often the best teachers work by provoking their hearers to think. The best-remembered lessons can be those which were a struggle to grasp. The conversation with the disciples converges in the end, and they eventually understand what Jesus means. The teaching of his enemies could have a yeast-like effect, expanding to fill the minds that absorbed it, influencing habits and outlook. So Jesus warns his disciples that much is at stake. Are they prepared to listen to him as their teacher, and follow his view when it differs from more popular or respectable opinion?

FOR THOUGHT AND PRAYER

Most of us are shaped by the thinkers and attitudes we follow. In Matthew's Gospel one of the most vital tasks of the Church is to heed and pass on the teaching Jesus has given (28:20). This Gospel reminds us to weigh everything that invites our loyalty against his words and outlook. The teaching of Jesus is still a solid basis and a wise guide for living, for people who are ready to take it seriously.

ROCK FORMATION

Jesus' relationship to the leaders of his own nation is under strain. There are hints already that he is shaping the community which will become the Christian Church. Now we start to see this community more clearly, and hear of Jesus' own plans and desires for its life.

Question time

The zig-zag movement around Galilee continues. Caesarea Philippi is in the far north of the area, out of Herod's territory. Again we get the impression that Jesus wants some quiet time with his disciples. His opinion poll (v. 13) receives a range of answers. All of them cast Jesus as a prophet, returned to minister to God's people.

When Jesus asks for the disciples' view, then Simon Peter's ringing affirmation (v. 16) confirms and expands what they began to see before (14:33). Peter recognizes Jesus as much more than just a spokesman for God. For him, Jesus is Israel's promised Messiah, bringing the life and presence of God to his people with new depth and power.

First base

Although verses 13–16 are also in Mark and Luke, the next snippet (vv. 17–19) appears only in Matthew. It makes several points:

- Simon's faith is a gift of God. Only God gives that sort of insight.

- From now on, Simon will be called 'Peter', the rock-man. There is a word-play in Matthew's Greek: *petra* means 'stone' and *Petros* is 'Peter'. And in Aramaic, the language most Jews spoke, the link is even more direct. The name given to Simon is *Kepha*, the exact word that means 'stone'.

- On this rock Jesus will build the community he is shaping. Peter and the faith he has declared will be the base on which the Church will grow and stand.

- Forces of evil will not destroy the Church. It will have the life and strength to prevail against all assaults and trials.

- Peter will lead the Church as it opens the kingdom of God, drawing many in, but also 'binding and loosing', setting out the way that believers should live. (See also comment on 18:18, p. 155.)

Splintered rock?

I am writing this as a Reformed Christian in the cordial hospitality of a Roman Catholic college. The Church is divided, and our understanding of these very verses reflects some of these divisions.

- There is an old-established view in the Greek-speaking churches, going right back to the third century, that the 'rock' is Peter's faith, and that he stands for the typical Christian believer.

- The idea that the 'rock' is Jesus, whom Peter has just confessed, comes from the great African theologian Augustine (about AD 400), and was taken up strongly by the 16th-century Reformers.

- The understanding that Peter himself is the 'rock', and that his authority has been handed down to his successors, the Popes, has been held by many Roman Catholics since the fifth century.

Digging in the Bible

So what is the text saying? I think the word-play on Peter's name is important—it does suggest that Simon Peter himself is the 'rock'. Then there is an echo of an Old Testament passage, Isaiah 51:1–2, which describes Abraham and Sarah, the father- and mother-figures of Israel, as the rock and quarry from whom the nation's life was cut. They were founders and prototypes of faith, who could hand on to others the heritage of grace and trust into which God had drawn them. That is Peter's position: the prototype Christian believer, the new Abraham of the Christian Church, the rock of a new community.

Finally, it is important to me that Jesus does not say 'churches'. The Church is one, even though it has been hard to live by that ideal. All Christians—whether or not we take communion together, and however we interpret Matthew 16—belong to the one family of faith that started to find its identity in the far reaches of Galilee when Peter said, 'You are the Christ, the Son of the Living God.'

PRAYER

Thank God for the firmness of his purpose, for the faith he has given the Church, and for the promise that no evil will destroy this worldwide fellowship, in which Jesus is known as Son of God.

61

SOLEMN DEPARTURE

'Don't tell anyone,' says Jesus (v. 20). He is keen not to be misunderstood by the crowds, careful not to give opponents any grounds for acting against him. He did not want the wrong kind of acclaim (see also comments on 9:27–31 and 14:15–21, pp. 78, 126–127). The disciples too would have to learn that his kingdom involved suffering and a cross.

New direction

'From that time on, Jesus began…' (v. 21) matches the wording of 4:17. That earlier text led the way into the Galilean ministry; this verse points the road out of Galilee to Jerusalem and crucifixion. If the stretch from 4:17 to 16:20 is Jesus' mission, then 16:21 onwards is his passion, his long journey to the cross. From Caesarea Philippi in the extreme north of Palestine, the movement is southwards, with a consistent focus on the holy city.

Unexpected rejections

Jesus' words (v. 21) are solemn and shocking. The earlier hints of trouble brewing have not seemed as harsh as this. Jerusalem is far from these Galilean hills and shores, and rejection so bitter and final by the central authorities of his own people seems a wretched and worthless end for God's Messiah. All Peter's loyalty and emerging faith rises up in protest and pain (v. 22).

Then suddenly the rock-man feels himself reduced to dust (v. 23). His attitude is wrong. His perspective is human, not godly. He is an obstacle in Jesus' path. He is the summons of Satan, beckoning Jesus aside from the way he must take, like the enticing words of temptation in chapter 4.

What about Peter's statement of faith, from just a few verses ago? Was it real? Surely it was, but it was fragile too. Peter, like the other disciples, was a person of 'little faith' (16:8), keen to believe, though not always alert to what faith means in practice. His failure here does not rub out his earlier gain. In the realm of faith, as with so many other activities, progress can be slow and painful. Growth often leads to new challenge, to fresh struggle and to deeper learning.

The 'must' that Jesus speaks (v. 21) is a deliberate commitment to a path laid out for him. In his own prayers, in his reflection on scripture, in his sense of God's calling, has come the conviction that he must suffer and die in the service of the kingdom. Yet he also believes that God will prove faithful, that he will be vindicated, that beyond death will be life. Along this road he takes his followers.

Following hard

Verses 13–20 showed the Church's faith, its privilege and final triumph; here we see the hard way of discipleship along which faith must walk. Jesus called his friends to costly obedience. Matthew's readers would realize that they too were summoned to a life of demanding service. And so are we.

Verses 24–25 are very similar to 10:38–39 (see also comments there, p. 88). 'Carrying the cross' will mean different things for different people—it depends on our circumstances. But whoever we are, and whatever the life we lead, we have not signed up for a cost-free Christianity. Faithful service is always likely to involve sacrifice, which may be unpredictable, inconvenient and intrusive. Jesus asks us for a basic decision to put him ahead of our own interests or desires. Only then will we 'find our life', in time and eternity.

Kingdom coming

Verse 27 offers assurance to fearful disciples. The Christian road has a destination. It is not just a journey of suffering. Faithful following will be gloriously and lastingly worthwhile. Jesus will honour the commitment his disciples make to him.

Verse 28, about the 'Son of Man coming in his kingdom', is difficult. It may refer to the destruction of Jerusalem in AD70. As God's judgment on the city that condemned Jesus, that could be seen as a vindication of Jesus and a pointer to his final coming in heavenly glory. But see further on chapters 24 and 25, where there is much material on Christ's coming and judgment.

FOR REFLECTION

'Carrying the cross means directing yourself to Jesus as your model for living… Self-denial means knowing Christ alone, instead of yourself, and watching him… rather than looking at the road.'

Ulrich Luz

MOUNTAIN-TOP EXPERIENCE

Jesus has spoken of the hard road he must take to the cross, and of his coming heavenly glory. Now comes an advance vision of that glory. He talked of founding a new community. Here he also stands honourably within Israel's ancient heritage of faith. In it all he receives the backing and approval of heaven. This transfiguration invites the disciples (and the reader) to follow Jesus without fear.

Speaking for the past

A riot of biblical connections link Moses and Elijah to one another and to Jesus (v. 3):

- One represents the law and the other the prophets—the two main portions of ancient scripture.

- Both were 'mountain men'. They met God on Mount Sinai—Moses amid cloud and glory, so that his face glowed with mysterious light (Exodus 24:9–17; 34:29–35); Elijah when the burdens of his ministry crushed him, yet God gave him assurance and encouragement (1 Kings 19).

- Both are, in different ways, forerunners for Jesus. Moses spoke of a coming prophet like himself (Deuteronomy 18:15–18), and Matthew has shown how Jesus takes up this mantle of Moses (see comment on 2:13–23, pp. 28–29). Elijah was expected by the Jews as roadmaker for the coming of God (Malachi 4:5–6; Luke 1:17), to bring reconciliation and peace to the nation. He stands for the dawning of promise, the coming fulfilment of Israel's hopes.

Together these two great figures bring the witness of the Old Testament to endorse the Messiah of the New. Both of them point to Jesus—Moses as pattern, and Elijah as herald.

Voice of God

Peter's offer (v. 4) is unnecessary, though well-meant. We cannot freeze-frame our deep experiences of God. Nor can we add anything to the sight of God's radiance. There are times, in worship and in our walk with Christ, when it is best simply to wait, to enjoy the presence of the Lord, and to relish this awareness of his greatness and love. Pray for those occasions, by all means. But do not try to preserve them. Let them be sufficient in themselves to sustain your journey ahead.

The cloud both reveals and conceals. God is present, in 'cloud and majesty and awe'. God's voice repeats the words of 3:17 (at Jesus' baptism; see comment there, p. 33). Jesus is God's anointed king, the sacrificial Son, and the Servant who will bring God's justice and victory to the waiting nations. The final command, 'Listen to him' (as at Deuteronomy 18:15), casts Jesus in the role of a new Moses. All the promise of the past rests on him as he goes humbly to the cross.

Quietly down

The three disciples fall to the ground and, as Jesus gently raises them to their feet, the vision has gone: they are there with him, alone (v. 8). As they walk down to join the others, Jesus presses them to say nothing of the experience—for the present. (Similar silence commands come at 8:4; 9:30; 12:16; 16:20.) Spreading their memories of this moment would cause confusion and trouble. Only after the resurrection will Jesus' glory be properly understood.

Gate of glory

By any reckoning the transfiguration is something of a mystery. What did the disciples see and how did they know it? What was Jesus expecting, and how did the experience help him? And how can heaven be revealed on earth?

Perhaps we are not going to find complete answers. There is majesty here that we cannot fathom. C.S. Lewis suggests (in *The Great Divorce*) that the stuff of heaven is not nebulous, elusive and shadowy, but firmer and more solid than our own world. We cannot yet know the full glory and grandeur of God. The depth and density in his being are presently beyond us. The disciples were allowed a brief and special vision. Yet the transfiguration is a glimpse of things to come, for the whole Church. For Christ is risen (v. 9), and all who love him will one day see him as he truly is (1 John 3:2).

PRAYER

God of time and eternity, all heaven praises you. Accept our praise
for all we have known of you, and for all you have yet to show us.
Through Jesus Christ our Lord. Amen.

FACING SUFFERING

This section could have been called 'Down to Earth'. However splendid the mountain view, you must eventually come back to the valley. As Jesus and his friends make their way down, suffering comes into sight, in two ways. First Jesus speaks about John the Baptist's suffering and his own. Then they meet a needy family, desperate for help. If the high-spots of our Christian life can help us to face the cost of our own discipleship and the needs of our neighbour, then they are high-spots indeed; if not, perhaps we should be a little suspicious of what they seem to offer.

Elijah incognito

The appearance of Elijah raises the question (v. 10; see comment on 17:1–3, p. 144), 'Is Elijah going to come back, then? Does the transfiguration give a new angle on that hope?' Jesus' reply is positive, but rather disturbing: 'Yes, the tradition is right. Elijah is meant to come, as a preacher of righteousness in Israel, just as the scriptures say.' But Elijah has come and the nation did not recognize him. It was John—the rough desert prophet—who took the role of Elijah (11:14). He had a strong popular appeal, but the religious leaders of the nation were not impressed (21:25, 32), and Herod killed him. 'They did to him whatever they pleased' (v. 12). His work was not given the attention or respect it deserved.

Then Jesus warns his friends that the Son of Man—Jesus himself—will suffer as well. Jesus' first direct prediction of his passion and death was at 16:21, and as the warning is repeated a number of times in these chapters (17:12, 22–23; 20:18–19, 28), it casts a shadow over this long journey to Jerusalem.

Son of God, Son of Man

This little conversation meshes with what has come before, to complete an interesting pattern:

Jesus as Son of God	Silence command	Jesus will suffer as Son of Man
16:13–19	16:20	16:21–28
17:1–8	17:9	17:10–13

Twice over, words of triumph are followed by words of tribulation—splendour by suffering. What holds all this together is that Jesus, the suffering earthly Son of Man, will also come as the glorious heavenly Son of Man (16:27). The glory of the transfiguration is not just a mist of summer, doomed to vanish in the heat of suffering. Both transfiguration and cross are the real Jesus. He is the Son of God, now ascended in glory. He is also the Lord who walked as one of us and died our death, sharing the pain and perplexity of human living. He has known the agony; he is no stranger to hurt and distress.

Helpless for healing

It is a fearful and desperate business to watch a sick child and be unable to heal or help. The father of this boy unloads his pain and fear before Jesus (vv. 14–16).

Jesus heals the child (v. 18). The verse says, 'The demon came out of him'; you may like to read the comment on 8:23–34 ('For clear minds', p. 71), on the issue of demon involvement. But verse 17 is strange: it seems that Jesus too has been drawn into the distress, and is frustrated that his disciples' faith has been unable to overcome it. Yet again the disciples are 'little faith people' (as at 6:30; 8:26; 14:31; 16:8). They have faith that 'understands and assents, but which does not trust God totally' (J.P. Meier). If only they had the tiniest quantity of true faith, it would have the expansive power of a mustard seed (13:31–32), and then obstacles would move before them.

(Note: verse 21, about prayer and fasting, is not in the earliest copies of Matthew, and is left out of most modern Bibles. But it may still have something to teach us.)

FOR PRAYER

Pray for children who suffer, for parents who fear for them and suffer with them, and for people whose work is to share the caring and try to help.

The COSTS of BELONGING

These two snippets have a common focus: the community of Jesus and its relationship to the central religious life of Israel.

Pilgrim people

'As they were gathering in Galilee' (v. 22) is the assembling of pilgrims before a journey. Many Jews, from throughout Palestine and from much further afield, travelled to Jerusalem for the annual Passover festival. Jesus and his friends are about to set off. We see the company moving on from Galilee at 19:1.

At the start of the journey, Jesus warns them that this will be no ordinary Passover (vv. 22–23). The disciples hear his sombre words, not with sharp contradiction (16:22), nor just with quiet understanding (17:12–13), but this time with deep sorrow.

I worshipped recently in a church with a giant wooden cross standing high and broad midway up the central aisle. In the looming shadow of the cross Jesus will speak to his friends about how to be Church (ch. 18), about the care, trust and mutual commitment they need, to live as his family.

Count me in

But first comes a question about whether Jesus and his company are committed to the religious life of the Jewish people. The temple tax required each adult male Jew to make an annual payment of half a shekel—about two days' wages. Although not compulsory, it was viewed as a patriotic duty. Capernaum was Peter's home town and was Jesus' base, if not his fixed abode. So the local collectors ask whether Jesus will pay or not (v. 24).

Jesus speaks about freedom. God is a Father to his people and does not tax them. The kingdom is a realm where God gives generously and his people respond with their grateful and glad commitment. Any sort of compulsory religious tax, the collection of an obligatory and measured slice of income, is a poor reflection of that relationship. This may also be the reason Jesus attacked the money-changers in the Temple (21:12–13). Money should not block or control people's access to God.

But Jesus will not cause unnecessary offence. He tells Peter to pay the tax—with a curious little saying about a coin in a fish's mouth.

Gold-fish

This saying (v. 27) is rather like the parable about treasure in the field (13:44). Routine daily work yields an extraordinary return. Some people think that Jesus was telling Peter to do a day's fishing, and so earn enough to pay the tax. But the language is very specific—'cast a hook, and take the first fish that comes'—and that suggests an unusual find.

So did Peter simply have an uncommonly good fishing expedition? Or did he manage to do what others have occasionally done, and hook a fish that had picked up a coin dropped in the water? Whatever Jesus meant, this little saying matches a regular theme of the Gospels. With Jesus, creation acquires a new generosity—bread and fish for thousands, water becoming rich wine (John 2), miraculous shoals of fish (Luke 5; John 21), provision from God (Matthew 6:31–33). The kingdom is about glimpses of light and generosity breaking through from heaven. And this fish saying points to an event on the limits of normality, 'a significant crack in ordinary experience… to enable us to glimpse… the dawning of the kingdom of God' (R. Bauckham, in *Gospel Perspectives*, Vol. 6, ed. D. Wenham and C. Blomberg, Sheffield Academic Press, 1986). God, for whose Temple the tax was gathered, provides the wealth for his children to pay.

FOR REFLECTION

While writing this, I spoke with a friend who is working to promote local development in a remote part of South America. For some of our neighbours, in many areas of the world, creation seems to have lost its generosity. Crops fail, health is hard to sustain and medicine difficult to afford, children grow weak, nature's resources are scarce. Christians may, in a small way, be copies of Christ if we will help others to discover and enjoy the wealth that God has put in his world. Let us thank God for the missions and relief organizations who help that to happen, on behalf of us all.

65

RECEPTION CLASS

Chapter 18 is the fourth block of teaching in this Gospel, and the theme is Christian community. Jesus speaks with his friends about their life together. Matthew is the only Gospel to use the word 'church' (16:18; 18:17); for him the Church is a strong, caring family.

Trouble with the ranks

Twice on this journey to Jerusalem, Jesus has to contend with his disciples' ambition (also at 20:20–28). As his own thoughts are drawn repeatedly to his coming suffering, his friends have not really grasped what it should mean for them too to take up the cross (16:24). So when they ask about rank and importance in the kingdom of heaven, Jesus leads their thoughts in a very different direction.

Small world

The word 'child' crops up repeatedly in the first few verses. Jesus calls a young child into the company and then says, 'This is how you have to be, to receive the wealth and dignity of God's kingdom.' The disciples, who are so concerned about position and precedence, must turn their attitudes right around and become like children.

So what was it about children that Jesus meant? Many answers have been suggested: children are innocent, gentle, uncomplicated, eager, expectant, receptive, humble, and so on. While all that is surely true (if not for every child all the time), it may miss the point. For children did not have much status in the ancient world; they were not thought very important. Jesus counters that view later (19:13–15), but here he uses it to explain the attitude that Christians should adopt.

The child-like attitude is to reckon ourselves truly unimportant, as 'less than the least of all God's people' (Ephesians 3:8), and genuinely to 'count others better than ourselves' (Philippians 2:3, RSV). Then we shall be small enough to know the greatness of God. Then we shall be 'great in the kingdom of heaven' (v. 4). Then we shall be generously open to Christ's other 'children' (v. 5), and in receiving them we shall be blessed by the presence of Christ himself.

Steps to stop stumbling

The first paragraph was about 'children'. The two words that appear next are 'little ones' (18:6, 10, 14), and 'stumble' or 'stumbling block' (six times in vv. 6–9). The nearest English equivalent to 'stumbling block' is probably 'banana skin'. But in these verses there is a moral aspect to making someone stumble: it is a wrong thing to do if it leads them astray and interrupts their walk with Christ.

The 'little ones' are other Christians, the people who are called 'children' in the preceding verses. Christians should recognize one another as fragile and vulnerable, as people to treat carefully. It is a fearful and serious matter, says Jesus, to drag a fellow Christian down. He warns his followers to be very careful of the effect our behaviour may have on others.

Strong language

Jesus makes his point forcibly and colourfully. A 'millstone' (v. 6) was the heavy top stone of a corn-grinding mill, that needed a donkey to drag it round. Jesus says it would be better to be sunk in the ocean by such a weight than to cause a 'little one' to fall. And it would be better to lose a hand or foot or eye than to be led by our own actions or desires into losing our faith (vv. 7–9).

What this means, so far as I can see, is taking care about how we live, and being watchful not to damage someone else's Christian life, or indeed our own. It is easy to be casual about conduct and lifestyle: 'Everyone has different ways of living these days… I'm an individual, I'll work it out for myself… God will forgive, that's his job.' This text urges a different approach.

Adrian Plass discusses these verses in his *View from a Bouncy Castle* (Fount, 1991). He tells of a woman who changed her regular commuting arrangement and started taking a different train. She was developing a friendship with a man who travelled with her, that looked as if it might encroach on her marriage. So without great guilt or anger, but decisively and calmly, she stopped seeing him. That's probably not your problem. But your Christian life is a precious thing too, and is worth making an effort to protect.

PRAYER

May God grant us vigilance, common sense, and a humble heart.
For Jesus Christ's sake. Amen.

SEARCHING QUESTION

One of the tragedies of church life, in almost every congregation, is the number of people who used to be heavily involved and have now stopped coming. Sometimes people fall suddenly out of the fellowship, as abruptly and visibly as mud flung off a wheel. Others drift away gradually: almost without anyone noticing, their enthusiasm for Christian worship and service seems to wane and wither. Matthew's Gospel sets that issue within the much broader commitment that we have to care for one another's Christian lives, and to support and sustain one another in our walk with God.

Looking down

Looking down upon other people, despising those whom we find difficult to get on with or who are very different from ourselves, is a real temptation even in the Christian Church. It is often easier to keep company with like-minded Christians of easy personality than to be genuinely receptive in spirit (18:5) to all the people of Christ. Verse 10 urges us to overcome that barrier, for the hosts of heaven look down in love on all Christ's 'little ones', rejoicing in our faith, not put off by our awkwardness, and glad when we love one another.

(Note: verse 11 is not in the earliest copies of Matthew, and was probably not written by Matthew. It comes from Luke 19:10, and may have been written into some copies of Matthew 18 because it connects so well with the story of the lost sheep in the following verses.)

Love that en-folds us

Jesus told a parable about a lost sheep in Luke 15:1–7, to explain his own habit of spending time with people who seemed far away from God. He wanted to help them find their way back. Here in Matthew is a very similar story, but with a different purpose to its telling. It urges the Church to give time and effort to seek wandering Christians, and to help them back into the fold.

There is a lively debate about why two very similar stories are used in two rather different ways. Did the early Christians use a parable of Jesus that was originally about himself, and give it a different twist, so that it applied to their own church life? Or did Jesus, like many an itinerant preacher, use the same story more than once, for rather different purposes? Either way, the Church is to do what Jesus did, and seek the wanderer in patience and love.

Some people wander away because of 'stumbling blocks' (18:6–9). They make a serious mistake and then find it hard to hang on to their Christian commitment. Or somebody else leads them off the tracks and they are not confident enough to make their own way back. Whatever has happened, none of us has the right to 'despise' (v. 10), and many of us may have a part in the gentle friendship, help and prayer that lead the wanderer back. It could have been—perhaps it once was, or it could yet be—us.

Searching question

The searching question is at the start of verse 12: 'What do you think?'

Is it not risky to leave 99 sheep on their own in the open country? This is not the cautious approach of percentage farming. Is there not a trace of favouritism in rejoicing more over one that returned than over 99 that did not stray? What balanced and sensible community does that?

Again Jesus is using picture-language to make a point that could be stated a good deal more plainly. The Church is not like any other community. People are more than percentages. Every one is important. This is a community where the last, the least and the lost can be first, favoured and found.

What do you think?

FOR PRAYER

Thank God for the people who have helped you to find the way of Christ, and to stay on the Christian road thus far.

Pray for the people who look to you for guidance, leadership and example.

Pray for anyone you know who has dropped out of church life, that they will come into contact with friends who can help them back.

67

RESTORING PRESENCE

The Christian denomination I serve has, like many other churches, a procedure for dealing with serious breaches of good conduct and trust within our fellowship. This may involve honest and frank facing of difficult issues. At times, no comfortable or tidy resolution can be found. But the predominant aim is always to bring reconciliation and restoration, as fully as possible, of trust, fellowship and service. There is a similar spirit in this section of Matthew 18.

The word 'child' ran through verses 2–5; then in verses 6–14 Christians were 'little ones'. Now Matthew's word is 'brother' (twice in v. 15, then in vv. 21 and 35), properly translated in some modern versions as the inclusive 'brother or sister'. Church is family: even in times of dispute, we belong to one another.

Falling out

Verses 12–14 urge the Church to restore the person who has wandered away. But what do you do when there is deep hurt and tension within a local fellowship, so that people no longer feel confident to worship or work together? First, try to settle it privately (v. 15). Talk it over. You might turn out to be wrong, and find more good in the other person than you expected. Or you might be listened to. Either result would be a gain for you and for the whole congregation.

If the first stage leads nowhere, one or two other people can be drawn in (v. 16), primarily to listen, possibly also to advise, and to bring some balance and perspective to a stubborn disagreement. The reference to 'two or three witnesses' comes from the Old Testament (Deuteronomy 19:15), where a person could not be judged on the word of one witness alone.

A third stage involves the whole congregation (v. 17). This passage seems to assume that a local church will be small enough, and well-enough known to one another, to be able to help. Perhaps any company small enough to be damaged by a personal dispute also has a responsibility for helping to sort the problem out. The last resort seems to be exclusion of the offending party. But that need not be the end of the matter, for there is always the hope of restoration (18:12–14).

Binding rules

Verse 18 is very similar to 16:19. What was said of Peter there now applies to the whole Church. 'Binding and loosing' probably means taking decisions about right and wrong, about how Christians should behave, and about what sort of practical commitment to godly living we owe one another.

The Church has a duty to its members, especially when disputes seem insoluble, to offer the security of guidance and judgment. When the Church accepts that responsibility with good conscience and care, then God honours and backs what we do. The considered guidance of our brothers and sisters comes to us as from God; only a very solemn matter indeed would justify our ignoring that wisdom.

Not on our own

Verses 19–20 support and encourage the Church as it takes up the duty of verses 17–18. Even in a small fellowship, if Christians can pray in agreement and common concern, God answers the desires of their praying and stands with them in what they seek to do. Jesus—Emmanuel, God with us—is a dynamic presence, constantly moving the Church forward in fresh hope, like the bright and tender company of God on the exodus journey (Exodus 13:21–22; 33:14).

In this together

Although I have never seen the three-stage procedure (18:15–17) followed right through, I have known the first stage—frank and private conversation—produce a surprising growth in understanding and trust. One would need to be deeply concerned about an issue, and feel that a lot was at stake, to go much further than that first stage.

The ability of the Church to handle difficulties of this kind appears to depend on three things: faith—a grain is enough (17:20); fellowship—the readiness of Christians to pray and act together (18:19); and forgiveness—the willingness to heed the next section of the chapter (18:21–35) and forgive without limit. Even to say the Lord's Prayer together requires a forgiving spirit (6:14–15).

PRAYER

God of peace and light, may our churches be places where quarrels can be settled, where prayer draws us together, and where love can grow. Through Jesus Christ our Lord. Amen.

FORGIVE US OUR DEBTS

As so often, especially in Matthew, Peter speaks out. He pursues an issue from the earlier verses. 'Suppose a fellow Christian offends me, and we sort it out. Then it happens again. How many times must I forgive? How far does Christian forgiveness stretch?'

Counting out

Peter offers a first bid, of seven. To forgive the same person the same fault seven times could well test our calm and courtesy. Seven times can seem quite a lot of forgiving, if we have to do it. Yet Jesus puts that figure in a very different perspective. 'Not seven,' he says. 'Many more times than that.'

Jesus' reply means either 'seventy-seven', or 'seventy times seven'. But exact numbering was not what he intended. He was taking the Christian duty of forgiveness right out of the realm of arithmetic. We are to stop counting, and simply get used to forgiving, for the forgiveness of God is loving and limitless.

Pass it on

Each of the five major blocks of teaching in Matthew ends with a solemn parable about judgment. The point in this parable (vv. 23–35) is that if we cannot pass on the forgiveness of God, we may find our own experience of it turning out to be hollow.

The parable pictures a king summoning his administrators to collect the proceeds of their work (v. 23). Galilee may have known just such a summons, after Herod Antipas visited Rome about AD29, and Jesus could be using that piece of news in his parable. A talent represented about twenty or thirty years' wages, the equivalent of a large mortgage. So the first servant's debt was astronomical (v. 24). No normal sum would be as large as this. The debt is utterly unpayable and the situation has gone far beyond recovery.

Yet the debt that could not be paid is pardoned (v. 27), and the servant goes free. Then he meets one of his subordinates, whose accounts are also out of balance (v. 28). A denarius is a day's wage, so this is a much smaller sum. But the servant treats his colleague harshly, and has him locked up until friends and family can settle the account (v. 30). He is totally unwilling to pass on his master's pardon to his fellow servant. The upshot is that the king withdraws the forgiveness he originally granted, and the story ends in bitterness and misery (vv. 31–34).

Copies of Christ

'So also...' says verse 35. We shall not enjoy the forgiveness of God unless we share it. We have not really grasped it unless we can pass it on. The Church has to copy Jesus in its pastoral care (18:12–14), and also in its willingness to forgive.

Unless we can forgive, we shall not know real security and acceptance with one another (18:5, 10). We shall not be very good at seeking the wanderer (18:12–14). Our grievance procedures (18:15–17) will be harsh, with no sense of reconciliation about them. Yet when forgiveness flavours all we do together, then the Church is a very special kind of community—truly the people of Christ.

Should you ever...

Should you ever not forgive? Are some deeds so bad that you cannot forgive? I can think of three limits that must operate in practice.

- If a person is unrepentant—say someone swindles us in business and is quite proud of having done so—we cannot really offer forgiveness and expect a positive response. But we may owe it to ourselves to forgive inwardly, before we are eaten up by annoyance.

- Jesus himself did not create unnecessary opportunities for people to sin against him—he dodged Herod, for example. There is nothing wrong with a proper caution when dealing with people who have hurt us or let us down badly.

- Some kinds of serious offence—for example, criminal actions against another person—do such severe damage that there is no satisfactory way for the people concerned to go on living, working or even worshipping together. Even then, wise Christian friends may have a role in helping all parties to find their separate ways and to live with the memories. We remain, even after unspeakable hurts, a family that cares for all its members.

PRAYER

Forgive us our sins, as we forgive those who sin against us.

CALLING *for* COMMITMENT

Jesus sets out for Jerusalem, travelling down the east side of the Jordan (v. 1). The concentrated instruction of chapter 18 is over, but teaching continues about the way Jesus' followers should live. In the Christian community, marriage and children are valued (19:1–15), commitment will often involve sacrifice (19:16–30), and some worldly values become strangely irrelevant (20:16, 27).

Designed for life

In Jewish society of this time, only the husband could initiate a divorce action. Deuteronomy 24:1 allowed divorce for 'a matter of indecency' and there were various opinions about what sort of grounds would fit this law. Stricter teachers believed that the law only applied to adultery. Others, freer in their interpretation, permitted divorce 'for any cause' (v. 3) that the husband thought fit. So Pharisees come to test Jesus. What sort of grounds will he recognize?

Jesus does not answer directly, but speaks first about marriage as part of God's design for human life. God made us male and female (v. 4); as male and female we bear God's image (Genesis 1:27). So when man and woman leave the parental home to marry, they forge a firm and solid unit, becoming 'one flesh' together (v. 5; Genesis 2:24). This bond is not meant for breaking (v. 6), either by the couple themselves or by intrusion on someone else's part.

Emergency exit

The Pharisees reply that Jesus has missed their concern (v. 7). He has not mentioned the divorce provision in Deuteronomy 24. So Jesus speaks about that text as God's allowance for human weakness. It was not God's first and ideal plan for our life (v. 8), but was a safeguard, to regulate and restrain our hardness of heart. It does allow divorce, but as an emergency exit—when the other partner has effectively ended the marriage already by forming another sexual relationship (v. 9).

So Jesus draws his teaching back towards God's first ideal: marriage should be treated as permanent. The exit is for emergencies only. Divorce is an obituary, not an opportunity—a sad acknowledgment that the marriage bond is already broken and dead, not a card up a husband's sleeve to be played as desired. Thus Jesus answers the original question (v. 3) by supporting the stricter view within Judaism.

Just one exception

The divorce sayings in Mark 10:2–12 and Luke 16:18 do not have 'except for unchastity', whereas Matthew (5:32 and 19:9) includes this clause. Did Jesus intend this exception or not? Was he so totally against divorce that he would not support it even after unfaithfulness —the impression Mark and Luke give us?

Many scholars believe that Jesus did indeed hold such an absolute view, stricter than any of his contemporaries, and that the exception clause has been inserted by Matthew to match the teaching of Jewish rabbis. Others think it probable that Jesus, along with most Jews of his time, assumed that adultery ended marriage, and—however unsatisfactorily—forged a new bond. If he did not actually say 'except for unchastity', he may well have taken this exception for granted. And the words in Matthew spell this meaning out.

Believing makes a difference

Divorce as a subject touches many raw nerves. The Church can make three important contributions.

- First, we believe in marriage—as Jesus did. Marriage is meant to last, as one of the building blocks of human living. We urge people who marry to embark on it carefully and thoughtfully—as well as joyfully.

- Second, we believe in forgiveness as pattern for all our relationships, and we try to practise it in church life. Married life too depends on willing and practical forgiveness in the small disagreements and irritations, not only in the major crises. Coping with divorce often involves some serious forgiving too—not least in forgiving oneself.

- Third, we believe that God's love reaches out to us not just when we prosper in faith and fortune, but also when we come badly unstuck. Our pastoral care can reflect that sort of love, for Christ's sake.

FOR REFLECTION

Marriage is a demanding and serious vocation. The next verses point out that single life can be testing too. Whatever our pattern of relationships, we need the daily grace of God if we are to be faithful to our commitments, and to the people who share them with us.

KINGDOM PEOPLE

Verses 10–12 continue the discussion about marriage that started at verse 3. Then comes one of the most memorable and moving incidents in the Gospels, as children are brought to Jesus for him to put a hand of blessing upon them.

Single-minded

The disciples' rather sceptical comment in verse 10 reflects the impact of Jesus' teaching on marriage. He has raised expectations, supported women's need for security and protection, and assigned to men much more commitment and responsibility than was customary. Marriage is a bond and one is bound by it, is his view. Suddenly the scales seem to be tilting, levelling out the rights and roles of husband and wife. No longer is it a man's world.

'Who is going to want a deal as tough as that?' say the disciples. 'It would be better not to marry' (v. 10). Jesus takes them at their word. 'Do you really mean that?' is his response. 'Not everyone can live up to that sort of commitment' (v. 11). The single vocation is not something that everyone can handle.

Jesus goes on to talk about 'eunuchs' (v. 12), applying that word in a broader way to mean people who do not marry and start a family, but live a single life. Some are made that way by nature: for whatever reason, they cannot seriously consider marrying. Some have been badly hurt by other people, and would now find it impossible to form a healthy marriage relationship. A third group deliberately adopt a single lifestyle because of the opportunities it will allow them for serving God's kingdom.

Perhaps Jesus was thinking of himself in the third group, and explaining why he lived the way he did. But he was also challenging the disciples. Commitment to singleness is a good choice, if made by the right people for the right reasons. But not everyone can or should take this path (v. 12). In any case, people who grumble about the binding ties of marriage may not be very well prepared for commitment to singleness.

Child allowance

Jesus has encountered children a number of times already in Matthew. For example, he has healed children (9:18–26; 15:21–28; 17:14–20), and used a child to illustrate God's kingdom (18:2–5). Yet strangely the disciples still think he might be averse to children's company (v. 13). In the event he turns out to be very welcoming. He overrules the disciples, and the children come to him (vv. 14–15).

'Of such is the kingdom.' The kingdom is for lowly people, who do not think too highly of their own place or position in the world. To children that often comes more easily than to adults. It is not so hard for them to enjoy God's grace, for they are used to receiving, to living by the plans and provision of others. Of course children have much to learn. But adults sometimes have much to unlearn, habits of thought and behaviour that make it harder for us to grasp God's love and follow his leading. A child comes without that luggage.

So children are welcome in the kingdom, to enjoy the love of Jesus and to help older people to enjoy it too. The story ends as it began, that children were brought for blessing and Jesus indeed blessed them. The last are becoming first (19:30; 20:16).

Children's church?

This story is sometimes used as an argument for infant baptism. I doubt very much if Matthew (or Jesus) intended it to be. The story is both simpler and more far-reaching than that. But it certainly encourages churches to take children seriously, as worshippers and learners of Christ and as people who have something to teach the rest of us. Children remind us not just of how we were but of how we could be.

A leader of Christian work among children recently said, 'I want our churches to be places where children are noticed, valued and protected.' Jesus would have agreed.

PRAYER

Pray for children you know, and for their steady growth,
in body, mind and faith.
Pray for your church, that within its fellowship
children may both receive and contribute.
Pray for yourself, for an open and child-like spirit
in your walk with God.

VALUING *the* KINGDOM

This incident, where Jesus tests the commitment of an eager enquirer, is reminiscent of 8:18–22. There are also a number of connections to the Sermon on the Mount, so that this passage brings a lot of the teaching of the sermon into focus. Keeping God's commands (5:21–47), being perfect (5:48), handling wealth (6:19–34) and squeezing through a narrow gate (7:13) all crop up in 19:18–24. The man in this episode has been described as a living illustration of Matthew 6:24, trying to serve the two masters of God and money.

Path to perfection

Matthew says that the man was young (v. 20) and rich (v. 22). Luke 18:18 calls him a ruler. He wants to gain the life of heaven and taste the blessings that only God can give. Jesus, however, talks about the kingdom in a different way. The man asks to 'have life' (v. 16), and Jesus tells him to 'enter life' (v. 17). We gain heaven by committed pilgrimage, not as an asset to drop into our investment portfolio.

Then Jesus directs the man to the chief commands of the Old Testament (vv. 18–19): to five of the Ten Commandments (Exodus 20:12–16), plus the command about neighbour love (Leviticus 19:18). The man knows these well, and supposes that he keeps them—although the reader, who has read through the Sermon on the Mount, will not be so sure. Loving neighbours, not infringing life, avoiding unfaithful relationships, are hard targets (5:21–30, 43–47).

But the man is keen to move the discussion on. There must be something else, he says (v. 20). What is it? So Jesus challenges him. If he wants to be 'complete, perfect, whole' (v. 21), there is for him only one way forward: to share all his wealth among the poor. At this point the conversation subsides into thoughtful silence (v. 22), and we are left to wonder—about him, and about ourselves.

Money makes the world go blind

Jesus accepted hospitality (Luke 10:38) and the help of monied friends (Luke 8:3). But he and his disciples travelled light, and his teaching on wealth carries a sharp edge. Whatever we have, and whatever we give time and effort to, can come between us and God.

The young man in this story seems a superficial character, not really recognizing the nature of the Old Testament law, and yet hoping to leap-frog into the kingdom. His wealth has clouded his vision. That, says Jesus, is always the danger. It may push this present world around, but money finds it desperately hard to wriggle into God's coming kingdom (vv. 23–24).

The camel is a fine long-distance runner on sand, but a total non-starter when it comes to sliding through narrow openings. Jesus seems to have found its irregular shape splendidly bizarre (see also 23:24), and here he offers the ridiculous picture of using a camel to thread a needle. All the probabilities are stacked against success. Rich Christians need a special kind of grace and wisdom, to steward humbly and generously what they have been given. (See also comments on 6:19–34, pp. 56–57.)

Possible with God

The disciples are amazed (v. 25). They presumably thought that a large fortune was a sign of blessing. If the rich cannot make it, who can? Humanly speaking, it is never possible, says Jesus. No one comes into the kingdom on their own resources alone. It always depends upon God, who is able to save all sorts of people, often in ways we would not expect (v. 26).

The discussion then runs on to Peter's question (v. 27). The rich young man's problem was an unwillingness to make sacrifices. But the Twelve have given up a lot. So, Peter asks Jesus, can they assume that they will be all right? See the next page.

FOR REFLECTION AND PRAYER

Money is a bad master. We only keep money in its proper place, as a good servant, if we are ready to plan our giving, sharing, saving and spending with Jesus Christ plainly in mind. When the offering is dedicated in church, can you dedicate to God the money you still have in your pocket and in the bank, as well as what you have given? Acknowledge inwardly that this money too is for God's use. You are the manager. Christ is the Master.

VINTAGE REWARDS

The two parts of this section speak, in different ways, about the same issue. Work for God can be tough: what will God give in return?

God is no one's debtor

Peter's question (v. 27) arises from the conversation with the rich young man. The Twelve have made big sacrifices. Will they squeeze into eternal life? So Jesus speaks of a new world coming (v. 28).

He had chosen twelve disciples to represent the new life of Israel (see comments on 10:1–4, pp. 80–81). Now he looks forward, and recalls the hopes of scripture. As Daniel prophesied the glory of the Son of Man, when kingship will be entrusted to God's holy people (Daniel 7:9, 13–14, 27), so Jesus' followers will share in his authority. They will make his glory and power known in Israel. A foretaste of the fulfilment of these words came in the period after Pentecost. The Twelve—who were witnesses of the resurrection—preached to the Jewish people the good news that Christ was risen. (But see also comments on chapters 24 and 25, pp. 196–211.)

Jesus then talks about sacrifices. God asks nothing that he cannot repay many times over (v. 29). Many Christians give up much to follow Christ or serve his Church: comfort, material prospects, friendships, home. Sometimes those sacrifices are foreseen and planned; on other occasions they come unexpectedly and painfully. God still honours what people offer him, and he still gives eternal life—yet not always in the way anyone expects (v. 30), as the next parable shows.

Clocking on

Jesus pictures the owner of a big vineyard recruiting day labourers to pick the harvest. Many people in rural Palestine had little or no land of their own, and needed casual work. A denarius was a typical day's pay, although it would buy only limited sustenance for a big family. Wages were paid daily, as the law prescribed (Deuteronomy 24:14–15); some families lived literally from hand to mouth.

Time is reckoned by a twelve-hour clock, from dawn to dusk. The first group of workers agree for the standard daily amount, and set to work (v. 2). Other teams of workers start later in the day, and there is an element of suspense about how they will be paid. 'I will pay you whatever is right,' says the master to the second group (v. 4), but we never hear what that will be. The hiring of the third, fourth and fifth groups heightens that uncertainty. How will they all be rewarded?

Settling up

The last group are paid first, and receive the normal sum for a whole day's work (vv. 8–9). We then skip over the three middle groups, and watch the first group rubbing their hands in anticipation. If this is the hourly rate, they will surely do nicely. But they too get just one denarius (v. 10).

So some grumbling follows. 'Favouritism, unfairness, injustice, idleness'—we can almost hear the rising tide of resentment and dismay. The master's reply makes two points. First, 'You got what you agreed; that's fair' (v. 13). And second, 'It's my money, and if I want to be generous with it, that's up to me' (v. 15).

Thinking it over

Jesus did not offer the parable as a regular agricultural management technique. He knew the master's behaviour was odd. This was part of his teaching method, to help the parable stick in hearers' minds. God is odd, by human standards. He does not always do what we expect or should do ourselves.

This brings us back to the last being first and the first last. The kingdom will bring glorious rewards that completely overshadow the sacrifices it demands of us (19:29). But if we think of those rewards as a right, we have some fresh learning to do (20:16). God will not leave himself in our debt, but nor will he come under our direction. Grace is not measured by hours of service, it is always a gift.

It is always good to see senior Christians, who have done much in their lives, coming alongside young people or newcomers to the faith in a pew or a queue, without any fuss about status or rank. Happy is the church where people mingle on truly level terms; that is one way of preparing for heaven.

PRAYER

*Teach us, Lord, the art of cheerful giving—of our service,
our substance, our selves—for the sake of your Kingdom.*

73 MATTHEW 20:17-28

SERVANT KING

Progress to passion

The pilgrim journey to Jerusalem, which started at the beginning of chapter 19, is moving towards its destination. For the fourth time Jesus tells his friends very plainly of his coming death (the other occasions were 16:21; 17:12 and 17:22–23). This is the most specific prediction of what will happen, and the first time the word 'crucify' is mentioned.

Crucifixion was a Roman punishment, though never inflicted upon Roman citizens. It was a humiliating and miserably extended form of killing. The victim was suspended from a rough wooden cross by nails through wrists and feet, and was then left until he was overtaken by pain, exhaustion and death. This is the way Jesus will die.

What might have led Jesus to expect a criminal's death? There are four likely factors. First, he knew what had happened to John the Baptist. Second, he had long been aware of growing opposition to his ministry. Third, he felt drawn, as part of his calling from God, to come to Jerusalem as prophet and challenge the leadership of his people. Fourth, there was deeply embedded in Israel's scripture the thought of one suffering for many (v. 28), a destiny which Jesus sensed as his own.

Eyes on the podium

A number of women (27:55) had joined Jesus' Passover pilgrimage, including the mother of James and John. Her sons are already part of the inner circle of Jesus' disciples (17:1), and all three of them hope for higher things still. Might they become Jesus' chief lieutenants when he is revealed as king?

Jesus must have groaned inwardly. Had they never listened? He responds by speaking of the 'cup' he must drink. In the Old Testament the image of a cup describes the bitter anger of God (Psalm 75:8; Isaiah 51:17, 22), and the suffering it brings. In Gethsemane Jesus speaks again of drinking a cup from God (26:39), and at the Last Supper this cup represents his shed blood (26:27–28). All of this suggests that the 'cup' means his coming suffering.

So James and John will suffer too. James died by the sword in AD44 (Acts 12:2). We think that John lived into old age, but he endured a good deal along the way. And their mother was one of the faithful witnesses who saw Jesus raised on to a throne (Matthew 27:55–56) very different from the one she first had in mind.

A different greatness

The anger of the Twelve looks to be a concern for their own places in the pecking order, rather than any support for Jesus' view. So he gathers them and talks about his style of leadership. Gentile rulers were strong on ceremony, dignity and pride. People quailed with terror when presenting petitions to the Roman Emperor. The Christian pattern must be very different.

The word 'servant' (v. 26) commonly meant someone who waited at table, bringing food and drink to others. A 'slave' (v. 27) was another person's property, with no rights, choices or freedom of his or her own. We have heard of Christians being 'like children' (18:3); this idea matches and meshes with that one. It is a position without status, indeed the last place in human rank and importance.

Yet the Lord took that last place, and died the slaves' death so that his people might live God's life. He lived out, in his journey to the cross, the lesson he taught. And his suffering was purposeful: it was a 'ransom for many' (v. 28). The same word 'ransom' is used to describe the Exodus (Deuteronomy 7:8), where the main emphasis is on God's power releasing his people. But a closer link to verse 28 is Isaiah 53:10–12, in the chapter about a Servant whose suffering brings healing and hope to many.

Jesus is the humble servant. He is the Suffering Servant. His service is our example for Christian living. It is also a sign that suffering borne for God need not be fruitless or futile, but may be far-reaching in the good it does and the grace it brings to others.

FOR THOUGHT

Jesus' servant life and death put into perspective the disciples' concern for status in the Church. Do you exercise any responsibility in your church? Pause to think about how you reflect the servant style of Jesus in the way you carry out that task. Then pray for grace to be consistent and humble as you continue in serving.

Compassion Road

Approaching the end

The pilgrim journey is nearing its completion. Jesus and his friends have travelled southwards along the east bank of the Jordan. Then they would have crossed the river a few miles north of the Dead Sea, and come to Jericho, a sizeable town in the valley. From Jericho a steep uphill road led south-west to Jerusalem, about fifteen miles away. As the group moved out of the town, and set off into the hills, they attracted quite a crowd (v. 29).

Royal mercy

The two blind people needed to shout. Someone must have told them that Jesus was coming by, and they had heard of his power. But they could not see him. So shouting was the only way to make contact, and no one was going to shut them up (vv. 30–31).

'Son of David' is an unusual greeting, cropping up in just a few of the miracle incidents (9:27; 12:23; 15:22). It is a royal title. These blind people think of Jesus as a new king. But their kingly hope is more than a political notion. Loaded into it are the promises and expectations that God's Messiah will be a figure of mercy, a worker of wonders, who sets suffering people free from their distress. Sight for blind eyes is the hope of Isaiah 35:5, linked by Jews to the ministry of God's Spirit-anointed Messiah (see Matthew 11:4–5). Similarly in Isaiah 42:7, sight comes through the work of God's Servant (Matthew 12:18–21). Jesus takes that double role, Servant and King, humble and afflicted for his people, yet mighty and majestic in what he brings them from God.

Son of promises

Many names and titles are used for Jesus in Matthew's Gospel:

- Jesus is Son of Man (20:18), a human figure, vulnerable as we are, destined to suffer and to pass through suffering to glory.

- In this passage he is Son of David, a name which stresses all he can do for God's people Israel.

- He is Son of God, revealing his Father's will and presence on earth (3:17; 17:5).

- He is Emmanuel, God with us (1:23; 28:20).

- Yet for many he remains only the son of a carpenter (13:55). They do not see. But the two blind people at Jericho see very clearly.

Asking and following

Nothing is said in this episode about faith. The way the blind people speak to Jesus is sign enough that they recognize God's work in him. They see spiritually, even though they cannot see physically. So they ask for 'open eyes', and Jesus gives them their sight. Then they join the crowd that is following him to Jerusalem (v. 34). There ought always to be a link between vision and discipleship. But how clearly will Jerusalem see?

Threshold of the city

This incident prepares the way for Jesus' entry to Jerusalem. There were many healings and wide public acclaim earlier in the Gospel. But for the last few chapters Matthew has concentrated our attention on the teaching Jesus has given his friends. Little has been said about miracles since he set his face to Jerusalem at 16:21. The main focus has been on the coming Church and its life.

This encounter at Jericho, reminiscent of an earlier healing at 9:27–31, resets the focus of the gospel story. Again Jesus is in contact with the public, with the wider Jewish community. As he approaches the capital city, this incident shows him as one who gathers a crowd, as Son of David, and as a healer whose praise cannot be silenced. All these themes will recur in the next few verses (21:8–9, 14–16).

PRAYER

Lord Jesus Christ,
light of the minds that know you,
life of the souls that love you,
and strength of the wills that serve you,
help us so to know you that we may truly love you,
so to love you that we may fully serve you,
whose service is perfect freedom. Amen.

COMING KING

Jesus has reached Jerusalem, the destination to which he has been moving since chapter 16. As he approaches the city, crowds greet him with loud acclaim.

Humble, riding on an ass

The road from Jericho runs into Jerusalem from the east. Bethphage was within a mile of the city wall, and counted as part of the city limits. From Bethphage the way led over the Mount of Olives, and down across the Kidron Valley to the city proper.

Matthew has not mentioned yet that Jesus had friends at Bethany, a village near Bethphage. So the fetching of the donkey has the feel of a royal command, as if the king commandeers any animal he needs. But it much more likely reflects an agreement with a sympathetic local contact. Even so, there is a curiously cryptic feel to the matter—almost like something out of a spy novel—and it may be that Jesus was even now being careful about how and where he attracted attention. Mark and Luke only mention one donkey, but John speaks of a 'young donkey', and Matthew's story indicates that the mother came too, to steady the young animal in unfamiliar surroundings.

So (v. 5) Jesus fulfils the prophecy of Zechariah 9:9. There are a number of links to Zechariah in Matthew's Passion account, to chapters of Zechariah that tell of a coming king and of a shepherd rejected by the Jewish people. Here Jesus comes as king of peace, riding royally into the city, yet showing a quiet and lowly spirit. He is not on a great war-horse, but on a donkey's colt. He is a meek and gentle Messiah (5:5; 11:29), accessible to humble people (21:14–16).

Loud hosannas

'Hosanna' is Hebrew and means, 'Come and save us!' The words are from Psalm 118:25, which was one of the regular Passover hymns. It speaks of a righteous one coming to the 'gate of the Lord' (118:20), and of a stone that is rejected by men and raised by God (118:22). Jesus comes now to enter city gates where he will indeed be rejected and raised (Matthew 21:42).

The spreading of garments and branches is a real celebrity

welcome. When Jehu became king over Israel (2 Kings 9:13), garments were spread before him. Much nearer to the time of Jesus, just a couple of centuries back, is an incident recorded in the Apocrypha, when the Jewish freedom-fighter Simon Maccabeus was greeted with 'palms and psalms' (1 Maccabees 13:51). Simon had driven out a foreign force, and went on to cleanse the city ceremonially to make it fit again for the worship of God. Jesus too will cleanse God's house, not from foreign pollution but from the way his own people have misused it. The freedom he offers will be very different from anything that military action could bring.

Shaken—if not stirred

There may be a deliberate contrast between the sympathetic crowd and the ripple of alarm that runs through the city (v. 10). Jerusalem was perturbed by Jesus' arrival once before (2:3), and he will be no easy company for many there. He is a prophet, coming to speak for God, and prophets do not always bring words of comfort. He is from Galilee, a stranger who will find much to disturb him here.

In our worship

This account of Jesus coming into Jerusalem has been used in Christian worship in two rather different ways. The regular tradition in Britain is to read the story on Palm Sunday, a week before Easter. We celebrate Jesus as the king who comes in peace, to die and yet to rise and reign. We join the crowd and sing their songs. Then as Holy Week goes on we follow the Gospel accounts through the solemnity of Maundy Thursday and the grim darkness of Good Friday to the light of Easter morning. We travel alongside the story.

There is another tradition, in some continental European churches, of reading in the Advent season about Jesus' coming to Jerusalem. The worshippers wait, as if they were in Jerusalem, to receive the Lord who comes to search and test his people. During the lead-up to Christmas we examine and hallow ourselves, in order to celebrate Christ's coming to earth. As a temple of living stones, we invite his cleansing, his challenging and renewing presence among us.

FOR REFLECTION AND PRAYER

Let me be your donkey, Lord.

Dom Helder Camara, Brazil

76

TURNING *the* TABLES

Falling market

The Jerusalem temple courts covered a vast area, roughly 400 yards by 300, with a high perimeter wall. The main buildings were in the centre, but the bulk of the space—called the Court of the Gentiles—was open to the sky, and available for people to move about and talk in. It was probably in this area that the traders were operating. The temple tax could only be paid in Tyrian coinage, which had no human images on it. If tax had been collected in other currency, then money-brokers would change it into Tyrian. Other dealers sold sacrificial animals, which had been approved by the temple authorities as blemish-free and fit for offering to God.

Jesus' action is abrupt and aggressive. It cannot have caused a widespread disturbance, for soldiers were stationed nearby at festival times and would have intervened quickly if there were major trouble. But those who caught the brunt of Jesus' wrath must have found it a fierce enough affair. What bothered him so much?

Crooked shepherds

Certainly Jesus was offended at the extent to which money surrounded and affected the work of the Temple. He had already taken a dim view of the temple tax (17:24–26). Nor would he welcome the official monopoly on sacrificial animals at inflated prices. 'The legitimate and necessary operation of the Temple was supported by a maze of intrigue, nepotism and corruption' (M. Bockmuehl, *This Jesus*, T&T Clark, 1994), and the wealth that accrued to the high priestly families would have been resented by many ordinary Jews. Jesus already felt that God's flock had no true spiritual leadership (9:36; 10:6), and the temple trade convinced him afresh that the people were being fleeced rather than fed (compare Ezekiel 34:1–6).

Clouds gathering

So Jesus is not opposed to the Temple itself, but his action is a protest about how it works—profit is obscuring the importance of prayer. Verse 13 combines two Old Testament passages, Isaiah 56:7 and

Jeremiah 7:11. The Jeremiah chapter came from a time of crisis and threat, and warned the Jews not to place a casual confidence in their Temple. It would not be any help, if their life was not right with God.

That may give another clue to Jesus' thoughts, for he too predicted the fall of the Temple (24:2). He took the view (as did some other Jews) that the Temple would have a limited lifespan. It was not doing what God expected, and God would one day bring it down and replace it with something more worthy. So Jesus' temple protest is also an acted symbol of trouble ahead, a small disturbance, as signpost and token of a coming great destruction.

Healing and praise

Jesus the king of peace has acted fiercely and forcefully. Yet he remains accessible, a man of mercy, healing the sick and receiving the praise of children. The approachable style of his ministry involves no tax or toll. He remains the gentle Christ, to whom the burdened and broken may turn (11:29).

High priests and scribes come to investigate (v. 15). Last time they checked up on Jesus, he was almost killed (2:4). We have heard of them on the way to Jerusalem (16:21; 20:18), and their arrival now is a portent of danger ahead. At the moment their protest makes little impact; but they will surely be back again. Meanwhile Jesus retires to his lodging at Bethany, a couple of miles outside the city.

Counter culture

How do we translate this incident into our time? Does it mean (some Christians ask) that a church should not sell fairly traded goods from Third World charities after Sunday worship? Is a church bookstall ruled out too?

I think the issue is more about attitude than rules. Certainly this episode suggests that money should not dominate our church life; that Christian giving should be genuinely a gift—not a levy; that church life should be as fully open to poor people as to rich; and that even the best-organized and most carefully budgeted church may learn from the simplicity and spontaneity of children's praise (v. 16).

PRAYER

Lord Jesus Christ, cleanse us and our worship
from all that obscures your love.

Hollow Hopes

Fruitless tree

The withered fig tree stands stark and alone among all the gospel miracles. Only this miracle is destructive. The others are positive and creative—healings, providing food, and so on. They make the world a fuller place. This incident takes something away. So what is it about?

The time of year is odd. The new spring figs would not be due for another month. All you would expect in early April would be small green figs, or old figs left over from winter. One writer points out that in a hot climate certain fruit trees occasionally burst into leaf at the wrong time, and look as if they are bearing fruit, though in fact they are empty. Whether that takes us nearer to knowing what happened, I am not sure. But it does help to show the meaning of the incident. This tree looked fruitful, but was not. It was worth Jesus' while to go to it, but it had nothing for him. Its fruitfulness was just a show.

House of disappointment

The tree, then, had the same problem as the Temple. It promised more than it could deliver. The Temple offered itself as a place of light and hope. Jerusalem was looked on as the 'navel of the world', the supply line of its life from God. Yet Jesus saw the Temple—Jerusalem's religious heart—as sadly introverted. For him, the Temple was a tree with no fruit, a dry oasis, efficient in securing its own preservation yet weak in presenting free and joyful grace to pilgrim and enquirer.

So Jesus' words against the tree indicate his feelings about the Temple. It has no life worth preserving, no goodness to nourish people with, and will surely come under the withering judgment of God. Jesus takes his place in the succession of Jewish prophets who spoke critically against their own people and their nation's religious life, often at considerable personal risk. Jeremiah had called the leaders and life of Jerusalem a basket of rotten figs (Jeremiah 24), and Jesus takes a fairly similar view.

Note: Mark (11:11–21) shows this link between tree and Temple more clearly than Matthew. The temple cleansing and the cursing of the tree are interwoven in Mark's account. But they stand side by side in Matthew, and there appears to be a close connection.

Motive prayer

The shrivelling of the fig tree leads into a conversation about prayer. The wording of verse 21 is fairly similar to 17:20, but the place where it is said gives fresh edge to the remark. 'Say to this mountain,' here sounds as if it means the temple mount. Faith could shift even this major landmark. Faith could be a stronger force than the Temple. The Temple may not stand for ever, but prayer can draw on the power of God to fulfil all that faith desires.

So the incident about the fig tree seems to be used in two ways. On one hand, the tree is an emblem of the Temple, and its perishing fore-shadows the Temple's own fall. On the other hand, it illustrates the power of faith and prayer. Though these sound like different issues, the two messages converge. For the Temple ought to be a house of prayer (21:13); it is not, and it will fall. Yet Jesus invites his friends to pray confidently. His example and his community offer a fruitful place of prayer, with open access to the power and love of God.

Praying with 'L' plates

Many other texts in the Gospels speak of answered prayer. See, for example, Matthew 7:7–11; 17:20; 18:19; John 14:13; 15:7; 16:23–24. It sounds very easy and straightforward. But prayer can be a difficult business to understand and practise. We cannot simply tell God how things ought to be.

I have no quick fix to offer, but I think these texts in Matthew offer some help. One point from chapter 18 may be worth repeating here: the word 'you' in 21:21–22 is plural. Learning to pray, growing in faith, listening to God, and dealing with the answers, are often better done by Christians together. Solitary prayer is a precious gift. So is praying with friends.

PRAYER

Give me the faith which can remove
And sink the mountain to a plain;
Give me the child-like praying love,
Which longs to build Thy house again.

Charles Wesley (1707–88)

175

PAUSE *for* THOUGHT

Now follow several pieces of teaching given by Jesus in the Temple during the days before the cross. He proves admirably nimble in the cut-and-thrust of debate, and all this teaching is directed, in one way or another, against the religious leaders of Jerusalem. This first conversation is with 'chief priests and elders'. Strictly there was only one high priest, but he was supported by a cluster of senior temple officials, and this will be the group involved here. The 'elders' are lay members of the Jewish ruling council, the Sanhedrin.

Questioning authority

'What right have you got to do these things?' is the first move in the exchange (v. 23). These men are responsible for the Temple. Jesus has caused a disturbance and is attracting attention. So they want to rein him in. But he wrong-foots them by answering their question with another one (vv. 24–25), which puts them in a quandary, and they pause to confer.

They cannot reply that John the Baptist was led by God, or Jesus will ask why they themselves took so little notice of John. Nor can they criticize John's ministry, for that would cost them popular support. So they stall, and in return Jesus declines to answer their question (v. 27). There the conversation might have stopped, except that Jesus now moves to take the initiative with one of his parables.

The lost shall be first

Jesus told a very famous parable about two sons (Luke 15:11–32). This story (vv. 28–32) is much shorter and quite subtle. One son seems an awkward, rebellious fellow, but eventually goes to work on the farm. The other sounds loyal and industrious, but does not do what he promises. What you see is not necessarily what you get. Minds can be changed. People can act in ways you did not expect.

That, says Jesus, is what happened with John the Baptist's ministry. Religious people, who appeared committed to God, did not respond. Yet many from the edges of society—unlikely people, you would think—believed John and started a new walk with God. That is the obvious application of the parable. But there is another angle, which pulls the whole of today's passage together. It is about people who change their mind.

Room to reconsider

Jesus' counter-question (v. 25) was not asked just to be awkward. He wanted people to think again about their attitude to him. For Jesus' own authority was linked to John's. The two men were similar in style, outlook and aim. They believed God was doing a new thing in Israel, that the kingdom was coming, and that people should set their lives in order (3:2; 4:17). The two ministries were closely linked. If people respected John, they would be more likely to listen to Jesus.

But these opponents in the Temple had not thought well of John. So Jesus tells his parable (vv. 28–32), in order to give them space to re-think. He invites them to act their part as Israel's religious leaders, to perform what they profess. 'Even when you saw, you did not change your mind and believe' (v. 32). But there is still time. If the shaft of this parable strikes home, if the questioners can review their opinion about John, then perhaps they can take Jesus seriously too.

The way home

A good parable has hidden layers. As the story rolls around in the mind, fresh meaning comes to the surface—rather like a cough sweet with a honey centre that seeps out as you suck. People would think about Jesus' words as they walked home, and would suddenly see the link to their own lives.

Some hearers that day might have thought poorly of John and been critical of Jesus. Yet here was a fresh opportunity, a chance to reconsider, to respond positively to Jesus, to find their way into the kingdom of God.

Not everyone in the Sanhedrin remained hostile to Jesus. Two of its members gave him an honourable burial (27:57–60; John 19:38–42). I wonder how many others came to think highly of him.

But the very first question about authority has been left hanging. Where does Jesus get his authority from? The next couple of parables offer an answer.

FOR REFLECTION

Do you meet situations where changing your mind would be a sign not of weakness, but of wisdom?

REJECTED & RAISED

This parable answers the question about Jesus' authority. He is the latest in a line of messengers from God, reminding the Jewish people of the love and loyalty they owe to God. Yet he is more than just one of the line. He represents God more intimately and directly than any prophet. They were servants; he is the Son.

Payment in kind

The fig tree incident portrayed the Temple as a fruitless tree. This time there is fruit in plenty, but the tenants keep it all. The picture is of a Palestinian vineyard, laid out by a landowner, then worked by tenants, who pay part of their harvest as rental. There is a clear resonance with Isaiah 5. That passage calls Israel a well-built vineyard, which does not bear fruit for God. All it produces is injustice and oppression. That, says Jesus, is the problem again. The tenants, who administer the nation's religious life, yield little by way of goodness. Prophets have brought this message before, and were treated roughly (for example, 2 Chronicles 24:21; Jeremiah 38:6). This time the owner has sent his son.

The tenants kill the son to get the owner off their back once and for all. If he has no one to leave the land to, they hope to gain it by default (v. 38). In fact the people around Jesus know very well that the reverse would happen (v. 41). The owner will install new tenants, whom he can trust to pay properly.

Rising s(t)on(e)

Of course Jesus knows he is on collision course with the powers of the land. He himself is the owner's son, who will be thrown out of the vineyard and killed. So he ends the parable with a text (v. 42; from Psalm 118:22–23) which switches the illustration from son to stone, and from dying to rising. In biblical Hebrew, the word for son is *ben*, and stone is *eben*. Jesus spotted that word-play and shared it with his audience. The rejected stone will be raised up high. The crucified son will be the capstone of the new household of God.

So Jesus' death will be a turning point in Israel's history. The people who have him killed will lose their tenure and trust. The nation's religious leadership will be displaced, and God's favour will settle elsewhere. God will shape a new people to bring him the fruit of obedient service (v. 43). Then Jesus, as God's honoured stone, will be a figure for all to reckon with. In him the power of God's kingdom will be known (v. 44, drawing on Daniel 2:44–45).

Home ground

The temple leaders take the parable personally (v. 45). Some rich Jerusalem families owned country estates themselves. They would know about collecting rent, and what to do if tenants were slow to pay. They could see the owner's point of view. But the parable has put the boot on the other foot. These men were used to owning; Jesus casts them as tenants. He points out, too, that their lease is running out. They have not been faithful to their trust. They have used their position to make themselves rich, but have not given God his due.

Building a people

Matthew's Gospel outlines how the Christian Church emerged from within the life of the Jewish people. There are three main themes:

- **Fulfilment:** This Gospel stresses fulfilment of the Old Testament (for example, 1:23; 5:17). Jesus, his teaching and his community are a faithful and sure expression of Israel's heritage and hope. The Old is being realized in the New.

- **Foundation:** God is building Israel's life around a new centre. Peter is the rock (16:18) of a new temple, made of living stones, with Jesus himself in the place of headship and honour (v. 42).

- **Forfeit:** Matthew portrays the leadership of Israel not only as self-serving and unfaithful, but as hopelessly out of touch with their own flock (21:26, 46). The crucifixion will be a turning point. There will be judgment, change and new fruitfulness (v. 43).

FOR REFLECTION

As a minister, I find that passages like this offer a sober warning. Religious leaders need to be vigilant about our attitude. Position, responsibility, habit, can all cloud our vision and tempt us to forget who we are working for. If you are a leader, will you search your own heart? If you are not, please pray for those of us who are.

80   MATTHEW 22:1–14

I Cannot Come *to the* Banquet

The last parable pictured the temple leadership as tenants who would not pay the master's rent. This story casts them as wedding guests who decline to turn up on the day.

Absent friends

In some countries a wedding in a rich family can last a week. The marriage of a king's son is more than just a social event. It is an occasion for leading citizens of the realm to show support for the prince and his future among them. Casual refusal would be more than rude, it would be a first sign of rebellion, as if to say, 'We will not have this man to rule over us.'

The sending of one group of servants after another (vv. 3–4) matches the last parable, that of the vineyard. Verse 3 uses the same word twice over: 'to *invite* those who had been *invited*'. These guests know what is expected of them. Like the son of 21:30, or the tenants of 21:34–38, they are going back on their word. Once refusal turns to murder, the king responds fiercely and promptly (v. 7). And there the parable could end. But it continues.

Out and about

The feast is ready to start, but all the places at table are empty. So the king sends servants out again. They go to the thoroughfares (v. 9): the word means the place where a town road runs out into the country. They search the streets and open land and gather everyone they can find, to fill the hall.

Thus far the parable is very similar to a story in Luke 14:16–23. The message is that Israel's leaders miss out, and a new people is gathered in, roughly as in the parable of the vineyard (21:33–43). The newcomers might be the poor and lowly in Israel (21:31–32), or even Gentiles (8:11–12). Grace lands in some unexpected places. There is more joy in heaven over unlikely people who come to God than over supposedly righteous people who turn away from his love. God's grace is free, but it does require a response. That point is made over again in verses 11–14, which seems to be a sort of postscript to the larger parable.

Dress for the occasion

The final scene (vv. 11–14) is unexpectedly severe. The king has a man thrown out because he is not wearing good clothes. That may seem unrealistic. After all, the guests have not had much time to go home and change. But the parable does not work in that tightly connected way. This last instalment has a message of its own—that we should respond to God's love with the fullest commitment we can. 'Wearing a wedding garment' (v. 11) means being properly ready to enjoy God's kingdom. The invitation to the kingdom is open, but God does expect a serious response. He wants people who will be glad to enjoy his company, honour his Son and learn of his love.

Three-course message

So there are three messages here, in the three stages of the parable.

- Those in Israel who scorn and ignore Jesus are in danger of missing out on God's grace (vv. 1–7).

- God gathers a new people. The Church arises as a mixed and motley company (vv. 8–10).

- The gospel requires committed response (vv. 11–13).

Looking at Luke, majoring on Matthew

Matthew's version of this parable is rather longer than Luke's, either because Jesus used the story in varied ways, or because the two Gospel writers have adapted it differently. The verses that come in Matthew alone are verses 7 and 11–13. Both these snippets emphasize the solemnity and, indeed, the severity of God. God is rich in mercy, but is not to be trifled with. Verse 7 in particular, with its talk of a burning city, might have made Matthew's first readers think of the fall of Jerusalem. We will hear much more about this in a couple of chapters' time.

FOR THOUGHT

The one thread that runs right through this complex parable is the word 'wedding'. God's banquet is indeed to be taken seriously, but is also spectacularly joyful. The kingdom is a place of rich love, full life, and holy laughter.

MAKER'S MARK

The discussions in the temple courts began with a challenge to Jesus (21:23–27). There were three parables in a row, all questioning the temple leaders' commitment to God (21:28—22:14). Next come three challenges to Jesus, from different quarters (22:15–40), before he takes the initiative himself (22:41) and the discussion ends.

Test question

By any reckoning this is a cunning question (vv. 16–17). We do not know anything about the Herodians, except that '-ians' is a Latin word-ending meaning 'supporters of'. The Pharisees were pious lay Jews, serious in their commitment to the law. They use honeyed words as a challenge to Jesus (v. 16): 'You're a plain speaker. You won't mind what people think of you. You just state your opinion.' They hope to draw him into an indiscretion.

The problem was money. Israel was occupied land. There were taxes on agricultural yield, and a personal 'poll tax'. That is why the Romans took a census (Luke 2:1–5), to count how much tax they could levy. Israel was also a nation with a keen sense of God's majesty. So paying tax in Roman coin was a threefold burden: no one likes paying taxes; Israel hated foreign rule; and the image on the coin was regarded as idolatry, breaking the command about graven images (Exodus 20:4–6).

So if Jesus supported paying tax, he could be criticized as unpatriotic. But if he opposed tax-paying, he could be reported as a troublemaker and rebel. The question has no right answer. Either reply is wrong. 'Yes' is religiously offensive. 'No' is politically dangerous.

Other side of the coin

One denarius per year, a day's wage, was the standard levy. This is the coin given to Jesus, and he asks his questioners to name the head on it. It is Caesar's. Jesus' next reply is sharp, but serious and searching too (v. 21).

The coin is Caesar's property. It bears his image. So they should give to Caesar what is his. The verb 'give' or 'render' means repaying a debt, settling what is owed, returning something to where it belongs. It is all right to give back to Caesar what belongs to him. It is his money, his stuff. Pay your taxes in the normal way. That is half of Jesus' answer.

The other side of the matter is that God should receive his due. Israel must offer God the worship and service he deserves. This is no limited tax bill, but a completely open cheque. There is only one proper way of responding to God's generosity—with the worship, love and service of our whole lives.

Costly commitment

So Jesus leaves his questioners with two challenges. First, what are they giving to God of themselves, their devotion and their obedience? Second, they must think whether their duty to God gets in the way of civic duty. Probably they would go on paying. Jews had been paying taxes to foreign governments for centuries. But that would be their own decision. In principle there is nothing wrong with returning to the state money it has minted, to support work it must do. In practice that always needs to sit within a greater loyalty and love.

What about us? Should Christians be obedient citizens and pay our taxes with an honest and ready heart? 'In general, yes, we should,' is the answer from this passage—unless and until it clashes with our commitment to God. That 'unless' is the reason we honour many Christians, all through history, who have suffered for their commitment to God and to right. In our own era there are Christians who confess Christ openly in lands where that is a crime, who defy unjust public policies, who support human rights, and who resist tyranny. They do it because they believe that Caesar's rights are limited, and that God's are not.

THINK ABOUT YOUR IMAGE

'Whose image is on the coin?' leads on to the question, 'In whose image have you and I been made?' We carry the Maker's mark. We bear God's image. Our life and first loyalty belong to him.

Father, please give me
love to serve others, in my service to you,
courage to stand apart from others, in my stand for you,
and wisdom to know which to choose, day by day.
Through Jesus Christ our Lord. Amen.

LIFE *to* COME

Once again, men confront Jesus with a thorny question. The last discussion, on tax, concerned Israel's relationship to her colonial lords. This next question is strictly within the realm of religion. Jews disagreed about resurrection. What happened to faithful people when they died? Could they expect any afterlife with God? Pharisees said 'Yes', Sadducees said 'No' (v. 23). What will Jesus say?

One bride for seven brothers

The Sadducees' argument is put forward in very biblical terms. The ancient Jewish law obliged a young widow's nearest male relative—normally her late husband's brother—to marry her (Deuteronomy 25:5–6). This offered the woman some protection, and gave her a fresh opportunity of becoming a mother. It also preserved her husband's memory, and kept his land and property within the family. This custom drives the plot of the book of Ruth, many centuries before Christ, but there is not much evidence of it being practised in New Testament times.

So the Sadducees sketch a rather improbable scenario, with a woman marrying seven brothers in turn, producing children with none of them and eventually outliving them all. So none of the seven has a stronger claim on her than his brothers do: none fathered a child by her; none lived with her to the end of her life. To which of them will she belong in the afterlife? Of course, the tale is designed to make belief in resurrection look ridiculous. Who could possibly take seriously a doctrine that produces riddles of this kind?

A greater world

Jesus replies that *he* takes resurrection seriously. The Sadducees' perspective is too narrow. They have not been biblical enough (v. 29). Jesus' direct answer is that the woman will be married to none of the brothers in the resurrection. Heaven is not that sort of place.

Some Christians would find Jesus' answer alarming. Will our closest personal relationships on earth count for nothing in heaven? Does Jesus mean that Christianity is really anti-marriage, so that the pure life of heaven will require us all to be single? Once our minds run along those lines, then, like the Sadducees, we are taking too narrow a view. Whatever heaven is like, it will not erase the goodness of earth but will gather it into the radiance of God's greater glory. Heaven will not be a poorer place than earth, but a richer, fuller, stronger, brighter place. If we insist on squeezing heaven into our earthly patterns of thought, it will simply not fit. That is where the Sadducees went wrong.

God of the living

Jesus now reaches for scripture himself. The Sadducees recognized the authority of the law, the first five books of the Old Testament, whereas Pharisees worked with a much wider range of scriptures. The two groups disagreed on resurrection partly because it was most clearly taught in books that the Sadducees did not use very much. Here Jesus manages to meet the Sadducees on their own ground, to produce an original argument and to explain his own views on resurrection.

He quotes (v. 32) from God's words to Moses in Exodus 3:6. By Moses' time the three patriarchs Abraham, Isaac and Jacob were long dead. Yet God says, 'I am their God.' Though dead to human eyes, they are alive to God. His relationship with them is not past and over, but present and active. Those who live by faith will die to God, and will rise to new and lasting life with God.

Clearer view

Christians believe in resurrection, not just because Christ taught it but also because Christ himself rose from the grave. We see more clearly, because of his resurrection, that God's power is greater than the power of death. We celebrate Easter, and in our Easter faith is hope and confidence for those who have died in Christ. We need not think of heaven as unrelated to the experience of earth. Jesus' words speak of real people, who have lived on earth, now living in the presence of God. But the vexing tangles of earth will not always help us to understand the radiant clarity of heaven.

·FOR THOUGHT AND PRAYER

Thank God for the people you have known who died in faith.
Thank God for people whom you have seen face weakness with
courage. Thank God for our Easter faith. Pray for grace that you
may live to God, live in hope, and live by faith in Jesus.

LOVE *the* LORD

Here are two short pieces of teaching, one about the Jewish law, the other about the Jewish Messiah.

Top of the orders

A challenge comes from Pharisees. They put to Jesus a question common in Jewish legal debate: 'Which is the greatest command in the law?' Jesus replies by quoting Deuteronomy 6:5, the command to love God with our whole selves. Deuteronomy says, '...with heart, soul and strength'; Matthew says, '...heart, soul and mind'; and slightly different versions come in Mark and Luke. The meaning is the same: all that we are, and all that we can be, is ours to give to God in obedience, service and praise.

Jesus then sets a second command beside the first—to love our neighbour as we love ourselves (Leviticus 19:18). This was a common technique among Jewish teachers. To explain an issue fully, they would string together scripture verses that had an important word in common. Loving God is the great command, but it does not stand alone because we are not made to be solitary people.

The command in Leviticus is very practical. It sums up a paragraph about helping weak people, about fair dealing and honest speech, and it means, 'Give your neighbour the consideration you would like to receive in their situation. Give a neighbour's interests and rights the respect you give your own.'

One breath for God

Verse 40 does not quite mean that two commands are all you need. But it does claim that everything in the ancient Jewish law leads towards those two commands and fills out their detail. Only Matthew words the verse in this way, reflecting his concern to relate Christian teaching to the ancient Jewish law (compare 5:17). And as followers of Jesus today, God still calls us to shape our life by these two great commandments—simple to say without even taking a breath, but utterly absorbing to live out, claiming every breath we take.

Royal issue

Jesus now takes the initiative in the discussion (v. 41), and introduces a new topic. He puts a question, and the Pharisees give the standard answer. 'The Messiah is son of David,' they say (v. 42). Jesus does not reject that answer, but he expands it. 'Son of David' is a true answer; the Messiah will be a royal figure, a ruler in Israel. But this is not the whole truth. Jesus invites the Pharisees to explore a text with him.

Psalm 110 is headed 'Psalm of David', and it says, 'The LORD [the Hebrew word for God] said to my lord, "Sit at my right hand…".'.

Jesus assumes that this psalm is talking about the Messiah: who else would sit at God's right hand? Then he points out how the psalm speaks with respect and humility, calling the Messiah 'my lord'. These are not the tones a senior ancestor would normally use of a young relative. The Messiah must be much more than David's son. His destiny, nature and rank far surpass David's. Israel's Christ is indeed a royal figure, but he is far greater than any human royalty.

Bigger picture

The first encounter asked Jesus to shrink the law to a narrow focus (v. 36). In this second exchange Jesus asks the Pharisees to expand their vision of messiahship to a broader horizon. The Messiah is indeed a special person, but he is more than a person. There is something profoundly God-like about him that no human title can fully describe. On a previous occasion when Jesus talked about identity, he accepted Peter's confession, 'Son of God' (16:14–16). This time he leaves broad hints, but in the presence of enemies he does not make outright claims. The time for that will come later (26:63–64).

Moving to crisis

The discussion is over (v. 46). Jesus came to the Temple as Son of David (21:9, 15). Now he leaves his enemies with the thought that he is much greater than this. From here onwards the Gospel moves steadily towards a harsh collision. Jesus' opponents will pursue him again. He himself talked of a burning city (22:7), and will speak in the next chapters about God's judgment on Jerusalem.

FOR THOUGHT AND PRAYER

People need to love and be loved. Never be frightened to tell God that you love him, and to rejoice that he loves you.

GRIEF & ANGER

This chapter is one of the most difficult in Matthew, and this page discusses some general points about it before we go on to read it, a section at a time, in the pages ahead.

Bridge of sorrows

Chapter 23 is a bridge in the development of Matthew's story. It spans across from the controversies of 21 and 22 to the teaching in 24 about the destruction of Jerusalem, and to the arrest, trial and cross in 26 and 27. It spells out how polarized Jesus and his opponents have become, and shows with painful clarity how far they are from reconciliation and how inevitable are the crises and calamities ahead.

Only Matthew

The matching sections of Mark and Luke are shorter than this. Hardly any material in Matthew 23 has a parallel in Mark, although quite a lot is in Luke, mostly in Luke 11:39–51. Many writers think that Matthew has assembled a quantity of critical comment that Jesus made about his opponents, and has included it all together here because it carries the storyline forward so effectively.

Others pursue that approach even further. They reckon Matthew had a reason for assembling this critical material about scribes and Pharisees. They suggest that his own church was at odds with the Jewish leadership of his time, that Christians were being elbowed out of Judaism. So this material expresses Matthew's own viewpoint, his unease and anger at his church's troubles.

I reckon it quite possible that Matthew gathered material. Like all this Gospel's blocks of teaching, the chapter has a single consistent theme. But I am inclined to trace the main thrust of this criticism back to Jesus. The Gospels record some very sharp differences of opinion. Jesus' style and approach differed quite widely from the formality and legal focus of the Pharisees' piety.

Hard words

If we judge the language of this chapter by modern Western standards, it seems very harsh. But these words relate more easily to the customs of their own time and place. Polemic (argument between different groups and parties) was pretty sharp in the first century: 'one's opponents were, as a rule, blind, foolish, impious, hypocritical' (Davies and Allison). This polemic does not aim to be balanced. It does not pick out the best points in Pharisaism. It intentionally draws attention to division, dispute and difficulty.

The same sort of thing is found elsewhere in first-century Judaism, for example, the Dead Sea Scrolls and the writings of Josephus. It is plentiful in the Old Testament prophets. Jews could speak to Jews in this way when serious questions of loyalty, faith or tradition were at stake. That leads on to the next issue.

Matthew the Jew

As the Jewish people have spread through the world, over the last 2500 years or so, they have met appalling hostility and cruelty in many lands and times. The horror of the Holocaust in the 1940s has moved many Christians to reflect on Christian anti-semitism across the years, and to do all they can to prevent any re-emergence of that spirit in our own day. We are rightly suspicious of anything anti-semitic. So what about Matthew 23?

This material was surely not intended by Matthew (nor by Jesus) as anti-semitic, although it has been used in that way since. Matthew was a Jewish Christian, a member therefore of a small but significant group within Judaism, trying to explain and justify his church's faith by writing a Gospel. That Gospel naturally shows some of the pressures and conflicts that have arisen, reasons why Christianity has diverged from other streams within Judaism. But Matthew would never have thought of Christianity (or himself) as un-Jewish. Open to Gentiles, yes; but un-Jewish, no. Matthew 23 is polemic, but it was not written as racist polemic.

TAKE TO HEART

Some Christians have used this text to fuel anti-Jewish prejudice. There is surely a truer approach. Matthew 23 shows some of the faults into which religion—even well-meaning religion—can fall. If we listen to it with ourselves in mind, we can gain much insight.

LEADING QUESTIONS

This section speaks of the servant lifestyle that Christians should adopt, along lines we have already met in 20:24–28. It targets especially those who teach and guide others in faith, and so offers a checklist for how leadership is exercised in the Church.

Sitting still

Matthew has pointed out several times that the Jerusalem crowds were more receptive to Jesus than were some of their teachers and leaders (21:15–16, 26, 46). Here Jesus talks to the crowds and criticizes the scribes and Pharisees, men who studied the law and encouraged others to observe it.

'Sitting on Moses seat' (v. 2) means exercising a teaching role within Israel, interpreting the directions and duties of the ancient law and applying it to people's needs and lives. 'Do whatever they teach' (v. 3) is difficult. It could be saying, 'When they teach the law truly, then take it seriously.' For Jesus valued the law, though he disagreed sorely with some of its interpreters. Or it could be rather ironic: 'You are welcome to observe what they say—but you really must avoid what they do!'

Either way, Jesus' criticism (v. 4) is that these teachers expect too much from others. Their legal rulings cut deep into daily life, yet they show little awareness of the practical effect these teachings have. Jesus, by contrast, offers an easy and bearable yoke (11:28–30).

The preachers who are heard most clearly today are usually those who know their people well and who share the burdens of their lives. A preacher may live largely among fellow Christians, but must still be sensitive to the pressures and perplexities facing Christian people who live and work in less sympathetic or supportive places.

Showing up

Most people enjoy attracting the good opinions and attention of others. We easily forget that good opinions and attention are worth little unless they have been patiently earned and can be accepted humbly. 'Phylacteries' (v. 5) are small leather boxes containing scripture texts, that were strapped to the forehead and arm (Deuteronomy

6:8). The 'tassels' were blue cords that hung from the four corners of a Jew's robe (Numbers 15:38–39). Perhaps a modern Christian equivalent would be carrying a large and well-worn Bible, in the hope that people will notice our piety and learning.

The word 'rabbi' (v. 7) appears here for the first time in Matthew. Literally it means 'my great one', 'my master', and was applied to Jewish teachers from about Jesus' time onwards. Enjoying titles and places of honour, basking in public regard and revelling in social opportunity are not ideal character traits in a Christian leader. The deepest work is sometimes done by those who are noticed the least.

Levelling down

In the Christian community, no one is any greater than the rest. All are brothers and sisters under the sheltering fatherhood of God. All of us are learners, following the one teacher, Jesus Christ (vv. 8–10). The Church has found these verses hard to take literally. Concern for responsible leadership has proved hard to manage without names, offices and titles. Possibly you carry one or other of these—as I do. So what does Matthew 23 ask of us?

- It asks those of us called 'Father' or 'Mother' to be rightly child-like in spirit, to serve like an older brother or sister who is caring for younger ones while our heavenly Father is out of sight.

- Teachers must carry on learning of Christ, and in particular should learn from the Christian experience of the people we teach.

- Any among us who are thought great must work hard to sustain the virtue of humility.

Authority in the Church is always loaned and delegated, held on trust rather than owned and possessed. Leadership is a temporary role. In heaven there will be no ranks, only worshippers. Dignity and achievement are found in some unlikely places, often among people who work steadily at a humble task and expect little in return, except the satisfaction of knowing that their work is worthwhile.

PRAYER

Lord, help me to take pleasure in applauding the successes of others, in learning from the people around me, in sharing the burdens of friends. Through Jesus Christ our Lord. Amen.

RELIGIOUS AUDIT

Jesus' public teaching in Matthew opens with a series of beatitudes (5:3–12), declaring the blessings of God's kingdom on people who are poor in spirit, meek and pure in heart. His public teaching ends here in chapter 23, with seven woes. Jesus grieves that his opponents are so far from the kingdom, so alien to it in the way they behave and think. The woes stand as if facing the beatitudes, like two avenues of great trees, at either end of the Gospel.

There is something similar in the Old Testament, in Deuteronomy 27 and 28. When Israel came into the promised land and committed herself afresh to God, she was to recite the blessings and curses of God's covenant from opposite mountain-sides. Matthew writes of a new covenant, of God's covenant with Israel, renewed in the death of Jesus (26:28). He knows of many who have come into that new covenant, and of others who have resisted and resented the good news. These markers of blessing and woe are invitation and lament, challenge and warning, bright hope and bitter sorrow.

Roughly speaking, two of these seven woes are about the scribes' and Pharisees' activity, two about their teaching, and two about their character. The seventh (23:29–33) we leave till later.

Unmaking converts

The first two woes (vv. 13 and 15, leaving aside v. 14, which is not in the earliest manuscripts) concern the kingdom. The Pharisees will not enter themselves, they discourage others from doing so, and they make strenuous efforts to win people to their own religious views without bringing them any nearer to God.

The issue here is spiritual growth. Are we serious in trying to get nearer to Christ? How do we react when someone else shows more enthusiasm for the gospel than we have—do we try to rein them back? Do our efforts to win people really help them to open their lives to God, or simply draw them into our habits and prejudices?

Hard to swallow

The next two woes are about finely tuned legal teaching, rules that seem splendidly detailed but which miss such great and obvious truths that they are almost useless. The third woe (vv. 16–22) is about oaths. Jesus has already taught that simple and consistent truthfulness is better than elaborate oath-taking (5:33–37). Now he attacks the idea that oaths could be split into two categories—those you needed to keep, and others you did not. His point of view is much more direct. Promises that sound serious should be seriously kept; there is no honest or godly way of getting round that.

The fourth woe (vv. 23–24) is about putting first things first, letting the most important matters in religion and life be those we take the most seriously. If we spend so much effort on the finer points of church affairs that we never take time to 'stir one another up to love and good works' (Hebrews 10:24), we could be in danger of swallowing the same camel.

Beneath the surface

The fifth and sixth woes are about the falsity of life that looks religious on the outside but lacks a deep vein of goodness within. Jesus knows that the Pharisees were careful to wash eating and drinking vessels. But he says that they themselves are like half-washed cups (vv. 25–26). Their formal and dutiful piety, he says, camouflages flaws in their practical and personal lifestyle. If they are so zealous for cleanliness, let them clean up their own lives, on the inside.

The sixth woe (vv. 27–28) compares Jesus' opponents to a painted tomb—either a white-marked grave, so that passers-by did not tread on impure land, or possibly an elaborately decorated and wealthy tomb. The point is the same in either case. The clarity and apparent innocence of the markings conceal the grim decay of death.

My family once bought a tin of peas that looked fine outside but had an insect inside. It must have flown in at the critical moment, after the peas were poured in and before the lid was clamped on top. It was there to greet us, very dead, when we opened the can. We have not much enjoyed tinned peas since. What is there within your life, or mine, that could put someone off the Christian faith?

PRAYER

Search me, O God, and know my heart. See if there is any wicked way in me. And lead me in the way everlasting.

Psalm 139:23–24

DIVISION & DESOLATION

The last woe (23:29–33) is the harshest of the seven. It tells of martyr-dom and crucifixion, of hatred and violence, of jealous and angry faith, and of the ugly consequences of rivalry and fear. Yet as it runs into the final verses of the chapter, righteous anger mingles with tears, and des-perate grief speaks one last word of compassion and love.

Trail of death

Verses 29–32 take up a theme from the vineyard parable (21:34–39). God sent prophets to Israel across the centuries, and many of them were treated harshly and cruelly. Finally God has sent his Son, and in his coming the whole wretched history will be summed up and brought to a point beyond repair or return.

If Jesus' opponents honour the tombs of prophets, he says, let them examine their own attitude. They are—at least in spirit—the heirs of those who did the damage, who resisted the message the prophets brought. For God's final and greatest prophet stands among them, and they resent him and his word. There will be an awful 'fulfilment' (v. 32) of this shadow side of Israel's tradition, in the wrath that will be mea-sured out to Jesus.

No meeting place

Yet still God's gospel will go out to Israel. Christian messengers will bring the word but will not always be well received. There will be a solid core of resistance among the religious leadership of the nation (v. 34). Finally and climactically, the events of 'this generation' (v. 36), in the lifetime of Jesus' hearers, will sum up a long history of conflict and gather to a focus the judgment of God.

Abel was the first godly martyr in the Bible (Genesis 4). 'Zechariah' (v. 35) may refer to 2 Chronicles 24:20–22, regarded as the last mar-tyrdom of the Old Testament. (In the Hebrew Bible, Chronicles comes last.) The death of Jesus, and the harassment of his followers, will bring this history to a head, and 'this generation' will feel the recoil.

Yearning love

Jesus holds out his arms in sorrow for opportunity lost. He had longed to gather Jerusalem into the gentle grasp of God's kingdom. Like the sheltering wings of a mother hen, he had tried to reach out in love (v. 37). But love had met with refusal, and is now moving on.

The Temple was seen as God's dwelling place, the house where God was known in an intimate way (23:21). Now Jesus speaks of an awful vacuum, of the Temple becoming empty and desolate (v. 38), a sort of anti-Emmanuel, the house of God's absence.

The last verse turns again to Psalm 118, to the words that greeted Jesus when he came into the city (21:9). Now the wheel has turned full circle, and his time in the Temple is over. As the glory of God once left the city before (Ezekiel 11:23), Jesus too steps away and pauses on the Mount of Olives (24:1–3). One day he will be known again as king. But before that day dawns, tumultuous and terrible days will come.

Passage of time

These verses expect the summing up of Israel's history in Jesus' own generation. But that history, stretching through the Old Testament, contains both light and shadow, faith and unfaith. Jesus himself is the culmination of Israel's faithfulness, the godly prophet *par excellence*. The opposition that eventually engineers his death is the completion of Israel's unfaithfulness, of the strand of disobedience that runs through her scriptures. So this passage at the end of Matthew 23 speaks to its own time, and also to ours. Do remember:

- The distinction Matthew has often shown us between the crowds and their leaders. Jesus and the movement he launched found a good reception among many Jews.

- If God's public judgment on Israel's leaders came in the fall of Jerusalem in AD70, then it is over.

- This passage is also about you and me, about the dangers of bitterness in religion, and the terrible consequences of trying too hard to defend God. We are not immune.

FOR REFLECTION

A wise friend once told me, 'When I take holy communion, I ask God to show me if I have gone badly awry in my faith, if I have seriously misunderstood his call and love.'

LOOKING AHEAD

Starting to teach

The last verse of chapter 23 closed a circle: it echoed 21:9, and drew Jesus' time in the Temple to an end. Now he moves out of the Temple to a new venue. The Mount of Olives was just outside the city wall of Jerusalem, on the east side, looking across the Kidron Valley to the temple buildings. Jesus sits down—the position in which a rabbi taught—with his disciples around him. This is the fifth great sermon of Matthew's Gospel: it runs to the end of chapter 25.

Crumbling securities

The Temple was famed for its grandeur, size and light-coloured, gleaming stone. The Mount of Olives was an ideal place from which to view it. The disciples' first comment (v. 1) sounds like the admiration of pilgrims. But Jesus' words cut grimly and abruptly into their awe (v. 2): it will not last; it will be shattered. What has made him think this?

First, he has a sense of history. This prediction carries forward the teaching in the last three chapters. The rejection of the Son will mean the loss of the vineyard. The wedding guests refuse to banquet with God, and murder the messengers who summon them; that will cost them their city. The Temple has failed to deliver; Jesus' demonstration there was an acted symbol of trouble ahead. The lives of the martyrs will be charged to the generation that kills the Son.

Second, he reads the political mood. Israel was impatient under foreign rule. A rash of small uprisings was dotted through the first century. A little sober foresight could trace the likely consequences. Under Rome, Israel found it hard to live at peace but would surely fail badly if she went to war.

Third, he knows the scripture. Past prophets had spoken of God's judgment against Jerusalem (for example, Jeremiah 7:12–15; 9:11). The city was not overshadowed by a cosmic insurance policy, but was sustained only by its people's covenant obedience. When that obedience reached a low ebb, then the covenant was a positively dangerous relationship.

Thinking positively

Jesus looked ahead and saw gloom and sadness for Jerusalem. But he was also a man of hope. He believed that God's power and love would one day be known on earth in a much fuller way than even he had shown. His parables of growth look forward with great confidence. So although this chapter tells of catastrophe, it also reflects a belief that time is in God's hands. The disaster ahead is part of a bigger purpose of salvation and judgment, of righteousness, hope and love.

If you look at a range of mountains, the highest peaks may appear interleaved with the nearer and lower hills. It is hard to sort out the separate layers when viewing from far away. A map-maker finds that sort of thing annoying, and wants to fix accurate distances and positions. However, for a prophet, the nearer and more immediate purposes of God can be a foretaste, assurance and meaningful anticipation of God's greater and final work. A prophet can revel in the merging of two horizons.

There is a similar merging in some biblical texts that look forward. A conviction that God controls the final outcome of all things, and an awareness of God's work in the foreseeable future, merge into one forward view. It is right that the two do hold together, that the God of the ages is known as the God who acts in time. History is the place where eternity is made known.

Posing problems

The disciples' question (v. 3) weaves two issues together. Two horizons merge and fuse in their minds.

- 'When will all this be?' is a fair follow-on to verse 2, and is a reasonable and predictable question.

- 'What will be the sign of your coming?' picks up 23:39, that one day people would again see Jesus coming in the name of the Lord. Again that is an understandable reaction.

The disciples seem to assume that the fall of the city will be a sign of the presence of Jesus. It will surely also be a time of great change in history, the turning of an era.

FOR REFLECTION AND PRAYER

God of the ages, please teach your Church to meet the uncertainties of time without fear, and to greet the certainties of eternity in faith. Through Jesus Christ our Lord. Amen.

PANIC, PRESSURE & PATIENCE

Matthew's Gospel looks back, at the life of Jesus and at the disciples' desire to understand him. But for Matthew's first readers, and for Christians ever since, this chapter has been much more than history. It looks forward from the time of Jesus, and describes events to come. Christians through the ages have asked when all this will arise: 'Are these verses speaking of our days?' This part of the chapter urges Jesus' disciples—and Matthew's readers, and us—to be patient. Panic is not a Christian virtue.

False alarm

There were several small rebellions in Israel in the generation after Jesus. During the period from AD30 to 66, the temperature was rising, and nationalism was becoming restless and increasingly militant. Leaders emerged who attracted groups of followers and promised signs and wonders. So far as we know, none of them actually claimed to be God's anointed, but their style and appeal drew the loyalty and hopes of many. None of them succeeded.

When the news is filled with disaster, it is tempting to think that the world is shifting, that present troubles will be worse than any before and will allow no return to normality. Where communication is poor, such thoughts and rumours can carry an eerie power. Herod Antipas went to war with an eastern neighbour in the late 30s, there was an earthquake in Syria in 37, in 40 the Roman emperor outraged the Jews by trying to place his statue in the Jerusalem Temple, and there was a long famine in Palestine in the mid-40s. To a church expecting the fulfilment of Jesus' words, such events could be unsettling.

But any alarm would be false. Many Jews expected a time of suffering—sometimes called 'messianic woes'—before God brought his purposes to fruition. Jesus shares that view. The Church should see these distresses as the very first 'birth pangs' (v. 8), indications that there is new life ahead, but not yet signs of its urgent coming.

Church under pressure

In its early centuries, Christianity was a vulnerable minority faith, liable to bouts of harassment and persecution. In Judea itself there were three prominent executions in the first generation: Stephen, about AD33 (Acts 6—7); James Zebedee in 44 (Acts 12:2); and James the brother of Jesus, leader of the Jerusalem church, in 62. In such an environment, many ordinary Christians are likely to have come under pressure. The temptation to fall away will have been strong (vv. 9–10).

Yet even in those years, when the mother church in Jerusalem and Judea was under such strain, the faith was spreading wide (v. 14). In well under a generation it reached Rome, from where roads radiated across Europe. The New Testament shows us part of that spread, but there is much more about which we have only slight and sketchy information—the movement eastwards, for example.

Home truths

I am connecting this chapter to events in Palestine. Jesus' words relate most naturally to his own land and people. I think Matthew was writing from either Palestine itself, or from sufficiently near it—Syria perhaps—to be affected by the mood in the Jewish homeland. He was ready to write about events in Palestine; it would be helpful to his church. But these verses carry wisdom for the Church in every age and place.

Christianity is a hopeful faith. We believe that the God of Jesus Christ is Lord of time and eternity, God of the future as surely as of the past. We cannot help being hopeful. But Christians have often found difficulty in balancing hope with patience, in walking the narrow ridge between over-enthusiasm and exhaustion. Panic, prophets and persecution still tempt.

Panic leads us into burn-out—we run out of energy. False prophets beckon us into byways—to invest our faith in some wayward discovery or futuristic timetable. Persecution pushes us into backsliding—we lose ground as Christians because it is hard to hold on.

These verses urge a steady calm. This is a long-distance journey. Let us run with perseverance the race that is set before us (Hebrews 12:2). Out of the turbulence of his world, God is working in creative love to bring new life to birth. Through the trials of the Church, God is spreading the gospel to the nations. We may rightly travel in hope.

FOR REFLECTION

'I do not know what the future holds, but I do know who holds the future' (Anon).

TIME *to* RUN

The start of this section is sharp and urgent. Previous verses have been cautious and cool: 'Keep watch, look out, not yet.' Suddenly here is something to react to.

Tainted Temple

The key sign is 'the desolating sacrilege' (v. 15). This odd phrase comes from the visions and prophecies in Daniel 7—12. The main event they cover is the defiling of the Jerusalem Temple by the Syrian king, Antiochus Epiphanes, about 200 years before Christ. He set up an altar to the Greek god Zeus, on top of the sacrificial altar in the Temple. This is what Daniel calls 'the abomination that makes desolate' (Daniel 9:27; 11:31; 12:11). For the Jews this was a ruinous defilement of the Temple's life, robbing the building of its role and reverence.

So this phrase in Matthew 24 surely refers to something improper and unworthy in the Temple. Jesus speaks of its being defiled and compromised. Exactly what Jesus meant, and how much detail he foresaw of the events ahead, is difficult to know for certain. Perhaps the linking of word to fulfilment became clear to the early Christians only as events unfolded. The most likely 'match' to this text, so far as I can see, came in AD67–68. The Zealots, Jewish freedom fighters, adopted the Temple as their headquarters, and violently and aggressively disrupted some of its life and worship.

If verse 15 describes this occupation of the Temple, then the verses that follow speak of the distresses of the Jewish War, which ran to a bloody end in the early 70s. Meanwhile Matthew's aside—'let the reader understand'—suggests that the link to Daniel will be taken up again.

Hard times

The next verses urge the Christians in the Jerusalem area to run for the country. Times will be hard and conditions harsh. The language of verses 17 to 18—'Don't even run indoors or go back for a coat'—may be deliberately graphic and stark. But the point is clear. Once the Temple is tainted, it is no time to hang around. The writing is on the wall. It is far better to flee for safety.

Many Jerusalem Christians migrated at this time to Pella, beyond the Jordan, apparently in response to a prophetic message. These verses may be that message: the Church acted on its memory and record of the words of Jesus. The letter of James, which probably comes from Palestine a few years before this, also urges Christians to avoid 'conflicts and disputes' (James 4:1). Many Christians did not join the war. They were a peaceful group. They opposed rebellion, and reckoned it was not their battle.

There is a warning about 'winter or sabbath' (v. 20). Wintry weather, with rivers running high, would make hasty travel almost impossible. Sabbath travel would be resented by Jewish neighbours, and indeed the Christians themselves may have been reluctant to do this. Verse 21 refers again to Daniel (12:1). These will be terrible days, but they are under God's sight, and they will come to an end (v. 22).

Distractions and deceptions

The warnings in verses 23–28 match those of the previous section (24:4–5, 11). Even in times of fear and flight, the Christians should not be taken in by flimsy claims and wild rumour. They will not need to hunt for the work of Jesus. When it comes, no mistake will be possible. As when vultures gather round a corpse, you will not need to ask what is happening.

Forward look

I have suggested (p. 196) why Jesus might have foreseen the fall of the Temple. He must also have spent time learning from the book of Daniel. He had the vision to prophesy a crisis in the Temple and to warn his friends to flee. And amid all the words of chaos, he retained a sense that God would vindicate him and his cause.

FOR REFLECTION AND PRAYER

Many people in our times have to live through refugee experiences like those described here: urgent flight; concern for weak relatives; unpredictable weather; longing for it to end. Many kinds of troubles make people run. Ethnic rivalry, political power struggles, religious conflicts, revolutions and those who try to crush them can all cause fearsome consequences for humble and ordinary people. Pray for refugees, wherever you hear of them in the world today.

DAY *of* DARKNESS

As if time had stopped

Verse 29 is the awful climax of this prophecy. All the lights go out. The earth is shrouded in darkness and cold. The skies shiver and fall. A dreadful gloom covers every horizon. Every certainty and landmark is gone, as if the end of all things has come.

This language of cosmic collapse and falling skies describes the fall of the city. This was the city on which God had set his love in a unique way. For it to come to destruction, fire and slaughter, for Jerusalem to be reduced to ruins, for the nation to lose past, present and future in one awful bloody disaster, cannot be spoken of in measured and easy words. This is like the end of the world.

Kingdom coming

Yet in a grim and awful irony, this dreadful event reveals the kingdom and Lordship of Jesus. This was the city whose leaders resisted and crucified him, whose Temple drew and devoured the wealth of God's people, the city against which he had spoken in sadness and dreadful finality. Even this awful destruction is a sign that he is Lord. That moment in the book of Daniel when God confirms the authority and rule of the Son of Man is acted out once again, as the words of Jesus against the city run to fulfilment (v. 30; from Daniel 7:13). The 'tribes of the land', the people of Israel, weep at the fall of the city (v. 30). Yet the word of Jesus goes out across the world (v. 31).

These words and pictures burst the bounds of normal experience. Here is one of time's most bitter days, when the fragility and futility of the world, its judgment and its sorrow, are tasted to the full—truly a sign of the end of all things. Yet it will come to the generation to which Jesus speaks (v. 34).

Green shoots

The illustration Jesus uses is common experience (v. 32). A greening tree is a sign of summer ahead. Buds, leaves and shoots are nature's clock. They carry the promise of the year running forward to its next stage. So with the sequence of events in Matthew 24: the defiling of the Temple and the need to flee (24:15–22) show that the fall of Jerusalem is near (vv. 29–31).

For the person reading Matthew, the fig·tree is already a symbol of the fruitless Temple and of coming ruin (21:18–19). Now that sign is coming to fulfilment. The short fig-tree parable in chapter 24 is a solemn reminder of a falling Temple and of the city running into serious trouble. This will come within a generation (v. 34), under the sure word that Jesus has spoken (v. 35).

Yet as people observe the fig tree, and trace from Jesus' prophecy that one event leads to another, they should also look further forward. The fall of Jerusalem is the shadow of a greater day ahead, a time when all humanity will know the authority of Jesus. 'But of that day and hour, no one knows' (v. 36).

Certain yet not clear

You will see that I have applied these verses to the fall of the city, but as a foreshadowing of that final day which the Church knows as the second coming of Christ. Yet these are verses on which the wisest interpreters do not entirely agree. This chapter is unusually difficult territory, and there are two good reasons why.

First, Matthew's chapter differs in places from the parallel material in Mark and Luke. All three aimed to record the teaching of Jesus in ways that would be helpful to their own readers. They select and arrange rather differently, and this may arise in part from how near they were to the events described. This is Jesus' teaching about the future, written down by people who were living through it.

Second, we have already mentioned (at 24:1–3) the issue of merging horizons. When events lead towards and foreshadow one another, we may expect difficulty in fixing a precise perspective. Understanding God's future is always hard, and Christians in our own day have wasted energy trying to work out dates and details. This chapter urges care and confidence. We must not panic (24:6). We should not trust leaders who try to take the place of Christ (24:24). We need not hunt high and low to locate God's activity (24:26).

FOR REFLECTION

Wise discipleship involves a balance of calm scepticism (24:26) and confident faith (24:35). Pray for both.

WAIT, WAKE & WORK

There is a shift of focus between 24:34 ('all these things') and verse 36 ('but about that day'). Up to 24:34, the main emphasis of the chapter is on the stresses and distresses that will afflict the Church in its first generation. After verse 36 there is a wider view of the Church waiting and serving until the final judgment of Christ. The parables that follow, here and in chapter 25—though they surely spoke to the first generation of the Church—have something to say to Christians in every age.

Flood warning

The theme that runs to the end of chapter 24 is of normal life being abruptly interrupted. God's timetables are not easily read. His plans can take the world by surprise. The disciples' last question in 24:3, 'What will be the sign of the end of the age?' does not have a direct answer. The events that usher time to its final destination, the processes by which the kingdoms of this world become the kingdom of our God and his Christ, are not easily discerned.

The story of Noah (Genesis 6—9) is an account of normal life being utterly submerged by the intervention and judgment of God. The message here is that we should not take God for granted. The world is not so fully under our control as we often imagine (vv. 37–39). However usual business may appear to be, there is a greater issue that should always concern and shape the Church. How ready are we?

Crime watch

The picture in verses 42–44 is of Jesus coming quietly and unexpectedly, like a thief in the night. When a householder expects a burglary, it is well to stay awake. If the burglar knows we are asleep, he will have the advantage of surprise. The only way to prevent that is to be constantly on the alert. This parable is about living the sort of spiritual life that is vigilant, involved, alive to the work of God in our world. It speaks against a dozy, careless and casual faith. Again, do not take God for granted. Do not drift or despair. Patience, persistence, prayer—these are basics of Christian readiness.

Service charge

The next parable (vv. 45–51) has a particular message for Christian leaders, and it may be that Jesus had the Twelve in mind. But it applies to any Christian whose responsibilities involve other people. The point is simple: be faithful to your work, keep at it, do it properly, treat other people with care and respect. That is readiness. The Church does not need to run to and fro looking for Jesus (24:23–28). Steady commitment to the work of God, to love and care, to faithful responsibility and patient service, is the way to honour Christ.

Apparently Martin Luther was once asked what he would do if he thought Christ would come back the next day. He replied that he would get on with today's work as normal. Daily life, regular activity, faithful duty, may be all the readiness Christ expects of us. So how do we do our work? Is it work with which Christ can be pleased, and do we go about it in ways that honour him?

Ready, steady

As in so many aspects of belief, we need balance in our Christian hope. The history of the Church is littered with disappointed people who thought the coming of the Lord was near. Some dropped normal responsibilities, some travelled to out-of-the-way places to greet the coming, some flamed with zeal and then burned rapidly low. But God is not a railway company, and the gospel is not a timetable.

The opposite fault is to lose hope. It does not all depend on us. God holds the issues of time in his hands: as he created, he will complete; as he commands, he will judge; as he sent Christ, he will save through Christ. 'Fog in Channel. Continent cut off,' said one newspaper headline of a century ago. We may feel as if the cloudiness in our vision and faith pushes God to a distance. But God is there, as solid and as near as ever, seeing through the mist with purpose and love.

PRAYER

May the God of hope fill us with all joy and peace in believing, that by the power of the Holy Spirit we may be filled with hope.

From Romans 15:13

OUT *of* OIL

The last parable was a call to patient readiness, to the sort of faithful service that will not be surprised or embarrassed by the unexpected coming of the Lord. This parable of the ten maidens gives the other side of that same message. The time will come when it is too late to repair or restore what we have neglected to do and to be for Christ. Sudden retrieval of the situation may not be possible. As with a lot of human activity, you need to get ready when you have the chance. Then, even if the timing of God catches us by surprise, it need not find us unprepared.

A Jewish wedding

We have already met the idea of Jesus as God's bridegroom, come to claim his people (9:15; 22:2). Here he again appears as the bridegroom, but before he does we have an inside view of some Jewish wedding customs. In Britain it is often the bride who keeps everyone waiting. In first-century Palestine it appears that the wedding started when the groom and his company arrived. These girls with their lanterns appear to be all set to give the wedding party a ceremonial escort, as a sort of guard of honour.

Beyond that, the details of the situation are not fully clear. Why did the groom not come until nightfall? Had the girls left their lamps burning constantly, or did they try to light them up when the bridegroom came? Why could the wise girls not share what they had? Why are the foolish girls shut out so abruptly at the end—is that realistic?

As so often with parables, the detail is not all meant to be interpreted, nor is it all realistic. There is a main thread, about readiness, and that is what the reader or hearer should take away. We should take the opportunities we have, and respond faithfully and readily to the love and call of Christ, as we hear them. That is the only sure way to be ready for what is ahead.

The parable teaches that readiness is really an individual matter. We can help one another in the Christian life, but ultimately we have each to take responsibility for our own spiritual life and service. Commitment to Christ is one of the things that no one else can take on for us.

Time lapse

This parable and the previous one both feature a delay. The wicked servant (24:48) expects a delay, and then finds himself overtaken by the master's sudden arrival. The foolish girls seem not to reckon on a long wait, and are caught out when things move slowly.

The Church has to be committed to the long haul, but also to make every day's activity fit for Christ. Church history may last much longer than we can foresee. But God is never so slow that we can afford to be slack in our service. It is that balance again, between hope that is ready and hope that is not afraid to wait.

Pictures of today

People who preach on parables sometimes try to be creative, in updating the story to fit something from our own society or experience. A modern parallel may help hearers to get their minds inside the message of the biblical story.

By all means think of your own examples. One that occurs to me is the work of the wedding photographer, who has to capture the day as it unfolds. 'There were ten photographers at a wedding. Five had brought a spare roll of film and five had not...'. Jesus had an inventive mind and used stories from his own time and place to explain the message of God's eternal kingdom. Good preachers should not be afraid to do the same.

FOR REFLECTION AND PRAYER

'Time is more important than all eternity. Here you can prepare for the Lord. There you cannot.'

Anon, from the Middle Ages

Lord Jesus Christ, may your Church be ready to meet your coming, with the lamps of faith burning sure and strong. Give us the bright eyes of hope, the steady gaze of faith and the caring look of love.

HIDDEN TALENT

This is the third parable in a row about waiting for someone to appear. Three servants are entrusted with their master's cash, to invest and do business until he returns. As with the ten virgins, this parable is about right and wrong responses: five virgins were wise and five foolish. Here it is two against one: two servants are active and successful, while the third is an ineffective and unhappy figure.

A similar parable occurs in Luke's Gospel (19:11–27). There are many differences of detail, and it is hard to know whether it is the same story or not. Did Jesus tell it more than once, in different ways? Or were details adjusted as different groups of Christians used the story? Certainly the parable fits well in this part of Matthew, and connects with the material around. It provides a lesson on Christian stewardship and service in the face of the coming judgment of Christ. It urges Christians to be diligent, energetic and confident in working for God, and in seeking to advance his kingdom.

Capital gains

The parable pictures a wealthy businessman entrusting slaves with large sums of money while he travels. While many slaves in the ancient world had very harsh lives, some rose to high positions in their owner's household and exercised considerable responsibility. That is the picture here. These slaves are expected to be active stewards, managers and entrepreneurs. The first two slaves act with alacrity and judgment, and make solid gains for their master (vv. 16–17). He responds with praise and enthusiasm: 'Enter into the joy of your master' (vv. 21, 23). The slaves are promoted, no longer simply to work for the master but to share his friendship. The thought that faithful Christians will be gathered into the eternal joy of Christ is peeping through the parable: the 'application is creeping into the telling of the story' (R.T. France). Thus far, all seems to be well.

Losing interest

The third servant has an unsatisfactory tale. Fear of his master or lack of confidence in his own ability paralysed him, and he took the easiest route available, involving no risk, no imagination and no work.

The master is not impressed. The servant could surely have done better. Even a bank deposit would have produced some visible return. So his one talent is passed on to the servant who started with five, and he himself is thrown out of the security of the master's house.

Parable of application

Christian obedience is meant to be active. The Church is not called simply to be, but to obey. We are meant to apply ourselves and achieve something for Christ. To sustain our own faith and Christian outlook is right. But we are Christians not just for our own spiritual survival, but in order to serve God, and to use the gifts and opportunities he has given us.

The English language has adopted a word from this story: talent, which originally meant a weight of silver. We use it nowadays to mean a personal gift, ability or skill. Here are two thoughts from the story.

- First, a talent is a very large sum. Personal abilities are precious: though often given for nothing, they are rarely developed without great effort. Treasure what you have been given. Treat it as valuable. And let us also value one another's gifts. Many people are far more gifted than they realize, but lack of opportunity or the doubts of others have choked the gift, and now they lack confidence to launch out. Part of the privilege of being Church is that we believe in one another, and we encourage and enable the talents of each, for the good of all and the glory of God.

- Second, the talents in the story 'belong to someone else' (R.V.G. Tasker, *Matthew*, Tyndale New Testament Commentary, IVP, 1961). A Christian is steward and servant. Our lives and abilities are to be used for God, not just for ourselves. Whatever your calling—secular employment, voluntary service, family care, church duty—if it is worthwhile work, and you can do it honestly and effectively, then be proud to do it as service to Christ.

FOR PRAYER

Pause to reflect on what you have been given: abilities, time, friendships, energy. Then consciously and deliberately offer yourself to Christ, not just as a bundle of talents but as a loving disciple and willing servant. Ask that your life may be truly effective for him.

JUDGED *by* CHRIST

This solemn and humbling passage is a dramatic display of Jesus Christ in judgment. As Son of Man he has authority over the nations (Daniel 7:13–14). Here he exercises that authority with all-seeing eye, tender heart and frighteningly powerful word.

Division according to kind(ness)

Strictly, verses 32–33 are the only part of the passage that is really a parable: '…as a shepherd separates the sheep from the goats'. It seems at first rather similar to the parables of the wheat and tares, and the net, in Matthew 13. What is very different here is the explanation that follows, of the division and judgment of the two groups.

Judgment is based on deeds of mercy to the 'least of these who are members of my family' (v. 40). It is all very practical, concerned with the basic requirements for human survival—food and water, warmth and shelter, and the provision of practical help and supplies to the sick and prisoners. But who are the 'members of my family'? Two opinions exist.

The least of my people

One view is that these are all poor people, of any race or religion. The whole human race is judged by its response to people in need. Christ is present everywhere, in the face and form of poverty and suffering, and even the simplest act of relief can be service to him. Jesus' teaching on neighbour love is not only the heart of the Jewish law (7:12; 22:39), but is also the standard by which the true humanity of every person and nation will be tested.

A second view connects the parable to other material in Matthew. Jesus speaks of his followers as his 'brother, sister and mother' (12:50). The 'little ones' are members of the church (18:6). In a verse that hints at the teaching of this present scene, the 'little one' is helped as a disciple of Jesus (10:42). So, it is suggested, the 'least of these' are Christians, and this separation of sheep and goats is the judgment of the nations according to their treatment of Christ and his followers.

Able writers on Matthew are evenly divided between these two views. Where does that leave us?

Right responses

The issue with all Jesus' teaching is not just what we think but what we do. Matthew's Gospel is clear that Christians will be judged, that faith should be expressed in obedient and loving behaviour, and that we should not confine our love to the people we like (5:43–47; 7:21–23). Those teachings push us to take this judgment scene seriously, to weigh our own lives by the marks of kindness mentioned here, and to love others genuinely and generously for Christ's sake—wherever we find them.

Some people ask how grace and faith fit into this picture. Does not this passage tell of judgment by works? Yes, it does, but faith ought to produce good works. That was the message of the last parable, about the talents: faith should aim to be active for God; otherwise it loses the right to count as faith. Then this parable fills out that picture: the main thing faith should do is to care, practically, sympathetically and readily. Jesus Christ is 'God with us'. He cares for us despite our own 'little faith'. He also leads and teaches us to serve the needs of others. Here is the grace of Jesus Christ, alive within the Christian and touching the world through the care given in his name.

Suffering shepherd

This is the end of the last great block of teaching. Jesus is moving on.

- The shepherd who divides sheep and goats is the same one who looked lovingly upon God's wandering sheep (9:36). Now he goes to his last and greatest act of care.

- The Son of Man who will one day sit in heavenly power (v. 31) will first hang in humiliation and pain (26:2).

- The Christ who identifies with the naked and the prisoner, with the famished and thirsty, with the weak, estranged and despised, is the Christ who will be subjected to all this himself.

- The Lord who speaks judgment now goes to bear it.

FOR REFLECTION

Jesus Christ invites us to know him in his weakness, that we may serve him in our neighbours' needs.

ANOINTED *for* BURIAL

The teaching is over (v. 1), and we return to the unfolding events of Holy Week. As we enter the Passion story, all the lines start to converge, to gather our thoughts and expectations. It is like a well-designed garden, where every stretch of path directs the visitor's eye to a distant central tree. Each of four short scenes (26:2–16) points us in the same direction—to the cross.

Time for sacrifice

Passover is at hand—the Jewish springtime festival that celebrated the people's rescue from Egypt over a thousand years before. Again Jesus predicts his coming death (v. 2), as he did on the journey to Jerusalem. Matthew's story does not yet show us that Jesus himself will be the great Passover sacrifice. That will come later. But we do see that he goes to death knowingly and willingly. He accepts obediently the 'must' (16:21) that is the destiny and plan of God.

On the quiet

Once again (as at 2:4) religious leaders of the nation gather, and again Jesus' life will come under threat. Caiaphas was high priest from about AD18 to 36. He must have been a politically skilful man, for he had difficult responsibilities to balance. His father-in-law Annas, who is mentioned in Luke and John, and had served as high priest from AD6 to 15, was still an influential background figure.

The leaders plan to 'arrest Jesus by stealth' (v. 4). This contrasts with the theme of Jesus' innocence, which will be important in the coming trial. But only by a quiet capture would they avoid a riot. Jesus has won the sympathy of many in the festal crowd, and direct action against him would be very risky.

Praise flowing freely

The woman's action seems to be entirely her own initiative (v. 7). It is demonstrative, lavish, devoted, intimate and moving. It also proved somewhat embarrassing, though not necessarily for the reasons that would apply in our culture.

The disciples start reckoning the cost involved. Their explanation sounds quite creditable. After all, Jesus has encouraged people to sell and give (19:21). But they miss the point. Worship has a value of its own that cannot be easily rated and measured. This act of worship is uniquely precious: the poor will always be there (Deuteronomy 15:11), but Jesus will not.

He senses the cross looming over him, and accepts this woman's worship as a kind of funeral ceremony (v. 12). As dead bodies were buried with spices and perfume, so Jesus receives this myrrh as a burial anointing ahead of time. He goes forward from now as the anointed one, named as the Christ and marked out for death by the silent worship of an unnamed woman. In the reading of the Gospel, her action has become known across the world (v. 13). Her memorial of the Christ, and his of her, lead the Church's worship towards his coming death.

The lines that converge on the cross are of many kinds. Jesus' steady commitment to God sits strangely beside the worldly cunning of the priests. The generosity of the woman's worship contrasts with Judas' actions in the next short scene. Sin and sacrifice, deceit and devotion, generosity and greed, all come together at the place where the love of God meets the suffering of earth.

Worthy worship

Worship in most of our churches is quite well planned and controlled. The woman's action at Bethany was unexpected, unusual, lavish and emotional. We use the order of a service to help worshippers offer their whole selves to God. This woman's worship seems to have been more spontaneous. So perhaps this passage invites some gentle reflection on how we worship. How much room ought we to leave, even occasionally, for the unscripted praise of the heart?

Jesus sees no clash of loyalties either between costly and committed worship and care for the poor. When we worship gladly and gratefully, God can deepen our love for others in ways that will affect all our living. Good praise is practical: it produces good practice.

FOR PRAYER

*Thank God that he accepts the worship of your life, as you are—
your prayer and practical service, your thoughts and emotions, the
order of your life, and your spontaneity.*

The TRAP IS SPRUNG

Matthew's narrative moves on two parallel tracks. On one hand is the priests' desire to have Jesus arrested, and their scheming to that end. The other movement is the path taken by Jesus as he goes with his friends to the Passover table, then out to the garden (26:30, 36). The go-between from one line to another is Judas Iscariot.

Man of mystery

I cannot read the mind of Judas. There is too much darkness to see clearly: the darkness of deceit, the darkness of death, and the darkness of our limited knowledge. Had he expected Jesus to be a different kind of leader, and was his betrayal the reaction of a disillusioned man? Was he trying in some perverse and ill-judged way to force Jesus into more aggressive action, by putting him in a tight corner? Had his facility with money caused him to be just too eager for one lucrative opportunity—as a person's greatest strengths may sometimes be the cause of great sins? However tangled his motives, his name has now become a byword for treachery, and one cannot help thinking that he should have known better. Nothing is unforgivable, but for some actions there is no real excuse.

So Judas watched for an opportunity (v. 16). What he eventually betrayed was the meeting place, the garden where Jesus and his disciples would go after the meal. That gave the priests their opportunity to take Jesus quietly, to try him quickly and to have the matter in the hands of the Romans soon after dawn. The popular tumult they feared (26:5) never came. Events moved too rapidly for that.

The figure of thirty silver coins is mentioned only in this Gospel. It echoes an Old Testament text (Zechariah 11:12–13) which Matthew takes up later (27:3–10). Judas' request for payment (explicit only in Matthew) contrasts with the free and generous worship of the woman at Bethany. Clear light and deep shadow set one another in sharp relief.

Setting out

The whole Passover festival lasted a week. This 'first day of Unleavened Bread' was the day for the festal meal. Once again (as at

21:2–3) there seems to be a prior arrangement, this time concerning the room. Even so, the story suggests that Jesus is in command. He knows; he arranges; he orders. As Judas seeks a moment of 'opportunity' (v. 16), Jesus prepares deliberately for his 'time' (v. 18), the critical hour to which he has long been drawn, and which now comes very near. The disciples go off to the city to prepare the room and meal as they are bidden.

Tension at table

The little group take their places at the Passover table, but the atmosphere is strained. As Jesus speaks of betrayal, the disciples search their own hearts. They have stumbled and misunderstood often enough, but to betray Jesus would be far worse. The word about dipping in the dish (v. 23) may be enough to alert Judas. Jesus knows his secret. He asks his own sad question (v. 25), there is a terrible moment as he feels Jesus looking right into him, and we do not see him leave.

Only Judas calls Jesus 'Rabbi' (v. 25). The other disciples say 'Lord' (v. 22). The different name seems to set Judas apart from the group. This is the language an outsider would use.

Destiny and despair

There is tension in this whole matter. Jesus' destiny is inevitable. This is the road he must take. But the people who bring him there, and especially Judas, remain responsible for what they do. Though the cross was God's purpose, some of the human deeds that caused it were very ungodly. It is easy two thousand years later to say 'them'. But these people were not so different from us. Many of their faults were common human failures. It was not just *for* our sins that Jesus died; it was also *by* our sins that he died.

Even if there is no excusing Judas, to be caught without excuse is not his plight alone. Many of us have been there over one issue or another. The forgiveness of Christ is broad enough to cover even the most wretched sins. Judas' final misery—who knows?—may have been that he could not believe that.

PRAYER

May God forgive what we have been, sanctify what we are, and direct what we shall be. Through Jesus Christ our Lord. Amen.

BODY LANGUAGE

The Last Supper of Jesus has spoken powerfully and profoundly to Christians through two thousand years. The Church across the centuries is welcomed in holy communion to the quiet intimacy of the upper room, to sit as friends of Jesus and witness as if for the first time the holy words and actions. There are four records of these words in the New Testament. Many of us will know Paul's account best (1 Corinthians 11:23–26). Matthew's version, though very similar, also has a slant and power of its own.

Given for you

Jesus presides among his friends, and he shapes the course of events. Only in Gethsemane will he be overtaken by his enemies. His four actions with the bread—'took, blessed, broke and gave'—recall his two feeding miracles (14:19; 15:36). This meal also will be for the feeding of many. With the cup too, he takes, blesses and gives. Matthew shows the two actions, with bread and cup, as parallel: the same giving, twice over, of the signs of body and blood.

In a Jewish animal sacrifice, the blood was drained away. The flesh and blood were separated by death. So the elements Jesus shares with his friends speak of sacrifice, of the separating of flesh and blood, of life laid down as worship and gift. His dying is a new Passover. He is, though the words are not used, the Lamb of God. There are other Old Testament resonances too.

- **Covenant:** God's covenant with Israel was sealed with the sprinkling of blood (Exodus 24:8). So now that ancient covenant ceremony is re-enacted, by the shedding of Jesus' blood.

- **Hope:** This is, although Matthew does not actually say so, a new kind of covenant. Jeremiah (31:31–34) wrote of God remaking his covenant, and covering his people with forgiveness.

- **Suffering:** Here is a reminder of Jesus' servant ministry. The words 'poured out for many' echo Isaiah 53:12. The Lord gives his life 'as ransom for many' (Matthew 20:28).

Parted from you

There is a finality in this meeting of friends. They will never gather this way again. The bond they have shared is being broken by death. There is anticipation in Jesus' words, but no mention of his friends continuing the meal or commemorating him. He looks forward to a new meeting, in 'my Father's kingdom'. He expects to die, and yet he looks forward to sharing in the great feast of God, and to a greater fellowship that time and tribulation will not break.

Shared among you

Christians rejoice to share this feast, week after week and year after year. There are many aspects on which we may reflect. Matthew's account of the Last Supper suggests a number.

- **Covenant:** The bread and wine speak of the depth of God's commitment to us, and of the bond forged at the cross of Christ. Holy communion draws Christians into relationship with Christ and with each other.

- **Forgiveness:** Only Matthew's version actually says '…for the forgiveness of sins'. Jesus shared bread and wine with disciples who would desert and deny him. We come to communion not because we deserve to, but because we do not; to the God whose pardon is clear and complete, for Christ has died.

- **Separation:** If we celebrate communion at special gatherings—synods, conferences and so on—we may be well aware that this group will never reassemble in exactly the same form. But in any local church, on any Sunday, the company who gather at the Lord's Table may never be all together again. Life—and death—move people on. Communion is a sacrament of parting, of fragile and fleeting life. Yet it is a chance to share, in time, a taste of eternity. We do this together as a signpost to the life where there will be no more parting and no more pain.

- **Service:** Jesus and his company close with a Passover hymn, and go to the Mount of Olives (v. 30). For Jesus that will be a place of painful wrestling and costly commitment. Communion is not simply a withdrawal. It is also a sacrament of discipleship, beckoning us forward to the trials, decisions and service we undertake for God.

STRUCK & SCATTERED

The Mount of Olives (26:30) was a sizeable wooded ridge, a place where Jesus might hope to find some peace. Gethsemane (v. 36) means 'oil-press'. John (18:1–2) tells us it was a garden—perhaps a small olive grove—and that Jesus and the disciples often met there. According to ancient tradition it is on the lower slopes of the Mount, not far from the city wall.

Shepherd and flock

The eleven disciples have searched their own thoughts, for fear they might betray Jesus (26:22). They will not betray; but they will come under strain they cannot bear (v. 31). The arrest of Jesus will scatter them to the winds, like sheep without care or leadership, spread aimlessly across the hills.

Jesus had wanted to give the people of Israel a shepherd's care (9:36). He was able to gather a 'little flock' (Luke 12:32) around himself. Now he will be struck down, so that even the little flock will disintegrate for a while. Then afterwards he will be raised up. The scattered flock will be gathered again. Their leader will call them, and go ahead of them, as a shepherd walks in front of the sheep. In resurrection he will meet them in Galilee (28:16), to lead his people into new places under his ever-watchful care.

Cock-sure

As so often before (see comment on 14:28–31, p. 129), Peter is the first disciple to speak (v. 33). Not for the first time, his comments are wishful rather than wise. He wants to support Jesus all the way, but he completely underestimates both the severity of the coming trials and his own frailty and inexperience. He is a man out of place, a sailor in the city, an eager follower who cannot understand that the master has to take this journey on his own.

Jesus' words seem harsh (v. 34). The reader will take them seriously, but Peter cannot. He refuses to believe Jesus. 'Peter, crowing like a proud cock, rebuts Jesus' (Davies and Allison). He is impulsive and indignant, and the other disciples follow his lead. We shall start to see in Gethsemane how much stamina they really have (26:40–45).

As the little procession moves on to the hillside, Jesus' words 'this night' (vv. 31, 34) suggest an atmosphere more sinister than mere physical darkness. The shadows are dense and disturbing. There is evil abroad.

Shepherd and king

A couple of Old Testament episodes echo in these verses, one very clear, the other so faint that we might be imagining it.

• The faint echo is from 2 Samuel 15. David faces a rebellion by his son Absalom, and flees Jerusalem for a period. He makes his way over the Mount of Olives. Like Jesus in Gethsemane, he grieves bitterly, but lays himself open to the will of God (15:25–26, 30). Like Jesus, he has a turncoat supporter who ends up hanging himself (15:12; 17:23). So Jesus too is a king under attack, a new David harried and hunted by Israel. A major difference is that David's loyal friends stuck with him (15:21; 18:1), and helped to get him out of trouble. Jesus friends, despite all their confident claims, could not.

• The second and stronger resonance is in Matthew 26:31: 'I will strike the shepherd, and the sheep will be scattered.' This quote comes from Zechariah 13:7. A number of texts from this prophet figure in Matthew's Passion chapters—about a peaceful king, a stricken shepherd, thirty silver coins, and the Mount of Olives as a place of crisis and judgment.

There are many links to the Old Testament in all four Gospels, and Matthew surpasses the other three in the way that he emphasizes these links. I am sure the fertile mind at the root of it all is Jesus himself. He knew the Jewish scriptures, and understood his own work in relation to them. Son of Man, Servant, Shepherd—these were his links and his ideas. The early Christians, Matthew among them, rejoiced to follow the lead Jesus had given and to tell his story against an Old Testament background.

FOR REFLECTION AND PRAYER

Thank God for the unfolding of his purposes through the centuries, for the complex tapestry he weaves, yet with one design—love— and with one focus—Jesus Christ. 'Let us keep our eyes fixed on Jesus, the author and finisher of our faith' (Hebrews 12:2).

GARDEN *of* TEARS

For Jesus, Gethsemane was a garden of stillness, and of terrible turbulence. The night was quiet, but his spirit was tense and perturbed. His resolve and his relationship with the Father were tested to the limit. Yet he rose from his prayers a man deliberate and determined not simply to submit to fate, but to carry through his Father's will and work. He had been tried and had not drawn back.

With three disciples

Once again Jesus takes Peter, James and John, the same friends who witnessed the transfiguration (17:1–9). This experience too is about sonship, and the cross, and God's will. At the transfiguration in the light of the mountain-top the disciples saw Jesus, as he went towards the cross, as Son of God. Here in the darkness of the garden it is Jesus who understands, with fresh clarity and immediacy, that sonship and crucifixion will belong together.

If it be possible

Jesus has seen the Passion coming from far away. But as he looks the experience in the face, he is sharply aware of the awful cost involved. The 'cup' is his suffering (see comment on 20:20–23, pp. 166–167). Jesus expects this, but he cannot embrace it. He would rather God's will did not lead him this way, would rather he could express and exercise his role as Son without the cross.

Gethsemane is not cowardice, nor even natural strain showing in a tired and committed personality. Gethsemane is such a very intense experience because something more than physical suffering is involved. The suffering will be spiritual too. Up to now, Jesus' Sonship has been both a task for God and a tie, a bond, to God. Now, in finishing the task, he will break the tie. He has taken the role of Servant, the bearer of the sins of others; that is where the cost lies. To be a sin-bearer will mean separation and alienation from God, and dreadful darkness (27:46).

Jesus returns in prayer to words and ideas he has often used: 'Father' (v. 39), 'thy will be done' (v. 39), 'pray not to succumb to temptation' (v. 41). His own Lord's Prayer has within it words and concerns that shape his approach to God, even out of deep distress. A well-formed prayer habit is the resource he brings to this crisis. He is speaking to the God he knows.

Man alone

Gethsemane is a pivot in the gospel story. This is the moment when action becomes passion. Here Jesus becomes isolated from his friends, a man entirely on his own. He goes to the garden 'with them' (v. 36), but they cannot stay awake 'with him' (vv. 38, 40). They drift away, first into sleep (v. 40), then into the night (v. 56), and he passes into the hands of his enemies.

Up to this point, Jesus has been in control of the group, giving the lead, expressing his own will. From now on he is subjected to a very different will, by men who hate and hurt him. His transition point is the will of God (vv. 39, 42), which leads him from power into passion, from initiative into humiliation, from control to the cross. Jesus goes forward into that will—of his Father and of his enemies— willingly, knowingly and obediently (vv. 45–46).

Watch and pray

In Jesus' last great sermon, he taught that the Church should be a people alert, spiritually 'on watch', ready to meet the crisis of judgment (24:42–44). But here Jesus himself keeps watch alone. Gethsemane, and indeed the whole Passion story, is a kind of compression of many of the troubles and persecutions in Matthew 24. Jesus keeps watch, he is handed over to trial, others fall away around him, and yet he stays faithful to the end. The path that the Church must take, and the pressures they must bear, he takes and bears first. He goes through crisis alone, that his people may be able to go through it after him and with him.

FOR REFLECTION AND PRAYER

Gethsemane was not a public event. There are depths of Jesus' experience we cannot probe. But Gethsemane tells us that there is no uncharted territory. In our costly decisions; in our bitterest loneliness; in our wrestling with God; if friends should fail us— in all of this, Jesus has been there, and he understands, and we do not need to go through it alone.

Swords & *a* Kiss

The one I shall kiss

The armed contingent comes from 'the chief priests and elders of the people' (v. 47), the group we have already seen acting against Jesus (26:3–5, 14–16; see comment on 21:23, p. 176). These were the men who held power in Jerusalem. The Pharisees, who had given Jesus a good deal of trouble in Galilee, scarcely appear in these chapters.

The arresting party intend to capture Jesus on his own. They have no interest in rounding up the disciples. Jesus was not a typical rebel or guerrilla. His strength lay in his knowledge of God, not in an armed human following.

So finally Jesus is 'handed over' (26:45), as he said he would be (17:22; 20:18; 26:2). Judas is called 'the one who hands over' (26:46, 48)—sometimes translated 'traitor' or 'betrayer'—but he is also the man who fulfils what Jesus prophesied. He picks Jesus out of the group with a kiss. Again he calls him 'Rabbi', which is not a disciple's greeting (v. 49; see comments on 26:25, p. 215). Jesus acknowledges Judas as 'friend', but that need not be a very intimate term, as its earlier use in Matthew shows (20:13; 22:12). The kiss cannot really conceal the barrier of distrust between the two men.

Violence breeds

John's Gospel identifies Peter as the swordsman among the disciples. He was the disciple who had been keenest to support and stick by Jesus (26:33, 35), and he is the first to fight back when Jesus is arrested. His hasty blow must have come very near to killing the other man (v. 51). But Jesus will have none of it.

'Tit for tat' is often the way human life works. People who use violence generally reap violence in return. Peter is just following the usual pattern. But Jesus has already taught his friends to take a different path, to break the spiral of violence, to reply to anger with peace (5:38–42). Because violence breeds, it also breaks those who use it (v. 52), and Jesus does not want this sort of support.

Even in the grip of his enemies, Jesus commands the situation. He retains his poise, his penetrating facility with words, his ability to think clearly under challenge, his trust in God. He is committed to the path laid out for him in scripture (v. 54), to live out the roles of the Suffering Servant (26:28) and Stricken Shepherd (26:31). He does not want or need powerful defence, either from earth or heaven (v. 53).

Like a band of robbers

Jesus called the Temple 'a den of robbers' (21:13). Now the temple police come armed, as if Jesus is the bandit (v. 55). 'Could you not have arrested me in the Temple?' he asks. He was an easy enough target, surely. Of course they did not act against Jesus there, because of his popularity. A dark hillside is a much better and more discreet opportunity. But his challenge strikes home. Banditry is their role, and it seems to be their rule of operation.

Running out

The disciples show up badly, as Jesus said they would (26:31). For a while they were able to obey and follow (26:19, 30), but eventually they can only sleep and scatter (26:45, 56). Two of them stand out from the group.

* Judas has taken his own deliberate and fateful line of action, a course that will finally destroy him (26:14, 25, 47; 27:3–6).
* Then there is Peter, constantly overreaching himself (26:33, 35, 51, 58), until he breaks down in tears (26:75).

Christians often stumble. We mistake and misjudge many situations. We are often fearful, like the ten men who melted into the dark. We are sometimes foolhardy, like Peter. But we should pray to be kept from the deep and sustained falsehood of a Judas. The time may come when, for weakness or lack of wisdom, we cannot act for Christ. But let us at least avoid—at almost any cost—acting against him.

FOR REFLECTION AND PRAYER

'There are some pressures and pains to which the proper Christian response cannot be either fight or flight: either would amount to abandoning our discipleship.' (Alexander Sand)

Lord Jesus Christ, please give me the courage and patience to be steadfast and calm when I ought to be. Share with me your inner peace and strength, when I need it most. Amen.

The JEWISH TRIAL

Matthew's Gospel has two trial scenes, this one before the Jewish Sanhedrin and the second before the Roman governor Pontius Pilate. The Sanhedrin was the chief ruling body of the Jewish people, and had very wide legal powers. Only the Romans, however, could carry out the death penalty.

The two authorities had different concerns. What counted with the Roman governor was peace and order. The Sanhedrin was different: it was a religious court as well as a political body. So although the two trials face the same issue—Jesus' claim to be the Jewish Messiah —they deal with it in different ways. For the Romans, a man calling himself king is a potential threat to peace. With the Jews, the main issue turns out to be blasphemy.

It is odd to have a trial at night. This hearing may have been an initial investigation, to prepare a case against Jesus. Then a more formal sitting of the Sanhedrin followed the next morning (27:1–2).

Two good men and true?

A capital charge required at least two witnesses (Deuteronomy 17:6). The impression is that the court cast about for adequate testimony, and paid more regard to haste than truth. The stress on falsehood (v. 60) emphasizes that Jesus is innocent and does not deserve to die.

Eventually two witnesses report that Jesus declared himself able to demolish and rebuild the Temple (v. 61). Jesus never says exactly this in the Gospels. Matthew 24:2 is a distant approximation. John 2:21 is much closer, though with the aside that 'he was speaking of the temple of his body'. But his words and deeds have evidently been interpreted by the witnesses to produce a very serious charge.

Jesus' restraint may simply be shrewd (v. 63). The testimony is off-target, but if he tries to explain or clarify, that will only make the situation worse. Yet his silence hints, for the sharp-eyed reader, that he is fulfilling the Servant's role (Isaiah 53:7)—a suggestion that will become much stronger later.

Uttering the unthinkable

With the temple charge not settled one way or the other, the trial takes another tack. The high priest challenges Jesus (v. 63): his question almost exactly matches Peter's earlier confession of faith (16:16). Jesus' first cryptic reply (v. 64) corresponds to the English expression, 'You said it!' But he continues with words and images that are far from cryptic and that bring together two Old Testament texts.

- Psalm 110:1 pictures Messiah sitting at God's right hand.

- Daniel 7:9–14 shows the Son of Man coming with clouds.

So Jesus does not just accept the title 'Messiah'. He associates himself with the glory, majesty and power of God. Though being judged, he speaks as Judge. Questioned under authority, he asserts higher authority. Facing his nation's leaders, he claims to be their true leader.

Blasphemy and blows

Blasphemy had a pretty broad scope—anything that expressed contempt for the sacred. Jesus' words come far outside acceptable limits. The court is outraged. They hear what he says as a gross affront—to decency, to reverence and to God. The high priest tears his robes in disgust (v. 65). There may be a touch of irony here: high-priestly robes were not supposed to be torn (Leviticus 21:10). In rejecting the Messiah, the high priest denies his own role.

The court moves quickly to decision, and the final scene is ugly and cruel. Jesus is blindfolded (Luke 22:64): that is why they ask who has hit him (26:68). Again he fulfils the prophecy of the Suffering Servant, who was spat upon, insulted and beaten (Isaiah 50:6). More poignantly, Jesus acts out his own teaching about not resisting evil and aggression (5:38–42). Even here, in the face of scorn, he remains Israel's true teacher, in whom God's way is truly known.

FOR REFLECTION AND PRAYER

Jesus has been caught and cornered, physically and legally. There will be no way out, only a painful way through. Yet we may read this part of the Gospel with thanksgiving that the Lord came through this for us. And as part of our response, we may act to oppose injustice wherever we can.

NO FRIEND *of* MINE

Peter's denial is one of the best-known stories in the Gospels. He is no worse than the other ten disciples, who fled. But Peter's head-strong personality means that his failures are generally more dramatic and conspicuous than other people's. God does not love Peter any less for that. God can do business with honest failure.

Waiting to see

Peter follows the arresting party through the dark lanes and streets. He manages to get access to the outer yard of the high priest's house, where the hearing is being held. Now he waits to see how things will turn out (26:58). It is the best support he can give Jesus, but he must be tired, fearful and apprehensive. He sits among strangers, and tries to look as if he belongs there.

You were with him

Three times over, Peter is challenged, and three times he denies that he knows Jesus. The incidents escalate from one to the next. Each is more public and open than the one before. The stakes seem to rise, and so too does the intensity of Peter's denial. His mood gets more and more desperate, his words become less and less controlled, as the night wears on and one awkward conversation follows another.

- The first accusation is made by one person, directly to Peter himself. His answer is simple and straightforward (vv. 69–70).

- The second challenge comes from one person again, but her question draws a group into the conversation. Peter replies 'with an oath' (vv. 71–72).

- The third time a number of people confront Peter together. His accent gives him away. He 'starts cursing and swearing', and blusters his way through another refusal (vv. 73–74).

Meanwhile the reader has been counting, and recalling what Jesus said earlier (26:34).

Cock-crow and tears

Straight away after the third denial, the cock crows. It is Luke (22:61) who tells us that Jesus turned round and looked at Peter. Matthew simply mentions how Peter remembered that Jesus had said this would happen. Suddenly Peter cannot contain himself. It is all too much for him—the pace of events, dark sayings about death, Judas' deceit, Jesus' arrest, his own tiredness, and now this wretched failure. The sheer tragedy and helplessness of the situation engulf him, and he runs out to hide, alone with his sorrow and shame.

The strange purposes of grace

It is bitter indeed that just when the high priest challenged Jesus (26:64) in almost the very words with which Peter had once confessed his faith, Peter should deny he ever knew Jesus.

There is a subtle mockery in the words, 'You were with Jesus' (vv. 69, 71). For Peter had tried to stay awake with Jesus and there too he had drifted away from his best intentions. 'Could you not stay awake with me?' (26:38, 40). He could not.

It is ironic that while Jesus is taunted and goaded to prophesy (26:68), one of his prophecies is fulfilled through Peter's threefold denial.

Finally, it is strange and marvellous of God that he should choose a man who gets into such a miserable mess to be the Church's first leader, first evangelist, pioneer missionary to the Gentiles, and one of the earliest martyrs for the gospel. Our Church, yours and mine, is built on the rock of faith, not on the rock of perfect holiness and virtue. That could be God's way of reminding us not to think too highly of ourselves. It could also be God's assurance that however many disasters and tangles we manage to make, there is still a place for us in his will and work.

FOR REFLECTION AND PRAYER

In the times when tiredness and tension prove too much for you, when tears take over, when you aim high and sink low, remember Peter. God used him, loved him and stood by him.

BITTER END

There are two short paragraphs in this section. The first is a phase in the trial of Jesus, a process which is now starting to move rapidly towards the cross. But before we follow the legal process to the next stage, Matthew interrupts the sequence to tell of the death of Judas.

Case conference

This short account of a meeting of the Sanhedrin (vv. 1–2) is really just a link in the chain. We have already heard of the hearing they have given Jesus, of his claim to be the Messiah, and of the reaction he provoked. The outcome of this morning meeting simply confirms the view that he ought to die. Now they will need to put their case to Pilate, and secure his co-operation.

Pilate was 'Prefect of Judea' from AD26 to 36, appointed by Rome and answerable there. History has given us a good deal of information about him apart from what is in the Gospels. The overall impression is of an awkward and unreasonable man. He was a tough governor, inclined to use a firm hand, but without a sure touch or good judgment.

So Jesus is 'handed over', passed from hand to hand like a parcel: first by Judas to the high priests (26:15); then by the Sanhedrin to the Roman authorities (27:2), and finally by Pilate to the soldiers who crucify him (27:26). This handing over to the Gentiles fulfils what Jesus had said would happen (20:19). But before we go forward to the final stage, we step aside from the main line of the story.

Innocent blood

Once again we see Matthew's technique of putting light alongside shadow. Interrupting the trial of Jesus to show the remorse and death of Judas highlights Jesus as an innocent man. The relentless process of hearings and crucifixion is unjust and unfair. That same theme will return again in the coming verses (27:19, 25, 54).

Matthew's inclusion at this stage of the death of Judas enables him not to interrupt the story ahead. Jesus is the central character, and his cross and resurrection must command full attention. In fact Judas may not have died as soon as this.

The Bible records a handful of suicides—Samson, Saul, Ahithophel. In different ways these incidents speak for themselves. The death of Judas tells of bitter and unbearable remorse, of the terrible loneliness of a man who could not live with his own deed. Scripture makes no further comment about the morality involved. There is no word of judgment against Judas here, beyond what Jesus has already given (26:24).

Scripture does, however, affirm that life is a good and precious gift from God. The small number of extreme cases in the Bible—and all of them are extreme—have rightly led the Church to advise strongly and consistently against suicide. But there is more we may do than teach. Many people in our society live with grave remorse, and may for various reasons consider taking their own life. Some, of course, go through with it. Skilled pastoral care, patient sympathy and practical support may often be asked of us, from people who have to live with deep misery, and also from their relatives.

Tapestry of texts

The main burden of verses 9–10 is to link Judas' death to the Old Testament. This is the last of Matthew's famous fulfilment quotations. The purchase of the field is mentioned also in Acts 1:18–19, again with the name 'Blood Acre' (although the Acts account of Judas' death is rather different). The scripture texts come from Zechariah 11:12–13 (thirty pieces of silver), from Jeremiah 18 and 19 (a potter and a burial ground), and possibly from Jeremiah 32 (the purchase of a field). Matthew has plaited the texts together, seeing in each a foreshadowing of one aspect of this incident. Thus, he says to the reader, even this painful ending finds its place in the purpose of God.

FOR PRAYER

God of mercy, we pray:
For those who live with shame: may they know your forgiveness.
For those who live with sin: grant them amendment of life.
For those who live with sorrow: bring them your comfort.
For those who hate themselves: give them loving friends.
Through Jesus Christ our Lord. Amen.

THE ROMAN TRIAL

Pontius Pilate is involved all through this scene, and is responsible for the final outcome. At the very end it is 'the governor's soldiers' (v. 27) who take Jesus away. Yet Pilate seems strangely and unusually indecisive. Against this background of indecision, Matthew highlights the determination of the Jewish leaders.

First questions

Jesus' claim to be Messiah fell foul of the Jewish court as a religious blasphemy. Here the Jewish leaders present the same material to Pilate, but with a fresh twist. The Messiah is a royal figure. So Jesus claims to be 'king of the Jews', and that is politically dangerous. It marks him out as a revolutionary, a prince pretender.

Pilate asks Jesus if he is king of the Jews. Jesus replies briefly, but not directly (v. 11): 'You said it.' He is a king, though not the kind Pilate thinks. When Pilate presses him further, he stays silent, as he did during the Jewish trial. Pilate is amazed, and perhaps scornful. Jesus cannot have appeared a very threatening character.

This man or Barabbas

The custom of releasing a prisoner at feast-time is known in some ancient lands, although we have no other knowledge of this from Palestine. Barabbas was a rebel, a violent man (Luke 23:19), presumably awaiting crucifixion. Giving the crowd a choice strikes Pilate as a good way out of an awkward situation. He can save face without having to decide whether Jesus of Nazareth is guilty or not. And if the Jewish leaders have charged Jesus out of envy, then rejecting their request will be one more petty gain in the power-play of colonial administration (v. 18). Pursuing a compromise instead of taking a decision is often a risky strategy. It can rebound badly. None the less, Pilate finds this an attractive option. As we wait to hear which way the choice will fall, Pilate is called aside.

Warned in a dream

Only Matthew mentions Pilate's wife (v. 19). She is a counterpart to the soldiers at the cross (27:54)—a sympathetic Gentile. For Matthew, dreams can be God's postal service (as in 1:20—2:22). Romans too took them seriously. Pilate's handwashing (v. 24) suggests that he himself is unsettled by his wife's message, but her intervention is too late to affect the trial. The matter is in the hands of the crowd.

People's choice

For the first time in Matthew, the crowd turns against Jesus. It is difficult to tell how big this crowd was. They may not have been the same people who cheered Jesus into the city, for example. Matthew stresses that they were led into their choice, persuaded by the chief priests and elders. The shouting against Jesus gets louder, and Pilate eventually realizes that he has been pushed into a bad decision.

The end of the matter

Washing one's hands of something has become a casual proverb. But there was nothing casual about Pilate's mood that day. I suspect he was haunted by what his wife had said, confused by the strange calm of his prisoner, and rather ashamed of the mess he had made of the case. The hand-washing is a desperate but futile attempt to rid himself of guilt and responsibility.

Pilate's final reply to the crowd is, 'You see to it' (v. 24). 'It's your responsibility.' The high priests used exactly the same expression to Judas (27:4). As with Adam and Eve in Genesis 3, none of the main actors will accept the blame. So the people bear the burden (v. 25). Matthew highlights Jewish responsibility for the death of Jesus more than the other Gospels do. But the people's responsibility should be qualified in several ways: that the high priests led them; that Pilate let them; and that God still loves them. There is nothing in the crucifixion story to warrant anti-Jewish feeling today. (There is further comment on this at Matthew 23, p. 189.)

Finally Jesus is beaten. A Roman whip was made of knotted leather straps, sometimes with pieces of metal or bone driven through the leather. This is the start of the degradation of the cross. A beaten man would not take so long to die.

FOR REFLECTION

'Crucified under Pontius Pilate' means that the Son of God was subjected to the jealousy, folly and stubbornness of human power. Pray for people who suffer today through the abuse of power.

ROAD *to the* CROSS

The trial is over. Suddenly it is very certain what is coming next. Events have moved with frightening speed to this point. Now that the prisoner has been found guilty, the execution will follow without any delay. Jesus is weak and badly hurt from the beating he has been given, a soft target for the callous mockery of Pilate's soldiers.

A soldiers' joke

Jesus was taunted and spat upon after his Jewish trial (26:67–68). After the Roman trial the same sort of thing happens again. This seems to be a more elaborate mockery than the earlier episode; certainly Matthew describes it more fully.

Pilate normally lived at Caesarea on the coast, but at festival times he came to Jerusalem with a strong contingent of soldiers to contain any trouble among the crowds. The mockery takes place in his headquarters, with 'the whole cohort' (v. 27) taking part. A cohort was about 600 men, and would have been second-grade soldiers, Syrian auxiliaries rather than the élite legionaries. The men who were off duty gathered around for a bit of cynical sport.

The scene is a shallow copy of a king's coronation. A soldier's red cloak does duty for a royal robe, Jesus is crowned with a wreath of thorns, and a reed is put into his right hand as if it were a sceptre of kingly authority and power. The whole thing is a sarcastic humiliation. It mocks Jesus personally. Perhaps the soldiers were also mocking the Jewish nation: is this the best king they can produce—a broken, beaten, poor village carpenter? Of course the irony is really the other way round. These soldiers make sport of the man who will judge the whole world. They laugh at him now, but one day his authority will overshadow every human empire.

As he did before, Jesus remains silent. Yet these events fill out his earlier words (20:19). He goes to death as a prophet. He also dies as a king, ironically acclaimed with the same title given him at birth (2:2). Gentiles kneel to mock him, as the wise men once knelt in worship (2:11). He leaves Jerusalem as he came into it (21:9), to the sound of royal greetings. The cross will become a throne, and through his suffering the power of his love will be known.

Led out to die

The vertical stake of the cross would already have been in place, with a slot for the cross-bar to be dropped into. The condemned man had to carry his own cross-beam to the place of crucifixion. But Jesus was so weak from the beating that a passer-by was pressed into service (v. 32). Roman soldiers could press anyone to carry a load for a set distance (5:41). But there was never another load like this.

Simon came from Cyrene in north Africa, in what is now Libya. He may have been a Jew whose family had settled in Africa, but who was in Jerusalem for the festival. It appears (Mark 15:21) that his two sons were known to Mark's readers, and so Simon himself may have been a Christian too. It is intriguingly possible that he is 'Simeon called Black' (Acts 13:1), the first of many black African Christians.

Seeing and tasting death

Golgotha is Aramaic for 'skull'. The sinister name fits the atmosphere of the day, of cheapened life and stark death. Someone offers Jesus a drink of wine mixed with gall, a sour toxic stuff (v. 34). This may be yet another stage in the taunting and mockery, pretending to offer a drink, but giving only bitter acid. Or it could be a kindly gesture, an opportunity for Jesus to take poison and spare himself some of the lingering pain ahead. Jesus refuses the drink. Then they nail him to the cross.

PRAYER

Thanks be to thee, my Lord Jesus Christ,
for all the benefits thou hast won for me,
for all the pains and insults thou hast borne for me.
O most merciful Redeemer, Friend and Brother,
may I know thee more clearly,
love thee more dearly,
and follow thee more nearly,
day by day. Amen.

St Richard of Chichester

AROUND *the* CROSS

The four Gospels describe the scene at the cross in varied ways. Matthew's and Mark's accounts are closely similar, Luke is rather different and John is different again. Some well-known features of the story come in only one of the four Gospels. For example, only Luke (23:39–43) mentions the penitent thief. Only John (19:20–22) tells us that the inscription on the cross was in three languages, and that the Jewish leaders tried to get Pilate to change its wording.

As we think about the various differences, we may want to keep three points in mind.

- The four Gospels agree on the main aspects of the story: Jewish trial, Roman trial, crucifixion, death, burial and resurrection. They match in many smaller details too: for example, the group of women followers looking on, the soldiers dicing for Jesus' clothing, Joseph burying the body.

- The Gospel writers had to be selective. We should expect some variation between one Gospel and another.

- We should aim to read each Gospel on its own terms, and hear its distinctive tones and themes. They all help us to experience the atmosphere of the crucifixion, but in different ways. Matthew's main emphasis in this section is the sheer desolation and loneliness of the cross. Jesus is a man utterly on his own.

When they had crucified him

Crucifixion involved driving nails through the victim's wrists into a wooden beam. Then the beam was attached to the vertical stake of the cross, and the victim's feet were secured, probably again by nailing. Matthew says little about the physical aspects—everyone in the ancient world knew that crucifixion was horribly and excruciatingly painful.

The victim would be stripped naked, or nearly so. Any articles of clothing he had would fall to the soldiers who executed him. So the men raffled Jesus' garments, while they waited for his death (vv.

35–36). It was a day's work—normal, nasty, necessary. The title above Jesus' head labelled him a rebel, and this was how rebels died.

The foolishness of God

Either side of Jesus are 'bandits', men who have lived on the edge of society (v. 38). Whether they were driven by hunger and need, or were pursuing rebel aspirations, or belonged to an armed gang of thieves, we cannot tell. Whatever they have been and done has caught up with them. Jesus dies among criminals, keeping the company of 'sinners' right to the end (9:10–13).

In these hours on the cross, Jesus becomes a target for taunts and jibes from all sides. People can stare at him and scorn him as they choose. The Roman soldiers had their jest with him earlier. Now he is mocked by fellow Jews. Everyone seems to be involved: clerics and criminals—the highest and lowest in the land—and ordinary passers-by too. They scoff at his words (v. 40), his deeds (v. 42), his faith in God (v. 43). They look on him, they think of him, as a complete fool—humiliated, hanging, helpless, hopeless. Only later will the world discover that 'God's foolishness is wiser than human wisdom, and God's weakness is stronger than human strength' (1 Corinthians 1:25).

As it is written

Even in dying, Jesus fulfils scripture. There are three echoes of Psalm 22: passers-by shake their heads (22:7); 'If he trusts God, let God rescue him' (22:8); men cast lots for his clothing (22:18). This psalm was a prayer, a desperate prayer by a faithful believer, out of the depths of hurt and humiliation. Matthew shows the psalm coming to life again through the suffering of Jesus. The life and death of Jesus are a magnet, drawing out the meaning of ancient scripture. And the Old Testament is like a bank of floodlights, illuminating Jesus, showing his life in the light of God's long purpose.

FOR REFLECTION AND PRAYER

We may not know, we cannot tell,
what pains he had to bear,
but we believe it was for us
he hung and suffered there.

C.F. Alexander (1818–95)

108 MATTHEW 27:45–54

The SHAKING of the FOUNDATIONS

Matthew says little about how Jesus himself bore the experience of crucifixion. This Gospel is more concerned to stress what the cross achieved. The death of Jesus has opened up a new era in history, a fresh age of hope.

Darkness at noon

Dark covers the land 'from the sixth hour to the ninth'—from roughly noon until 3 o'clock. Matthew does not mention any natural explanation. That is not his concern. The accent in these verses is on the power and strangeness of the signs. Surely God is at work. Yet the earth is not bright with greeting: it is wrapped in gloom.

There is no light in the sky. There seems also to be a thick veil of darkness over Jesus' own spirit, blocking any awareness of his Father's presence. His loneliness now becomes a total separation, from human support and from heaven too. Jesus feels utterly forsaken. Only here does he say 'My God' (v. 46). Everywhere else in the Gospel, he says 'Father'. This is the separation that he has dreaded, the path he shrank from in Gethsemane (26:36–46)—the time when his faith and his Father seem utterly remote. This is the cost of bearing human sin—a fracture in the bond that links Father and Son, a cross in the very heart of God.

The words Jesus calls out come from the first line of Psalm 22. This psalm was echoed several times in earlier verses (27:35–44). It speaks of miserable loneliness, of a helpless and empty sense of forsakenness. But it also speaks in faith, that when God seems far away, even then only God can really help. Jesus' faith on the cross is not the comfortable faith of knowing that God is near and all is well. It is the faithfulness that hangs on to God even when it has no sense at all that God is still there to hang on to.

Last breath

The Aramaic for 'my God' is *Eli*. Some bystanders mishear or misunderstand and think that Jesus is calling for Elijah (v. 47). Elijah did not die, he was taken up into heaven (2 Kings 2), and many Jews expected him to return as an advance sign of the coming of God. But

Jesus looked on John the Baptist as God's latter-day Elijah (see comments on 17:1–13, pp. 144–146). He was not calling on Elijah from the cross, and Elijah did not come to rescue him.

The sponge soaked in vinegary wine (v. 48) appears to be a small act of kindness, to ease the dreadful thirst of crucifixion. But then the time for kindness is over. Jesus lifts his voice in one last great cry, and 'gives up the ghost'. His breath is gone. His work is done.

Judgment and resurrection

The Jerusalem Temple had two great curtains. One hung across the entrance to the main central building, the other covered the innermost shrine, the Holy of Holies. The tearing of either (v. 51) would be a mark of judgment, another warning of the destruction that Jesus prophesied. If the innermost curtain were the one torn—as Hebrews 10:19 suggests—this would also signal that God's presence is no longer shut away. Because Jesus has died, access to God is free and open.

When Jesus was born, a new light in the sky welcomed his coming. When he dies, creation groans, as if with the pain of childbirth, breaking open into new life. Rocks split. Graves open—not by any means unusual during an earth tremor. Only Matthew mentions the rising of the 'dead saints', and his account leaps forward here to speak of the aftermath of the resurrection. Because Christ is raised, the faithful dead shall rise too. Matthew's story expresses with graphic clarity the hope to which New Testament letters look forward (1 Corinthians 15:20–21; 1 Thessalonians 4:14). God has not forsaken Jesus: out of death comes new life.

God squad

As at the start of the Gospel (2:2), Gentiles recognize Jesus (v. 54). These soldiers do not have a carefully formed faith. They simply sense that God is present in this man. For them, even the darkness has brought a kind of light.

FOR REFLECTION

We only understand the cross if we feel both the darkness and the light, the absence of God from Jesus, and the presence of God in Jesus. Where was God on Golgotha? Nailed to a tree.

SHARING OUR DEATH

The burial completes Matthew's long account of Jesus' crucifixion. It seals and certifies death. Jesus has shared our human dying. But his story will not end there: the burial and the guarding of the tomb set out the stage for the next act—for resurrection.

Faithful women

This is almost the first time Matthew has mentioned women among the group that followed Jesus. Mary came from Magdala, a lakeside town in Galilee. Only in Luke (8:2) do we hear about Jesus healing her 'of seven demons'. There was another Mary, who was 'mother of James and Joseph'. There was also the mother of James and John Zebedee, who had hoped for great things from Jesus (20:20–21). The male disciples have scattered, but these women have found the courage and commitment to wait at the cross. The two Marys are last to leave the tomb (v. 61), and first to come back to it (28:1). They are the last witnesses of Jesus' burial and the first of his resurrection. At this key moment in history, they are the nucleus of the Church, the thin thread of its continuing faithfulness to Jesus.

Rich man's grave

A long day is drawing to an end, from the trial 'in the morning' (27:1), to this burial as the sun sinks towards evening. Jews believed that even a condemned man deserved a decent burial (Deuteronomy 21:22–23), but it was not common for a crucified criminal to be laid in a private grave.

Joseph was a rich man, and a follower of Jesus' teaching. Mark and Luke mention that he was a member of the Jewish ruling council, an exception to the steady opposition the nation's leaders had shown Jesus. John (19:38) says that Joseph had kept his discipleship secret until now, but this burial would surely make his loyalty obvious. Still, this was the last service he could offer Jesus and, cost what it might, it was a challenge he had to meet.

The tomb was fresh, never previously used (v. 60). It was a cave in a rock face, and had been cut ready for Joseph's own death. A heavy stone, the shape of a coin or a cheese, would be rolled across the front. The last act of worship—as it seemed at the time—was over.

As secure as possible

The alliance of chief priests (mostly Sadducees) and Pharisees is unusual. Their acting on the sabbath is stranger still. But these were tense times. Jesus had caused enough trouble already. It would be important to prevent even a whispered rumour of resurrection. The disciples might start some odd stories if they could spirit Jesus' body away. With that concern in mind, the Jewish leaders ask Pilate to post a guard. Only Matthew mentions this incident, and he takes it up again in the light of Easter Day (28:11–15). As before, he emphasizes the Jewish leaders' deliberate and determined opposition to Jesus.

Yet rarely can a security operation that seemed so easy have gone so badly wrong. We start to sense trouble ahead when Pilate says, 'Make it as secure as you can' (v. 65). But how secure can you be with the Son of God? Despite the stone, the seal and the soldiers, the only certainty is that God will have the last word.

Holy ground

The Church of the Holy Sepulchre in Jerusalem is built above the tomb where Christians believe Jesus was buried. This site has a good historical claim to be the right place. The evidence goes back a very long way. But Jesus' death hallows more than just one spot. He goes before us in human death. He stays beside us in our dying, and waits to meet us on the other side. The dust of our humanity and the earth to which it returns have been shared by Jesus, so that we may share his risen life.

PRAYER

O God, creator of heaven and earth,
as the crucified body of your dear Son
was laid in the tomb
and rested on this holy sabbath,
so may we await with him
the coming of the third day
and rise with him to newness of life;
through the same Jesus Christ our Lord. Amen.

Church of Scotland: Common Order, Collect for Saturday in Holy Week

110 MATTHEW 28:1–7

The PLACE WHERE HE LAY

None of the Gospels describes the resurrection itself. No one saw it happen. The first sign was an empty tomb, an open grave.

Light dawning

It is early on the Sunday morning. Jesus was crucified on Friday. Saturday was the sabbath, the Jewish rest-day, and now the sabbath is over there is opportunity for travel and activity. The faithful women who watched where Jesus was buried come back to visit the tomb. Mark (16:1–3) says they brought spices to anoint the body, and they wondered how they would shift the great stone. But Matthew concentrates on the strangeness of what meets them. He is keen to accentuate (more than Mark) the supernatural aura of this event.

The earthquake, the angel, the paralysis that grips the guards—all this is the stuff of theophany, of God's appearing on earth. We overhear echoes of the God of Sinai (Exodus 19:18) and of ancient visions (Daniel 10:8–9). The angel's radiant white clothing is like the splendour of Jesus' Transfiguration (17:1–8). This place is rich with symbols of the glory of God. Here is the dawn, not just of a new day, but of a new era and a new creation.

Fearing and fearing not

When God comes near, when earth is changed by his presence, people get frightened. When things happen beyond normal human experience and control, fear quickly asserts its presence. Sometimes fear is a proper response. But so often in the Bible we hear the words 'Fear not'. At Jesus' birth, on a stormy sea, on a mountain-top, comes the simple command, 'Do not be afraid' (1:20; 14:27; 17:7). The mystery of God is laden with grace and rich with promise.

There is irony in the guards' fearful collapse (v. 4). They had been posted to keep the dead body securely in the tomb, and now they are like dead men themselves. Armed secular power cannot contain and limit the power of Jesus Christ—as the witness of persecuted Christians across the ages has shown.

But the women are told, 'Do not be afraid.' They came seeking Jesus 'who was crucified' (v. 5). Their eyes are still blinkered by death.

It is too soon to grasp that he could be alive. But 'he has been raised, as he said' (v. 6). The tomb he occupied is empty. And they are ordered to bear witness to what they have seen, to be 'apostles to the apostles' (v. 7).

The women must go and tell the male disciples what they have heard and seen. A woman's testimony counted for comparatively little in Palestine. But these were the witnesses God used to let the Church hear the gospel. Jesus promised to meet his friends in Galilee (26:32), to go ahead of them there like a shepherd leading his flock. He is going to keep that promise. They will see him in Galilee, in the place where he first called them and spoke of God's kingdom. In Galilee, where he healed and taught, he will commission his friends to start again, to share his mission and to reach the world.

Celebration

Christians celebrate Easter—not just once a year, but every week. We worship on a Sunday because this is the day of resurrection, a weekly reminder that we live in a new era. The great brooding powers of death and decay have been disturbed. The normal physical order has been interrupted by the God of life. Christians rejoice in hope, because Christ is risen. We praise him for his cross, and we know him as risen Lord. The empty tomb is full with possibility and power. We live, even now, in the light of Easter morning.

FOR REFLECTION AND PRAYER

'If Christ has not been raised, our faith is futile, and we are the most pitiable people in the world. But the truth is that Christ has been raised. Thanks be to God, who gives us the victory through our Lord Jesus Christ.'

From 1 Corinthians 15:17–20, 57

APPEARANCE & DISAPPEARANCE

Two groups of people leave the graveyard, each with a story to pass on. There is quite a contrast between them. The women race to tell Jesus' friends about what they have seen and heard (v. 8). Their feet are light and their hearts are leaping with joy, whereas the soldiers go with heavy and dragging steps, shame-faced, embarrassed and worried, to report the failure of their mission.

Living Lord

The empty tomb was an important sign of mysterious and mighty powers at work. The angel's words sent the women running off, 'with fear and great joy'. But their meeting with Jesus is the vital moment of this whole experience. They have seen the place where he was (28:6). They have heard the promise of where he will be (28:7). Now suddenly he is there, with them, so solid that he can be touched and held. Fear and joy are overtaken by love, awe, worship and praise.

Once again the beginning and end of the Gospel meet. The combination of great joy leading into worship is exactly what was said about the wise men (2:10–11). The wise men worshipped Jesus at the start of his earthly life. These women are the first to worship him in his risen power.

Jesus' message underlines what the angel has said. The women should not fear, but should go and tell the eleven disciples to make their way to Galilee, to meet Jesus there. There is one important word that makes quite a difference. Jesus speaks of 'my brothers'. Though these male disciples have scattered and fled, he still counts them among his spiritual family, as people he relies on to do his will (12:46–50). He still trusts them, includes them and values them.

So the women go as witnesses. Their story, their sight of Jesus, will show the men the way forward so that they can see him too. As so often in the Gospels, one follower's testimony leads someone else to Jesus and to faith. People help one another towards their own encounter with the Lord. Christians who speak naturally and positively about what Christ means in their lives can still inspire others to find out too.

Missing person

The guards' short journey and report is less positive. They 'tell every-thing that has happened' (v. 11), but in truth they do not know half of it. They get a substantial bonus payment for failing in their task. They were sent to prevent grave robbery, but the eventual tale is that the grave was robbed. And if anyone asks why they are so sure about their story, they can say they were asleep. All very dubious—but perhaps the best that could be thought of in the circumstances.

Sadly, Matthew tells his readers, that is the story many Jews have heard and believed, right up to the time the Gospel was written (v. 15). The people's leaders have opposed Jesus in life and death; now they discredit his resurrection. But Israel as a whole nation is not completely set against him. There is a group of believing women, eleven 'brothers', and a rich man who buried the body. These are just the tip of the iceberg, a small selection of the followers Jesus already has, and the first visible instalment of a large Jewish church which will grow through the decades ahead.

Risen indeed

This episode with the guards is the first indication that the Christian Church's faith in resurrection will be hard for the world to believe. Right down to our own day, there have been many thoughtful en-quirers who have tested the evidence and asked seriously whether any other explanation fits the facts. So far as I can see, nothing comes near.

Suppose, for example, the disciples had stolen the body. That would mean that for years they preached and spread the faith, being persecuted and some martyred, and none of them ever let on—all for something they knew was a hoax. That really does not make sense.

Easter was incomparable. There is no natural and everyday explan-ation that fits. Something unique is here, an extraordinary event, the power of God breaking through human death. He is not here. He is risen.

FOR REFLECTION

The Church did not make Easter. Easter made the Church. So how is Easter—the message and presence of the risen Christ—shaping, influencing and inspiring your church and your Christian life?

112 MATTHEW 28:16–20

WITH YOU FOR EVER

This 'Great Commission' is one of the most famous passages in the Bible. Christians through two thousand years have read these verses as the Church's marching orders, our mandate for mission, a task that is always ahead of us.

Whole Gospel

The word 'all' comes up four times in just a couple of verses. Jesus has all authority. He sends his followers to all nations, to pass on all that he has taught. And he will be with them through all time.

There is no time or place outside Jesus' reach or care. There is no limit to his involvement in his people's lives. The details of Christian obedience may alter as times change, but the serious call to practical discipleship goes on. Jesus still wants committed people. There are four words in these verses that describe what his followers do.

- **Learn (v. 16)**: The word disciple means 'learner', someone who listens, watches and copies Jesus.

- **Worship (v. 17)**: A church that honours Jesus, that makes his life, death and resurrection the regular focus of our praise, will always be likely to grow in faith and love.

- **Doubt (v. 17)**: 'They (or some of them) doubted'. This is the word used when Peter tried to walk on water, and fell in (14:31). Not all Christians are successful and confident. Most of us are hesitant and cautious. Jesus often invites us to step beyond our inhibitions. But he never discards us because of our fears or failures.

- **Keep (v. 20)**: This is the other side of learning. Followers take Jesus' teaching seriously, and try to keep his commands.

End of the story

These few verses weave together threads that have been clear and strong throughout Matthew. Each of the five great sermons in the Gospel is reflected in this final commission.

- Matthew 5—7. The Sermon on the Mount showed Jesus as the great Teacher. His teaching is practical, involving lifestyle, relationships, wealth, words. Making disciples (28:19) means passing on the practice of the faith, helping people to act out what Jesus has taught.

- Matthew 10 was the Mission Charge. Jesus sent his friends out to gather the Jewish people, like a scattered flock of sheep (9:36; 10:6). At the end of the Gospel, he is still the great Shepherd, going ahead of his friends to Galilee (26:31–32; 28:7). But this time the flock is greater. The Church is sent to reach the world.

- Matthew 13 is the parable chapter. This small company of Jesus' followers will be like seed, like yeast, changing the world with their faith.

- Matthew 18 teaches about Jesus' community, the Church. The sign of baptism (28:19) marks this community. It is the family sign, the badge of belonging, a call to be committed to Jesus and to one another.

- Matthew 24—25 looked forward to the end of the age. Until then Jesus will be with his friends (28:20), guiding and helping them as they do his work. He has authority as Son of Man, to be Lord and Judge over all the nations (28:18).

Story without end

So the Lord dies, and rises. His work runs on and reaches out. This is the end of Matthew's Gospel. It is also a new beginning, of a world-wide mission. It is the next chapter in a continuing story. For the Jesus who came as 'God with us' (1:23) will still be 'with you for ever' (28:20), in the spreading life of his Church.

At the start of the Gospel Jesus was called 'son of David, son of Abraham' (1:1), a new king and a child born to reach the nations. At the end he fulfils all that destiny. His royal authority touches the whole world (28:18–20). His story goes on, until now it includes you and me. Like his first followers, we are sent—to serve, to share, to spread and to show the love and life of Jesus Christ.

PRAYER

Lord Jesus Christ, Lord of every far horizon and of every faithful heart, take our small service and weave it into your grand purpose. For your honour and glory we pray. Amen.

NOTES

NOTES

NOTES

NOTES

NOTES

NOTES

OTHER BOOKS IN THIS SERIES

All prices are correct at time of going to press, are subject to the prevailing rate of VAT and may be subject to change without prior warning.

For more information, visit **www.brf.org.uk/pbc**

PBC ORDER FORM

Please ensure that you complete and send off both sides of this order form.

Please send me the following book(s): **Quantity** **Price** **Total**

3145	Genesis (G. West)		£8.99
0663	Exodus (H. Page Jr)		£8.99
1929	Leviticus and Numbers (M. Butterworth)		£7.99
3183	Deuteronomy (P. Johnston)		£8.99
0953	Joshua and Judges (S. Mathewson)		£7.99
2421	Ruth, Esther, Ecclesiastes, Song of Songs and Lamentations (R. Fyall)		£8.99
0700	Chronicles to Nehemiah (M. Tunnicliffe)		£7.99
0946	Job (K. Dell)		£7.99
0311	Psalms 1–72 (D. Coggan)		£8.99
0656	Psalms 73–150 (D. Coggan)		£7.99
0717	Proverbs (E. Mellor)		£7.99
1516	Isaiah (J. Bailey Wells)		£8.99
0878	Jeremiah (R. Mason)		£7.99
0403	Ezekiel (E. Lucas)		£7.99
3954	Daniel (D. Ingram)		£8.99
2452	Hosea to Micah (P. Gooder)		£8.99
1912	Matthew (J. Proctor)		£8.99
0465	Mark (D. France)		£8.99
0274	Luke (H. Wansbrough)		£8.99
8508	John, new edition (R. Burridge)		£8.99
2162	Acts (L. Alexander)		£8.99
0823	Romans (J. Dunn)		£8.99
1226	1 Corinthians (J. Murphy O'Connor)		£8.99
0731	2 Corinthians (A. Besançon Spencer)		£8.99
0120	Galatians and 1 & 2 Thessalonians (J.Fenton)		£7.99
0472	Ephesians to Colossians and Philemon (M. Maxwell)		£7.99
1196	Timothy, Titus and Hebrews (D. France)		£8.99
0922	James to Jude (F. Moloney)		£7.99
3633	Revelation (revised edition) (M. Maxwell)		£8.99

POSTAGE AND PACKING CHARGES				
order value	UK	Europe	Surface	Air Mail
£7.00 & under	£1.25	£3.00	£3.50	£5.50
£7.01–£30.00	£2.25	£5.50	£6.50	£10.00
Over £30.00	FREE	prices on request		

Total cost of books £ _____

Donation £ _____

Postage and packing £ _____

TOTAL £ _____

Please complete the payment details overleaf.

All prices are correct at time of going to press, are subject to the prevailing rate of VAT and may be subject to change without prior warning.

PAYMENT DETAILS

Please complete the payment details below and send with appropriate payment and completed order form to:

BRF, 15 The Chambers, Vineyard, Abingdon OX14 3FE

Name _____

Address _____

_____

_____ Postcode _____

Telephone _____

Email _____

Method of payment:

Total enclosed £ _____ (cheques should be made payable to 'BRF')

Please charge my ☐ Visa ☐ Mastercard ☐ Switch card with £ _____

Card number: ☐☐☐☐☐☐☐☐☐☐☐☐☐☐☐☐☐☐☐

Valid from ☐☐☐☐ Expires ☐☐☐☐ Security code* ☐☐☐

Issue no (Switch only) ☐☐☐☐
*Last 3 digits on the reverse of the card. Essential in order to process your order

`1234 567`
EXAMPLE

Signature _____
(*essential if paying by credit/Switch*)

☐ Please do not send me further information about BRF publications.

For more information, visit **www.brf.org.uk/pbc**

ALTERNATIVE WAYS TO ORDER

Christian bookshops: All good Christian bookshops stock BRF publications. For your nearest stockist, please contact BRF.

Telephone: The BRF office is open between 09.15 and 17.30. To place your order, phone 01865 319700; fax 01865 319701.

About
brf:

BRF is a registered charity and also a limited company, and has been in existence since 1922. Through all that we do—producing resources, providing training, working face-to-face with adults and children, and via the web—we work to resource individuals and church communities in their Christian discipleship through the Bible, prayer and worship.

Our Barnabas children's team works with primary schools and churches to help children under 11, and the adults who work with them, to explore Christianity creatively and to bring the Bible alive.

To find out more about BRF and its core activities and ministries, visit:

www.brf.org.uk
www.brfonline.org.uk
www.barnabasinschools.org.uk
www.barnabasinchurches.org.uk
www.messychurch.org.uk
www.foundations21.org.uk

If you have any questions about BRF and our work, please email us at

enquiries@brf.org.uk